Destination:

MORGUE!

L.A. TALES

James Ellroy

arrow books

Published in the United Kingdom in 2005 by Arrow Books

1 3 5 7 9 10 8 6 4 2

The following pieces were published in American GQ magazine in slightly
different form: 'Balls to the Wall' (published under the title 'Bloodsport', July
2000), 'Where I Get My Weird Shit' (September 2002), 'Stephanie' (January
2003), 'Grave Doubt' (June 2000), 'My Life as a Creep' (October 1999), 'The
D.A.' (July 2002), 'Little Sleazer and the Mail-Sex Mama' (March 2002), 'Ive
Got the Goods' (March 2000), and 'The Trouble I Cause' (March 2000)

First published in the United Kingdom in 2004 by Century

Arrow Books Limited
The Random House Group Limited
20 Vauxhall Bridge Road, London, SW1V 2SA

Random House Australia (Pty) Limited
20 Alfred Street, Milsons Point, Sydney,
New South Wales 2061, Australia

Random House New Zealand Limited
18 Poland Road, Glenfield
Auckland 10, New Zealand

Random House (Pty) Limited
Isle of Houghton, Corner Boundary Road & Carse O'Gowrie,
Houghton, 2198, South Africa

The Random House Group Limited Reg. No. 954009

www.randomhouse.co.uk

A CIP catalogue record for this book is available from the British Library

Papers used by Random House are natural, recyclable products made from
wood grown in sustainable forests. The manufacturing processes conform to
the environmental regulations of the country of origin

ISBN 0 09 944674 X

Printed and bound in Great Britain by
Bookmarque Ltd, Croydon, Surrey

James Ellroy

Destination: MORGUE!

James Ellroy was born in Los Angeles in 1948. His L.A. Quartet novels—*The Black Dahlia*, *The Big Nowhere*, *L.A. Confidential*, and *White Jazz*—were international bestsellers. *American Tabloid* was *Time's* Novel of the Year for 1995; his memoir *My Dark Places* was a *Time* Best Book of the Year and a *New York Times* Notable Book for 1996; his most recent novel, *The Cold Six Thousand*, was a *New York Times* Notable Book and a *Los Angeles Times* Best Book of the Year for 2001. He lives on the California coast.

Also by James Ellroy

Early Novels
Brown's Requiem
Clandestine
Killer on the Road

L.A. Noir – The Lloyd Hopkins Trilogy
Blood on the Moon
Because the Night
Suicide Hill

The L.A. Quartet
The Black Dahlia
The Big Nowhere
L.A. Confidential
White Jazz

Short Stories and Collected Writings
Dick Contino's Blues
Crime Wave
Destination: Morgue!

Non-fiction
My Dark Places

Underworld U.S.A.
The Cold Six Thousand
American Tabloid

Destination:

MORGUE!

To Oscar Reyes

Contents

Part I

CRIME CULTURE/ MEMOIR

Balls to the Wall

oxing is:

Blood sport declawed and reregulated. Cockfights for aesthetes and wimps.

Boxing is microcosm. Boxing baits pundits. Boxing rips writers and rags them to riff.

Boxing taps testosterone. Boxing bangs to the balls. Boxing mauls and makes you mine meaning.

Mexican boxing is:

Boxing distilled. Boxing stoicized. Boxing hyperbolized.

Mexican boxing is machismo magnified. Mexican boxing is bristling bravado. Mexican boxing means you die for love and live to impress and subjugate your buddies.

Vegas boxing is:

Lowlife pomp. Westminster West. Best-of-weight class as best-of-breed.

Vegas boxing is Rome revived. Gladiators divert high rollers. Imperial goons exploit muscled maxi-men and mainline their money.

I got the word:

Erik Morales meets Marco Antonio Barrera.

Junior featherweights. Title tiff. Vegas.

I had to go.

■

I love boxing. We go back.

My folks divorced in '55. My dad got me weekends. We holed up. We watched the fights.

We had a bubble-screen TV. We snarfed Cheez Whiz. My dad rooted on race and "heart."

He liked white fighters best. He liked Mexicans next. He liked Negroes last.

Heart eclipsed race. Heart mitigated race. Heart gave Mexicans White Man status.

"Mexican" meant all Latins. Mexican meant some Italians. Mexican meant the Cuban Negro Kid Gavilan.

My dad fucked up race and geography. He was a Wasp. He hit L.A. and learned Spanish. He dug inclusiveness. He knew the White Man ruled. He knew the Brown Man craved in.

He wanted him in. *If* he kicked ass to his specifications.

Race. Heart. My early education.

I lived in L.A. I watched TV fights. I watched fights live.

The Olympic. The Hollywood Legion Stadium.

Smoke. Ceiling lights. Beer and crushed peanuts.

My dad took me. We sat with Mexicans. We watched Mexicans kick triracial ass.

My dad went chameleon. My dad gestured wild. My dad Mexicanized.

He talked to Mexican men. He slapped their backs. He translated for me.

Male-speak. My early education.

Headhunter. Go to the body. Cut off the ring.

Pendejo. Cojones. Maricon.

My dad divided Mexicans. Illegal immigrants were "wetbacks."

Wetbacks had heart. They swam the Rio Grande. They sought *trabajo*.

They scuffled. They worked hard. They craved White Man status.

Hoodlums were *Pachucos*. *Pachucos* lacked heart.

They oiled their hair. They overbred. They packed switch-blades.

They shivved cops. They smoked mary jane. They disdained White Man status.

I met two Mexican kids. Reyes and Danny. They came from T.J.

They saw T.J. fights. They saw the mule show. They loved Art Aragon and Lauro Salas.

We smoked mary jane. I was ten years old.

I got dizzy. I punched the air like a *maricon*.

My mother died. I bunked full-time with my dad. We watched fights. We snarfed TV dinners.

12/5/58:

Welterweights. Title tiff. Don Jordan versus Virgil "Honey-bear" Akins.

Jordan wins. Jordan's a Dominican *negrito*.

He's mulatto. My dad digs him. My dad grants him Mexican status.

He's psycho. He was a child hit man. He killed men at age ten. He killed thirty men in a month.

Mexicans were killers. My dad said so. My dad spoke Spanish. My dad saw the mule show. My dad knew his shit.

12/10/58:

Light heavyweights. Title tiff. Archie Moore versus Yvon Durelle.

It's Armageddon. Moore wins. Moore's Negro. Durelle's Que-becois.

My dad upgrades Moore's racial status. Moore gets Mexican-ized. My dad downgrades Durelle. Durelle gets Mexicanized.

Durelle "eats leather." Durelle "leads with his face."

5/27/60:

Welterweights. Title tiff. Jordan bows to Benny "Kid" Paret.

Paret's a Cuban Negro. My dad hates him. My dad gets his race right.

3/24/62:

Welterweights. Title tiff. Paret versus Emile Griffith.

Griffith's Negro. Griffith's island-bred. Griffith stomps Paret. Paret dies.

Paret trash-talked Griffith. Paret called him queer.

Sex hate. Revenge. My early education.

I went to fights. I watched TV fights. I read fight magazines.

I still lived in L.A. I bopped around. I dug racial stratification.

Negroes lived south. Mexicans lived east. Whites lived everywhere.

Negroes craved civil rights. Mexicans craved conflict and personal honor.

Mexicans grew small. Mexicans moved swift. Mexicans ran stoic *and* expansive.

Mexicans coveted. Mexicans aspired. Mexicans knew the White Man was El Jefe.

Mexicans hobnobbed with whites. Common tastes united. Common language flowed.

Chili con carne. *Una cerveza, por favor.* Hook to the liver.

I Mexicanized. I Mexicanized with Wasp circumspection.

I wore Sir Guy shirts. I provoked fights with little kids. I notched mixed results.

I lacked power. I lacked skill. I lacked speed. I lacked heart.

It showed. My defeats were ignominious. My victories were pathetic.

Summer '64:

I was sixteen. I stood 6'2". I weighed 120. My dad said I ruled the Toilet-Paper-Weight Division.

I challenged my pal Kenny Rudd.

Six rounds. With gloves. Robert Burns Park.

Cornermen. Ref. Five-dollar purse.

I had height. I had reach. Rudd had heart. Rudd had speed and power.

Rudd kicked my ass. Rudd fought barechested. I wore a Sir Guy shirt.

My dad got sick. He went to the hospital. He bunked with a Mexican guy.

They talked fights. I brought them cheese enchiladas.

My dad died. The Mexican guy recovered.

I lived by myself. I watched TV fights. I hit the Olympic.

I saw Little Red Lopez. I saw Bobby Chacon. I saw six million guys named Sanchez and Martinez.

I sat ringside. They bled on me. I ate cut residue.

I sat top-tier. I shared piss cups with Joses and Humbertos. They protested bum verdicts. They tossed piss cups. They doused *puto* officials.

I pulled some dumb stunts. I got in trouble. I detoured and paid.

I did county jail time. I talked fights with wicked Juans and rowdy Ramons. I fought a Mexican drag queen named Peaches.

Peaches squeezed my knee. I popped him. I aped Benny "Kid" Paret. I called him a *maricon*.

Peaches kicked my ass. Guards pulled him off. Triracial inmates cackled.

I dissected my defeat. I put something together.

Mexican boxing explicates the mind-body split for white wimps worldwide.

MEXICAN BOXING IS WORKMANLIKE. Mexican boxing is inspired.

It's savage emphasis. It's basic boxing retuned to short range.

You move in. You stalk. You cut the ring off. You intimidate with forward momentum.

You crowd your man. You eat right-hand leads. You counter and left-hook to the body.

You instigate exchanges. You trade in close.

You take to give. You forfeit your odds for survival. You eat shots. You absorb pain. You absorb pain to exhaust your man and exploit his openings. You absorb pain to assert your bravado.

You clinch when desperate. You backpedal when stunned or insensate. You fight coy to avert the brink and buy moments.

The body shots sap wind. The momentum saps will. The absorbed pain saps brain cells. The absorbed pain builds character and fatuous ideals.

Mexican boxing is lore.

Mexican fighters chew steaks. They drink the blood and spit out the meat.

Mexican fighters slurp mescal. They gargle and swallow the worm.

Mexican fighters do roadwork at 10,000 feet. Mexican fighters train in bordellos.

Mexican boxing is memory.

Fights in bullrings. Fights at weigh-ins. Fights at victory balls. *Fights.*

The Trifecta. '70–'71. Ruben Olivares and Chucho Castillo.

The Inglewood Forum. Sellout crowds.

Rockabye Ruben rocks. Chucho presses and bleeds. Round 3—Ruben rests recumbent. Ruben rises and rallies *rapidamente.*

Ruben takes tiff one. Unanimous decision. The mayhem mandates tiff two.

Ruben rips. Chucho chops and chisels. Ruben launches left hooks. Chucho counters contrapuntal.

Ruben cuts. His left eye leaks at the lid. The cut calls it. It's over. Chucho—TKO 14.

The rubber match rocks. It's all pressure. Chucho drops Ruben. Ruben rises and rebounds.

Ruben roils. Ruben wracks the ribcage. Ruben rules the ring. Ruben reigns in the rubber.

4/23/77:

The Forum. Nontitle tiff. Carlos Zarate and Alfonso Zamora. Seventy-two fights collective. Seventy-one KOs.

Round 1 goes slow. Zarate tests Zamora. Round 2 disrupts.

A geek jumps in the ring. Cops haul him out. Cops kick his ass.

Round 3. Zarate zips close. Zarate zaps Zamora.

One knockdown. Eight count at the bell.

Round 4. Zarate in close. Zamora's got zilch. Two-knockdown TKO.

It's over. It's not momentous. It's not competitive.

Zamora's dad's in the ring. Zarate's dad ditto. Zamora's dad zaps Zarate's dad.

It's instantaneous. It's Zarate–Zamora II.

Memory:

Zarate. Lupe Pintor. Rafael Herrera.

The great Salvador Sanchez. Julio Cesar Chavez—*el grande campeón*.

Mexicans. White Men all. Ask my dad.

Morales–Barrera vibed walk-through or war.

Morales was 35 and 0. He had the WBC belt.

He had youth. He had speed. He had a more diversified attack.

He had career momentum. He had an HBO contract. He had the Next Chavez prophecy.

Barrera was the last Next Chavez. He ate some right hands. He got de-prophesied.

He was 49 and 2. He had the WBO belt. Wags called it WBOgus.

Barrera *owned* the Mexican attack.

He closed in. He cut off. He left-hooked. He went downstairs.

He *had* career momentum. He *had* HBO ties. Junior Jones de-momenticized him.

Right hands.

One KO loss. A rematch. One loss by decision.

Barrera learns defeat. Barrera fugues out. Barrera regroups.

Barrera's a Mexican. Barrera's a Catholic. Barrera digs redemption.

Barrera's a rich kid. He hails from Mexico City.

Boxing ends someday. He knows it. He's eyeing law school.

Morales was middle-class. He hailed from T.J. His dad was a fighter.

He's a soft touch. He donates Christmas dinners. He won his belt. He banked the check. He stocked T.J. schools with computers.

They were good kids. "Good kids" is fanspeak. Good kids are killers who limit their rage to the ring.

VEGAS WAS T.J. UNCHAINED.

I hit T.J. in '66. I got a head job. I saw the mule show.

T.J. was scary.

I hit Vegas in 2000. Vegas was worse.

I stayed at the Bellagio. I heard it had "class." I heard right and wrong.

It featured an art gallery. It featured silent slot machines. It featured stretch limos.

License plates: Cezanne/Matisse/Picasso.

My suite was big. My suite had a church directory. My suite had cable fuck films.

I settled in. I walked the Strip. I misjudged distances.

Hotel facades streeeetched.

Medieval moats. Paris skylines. Mock Manhattans.

Street traffic crawled. Foot traffic gawked.

Folks carried kiddies and cocktails. Folks carried slot-machine cups.

I grabbed a cab. The cabbie was psycho. The cabbie vibed Klan.

He picked his nose. He picked his teeth. He slurped beer in a McDonald's cup.

He talked fights.

He liked Morales. Barrera was stale bread. J. C. Chavez was a punk. He lost to Frankie "the Surgeon" Randall. He trashed his suite at the MGM Grand.

He talked Mexican fights.

The cholos had heart. The cholos fought dirty. The cholos fucked goats.

He talked Vegas fights.

Morales–Barrera was small. Hipster stuff. Rap stars and movie shitbirds verboten.

Big fights rocked Vegas. Big fights flew on big money.

Site fees. Pay-per-view. Casino perks. High rollers lured in to lose.

Big fights drew big names. Ringside recognition.

Big fights meant heavyweights. Big fights meant Tyson and bad juju. Big fights meant Oscar de la Hoya.

Oscar was pretty. Oscar bruised pretty. Oscar magnetized chicks.

He ain't a real Mexican. You can't be real and come from L.A.

I FOUND a Mexican restaurant. It vibed L.A.

I ate a Mexican dinner. I schmoozed a Mexican waiter. He came from L.A.

We talked fights.

He liked Morales. Barrera was shot.

His wife liked Oscar. His daughter *loved* Oscar. He thought Oscar was queer.

I walked to the Bellagio. A waiter brought coffee up.

He was Mexican. He came from L.A.

We talked fights.

He liked Morales. Barrera was through.

His wife liked Oscar. He didn't get the allure.

The waiter split. I dug my view.

Ant swarms. Streeeetch facades. Seduction signs.

Caesars. The Mirage. Gay white tigers.

The swarms vibed migration. Peons with cups. Supplicants hot for cash and diversion.

I felt like El Jefe. Call me Batista. Call me Juan Perón.

I viewed my Third World. I dispensed benedictions. I scrutinized and exploited small men.

Sanctioning bodies ruled boxing. *Puto* patriarchs reigned.

The IBF got indicted. The WBC held in. A wag called it "World of Bandits and Charlatans."

The WBA. The IBA. The WBOgus.

The I's meant "International." The W's meant "World." It stressed dominion and shared thought.

Official judges judge fights. State commissions appoint them.

Sanctioning bodies court them. Sanctioning bodies corrupt them. Sanctioning bodies stress shared thought.

Fractured titles. Multi-championships. Two I's/three W's.

Titles mean money. Titles drive a fighter's momentum.

Judges judge off it. Judges vote what's perceived best for boxing. Judges know the formal rules. Judges know subtext. Judges enforce consensus thinking.

Not all judges. Not most judges. Some judges in key fights.

Bribery.

Implicit. Covert. Unindictable.

The migration continued. The light show blipped on.

I fucked with the TV. I hit HBO.

Wags called it Home Breast Office. I hit breasts and an end-title crawl. I hit a *Boxing After Dark* teaser.

Two days hence:

Morales–Barrera. *Sangre.* The Holy War.

BAD had it. *BAD should* have it. *BAD knew.*

BAD was the best boxing show in TV history. *BAD* broadcast great fights. *BAD* broadcast bravura.

Great blow-by-blow. Jim Lampley in tight. Pro scoop and malapropisms via Roy Jones and George Foreman. Larry Merchant on meaning.

Bad Boy Barrera top-lined *BAD* card #1. He KO'd Kennedy McKinney.

A fierce fight. A tuff tiff. A proud prophecy.

I went to bed. I slept late. A waiter brought coffee up.

He was Mexican. He came from Oregon.

We talked fights.

He liked Morales. Barrera was fucked.

■

The Mandalay Bay:

Slot-Machine Acres. Blackjack Estates. Keno Kountry forever.

I walked through it. I got lost. I gagged on smoke. I smelled spilled cocktails.

I rerouted. I trekked on.

Card-Table Terrace. Roulette Rendezvous. Blow-Your-Mortgage Mesa.

I hit a corridor. I saw directional balloons.

Tricolor. Mexican. Red, green, and white.

I followed them. I hit the press gig.

Dais. Lectern. Steam tables. Buffet in gear.

I mingled. I saw Wayne "Pocket Rocket" McCullough. Morales decisioned him. I saw Richie Sandoval. Gaby Canizales KO'd him.

He got hurt. He quit boxing. He went into boxing PR.

I saw Latin reporters. I saw Latin cornermen. I saw some Anglo press.

The room chowed down. The food was bad. All starch and grease.

I sipped coffee. I listened. I bootjacked conversations.

Male experts dueled. Male experts interrupted. Male experts riffed lore.

I was there. *I* saw it. Dig *my* perception.

The honchos hit the dais.

Lou Di Bella. Mr. HBO. State commissioners.

Morales. Barrera. Promoter Bob Arum.

Morales looked calm. Barrera looked drained.

Weight.

Stabilize. Walk at 135. Make 122 by tomorrow.

Weight.

Eating disorders. Boxing's dirty secret. *Cosmo*—take note.

Intros went around. Honchos sanctified. Arum worked the mike.

His cheeks glowed. Perfect circles. He Mexicanized.

His kids spoke Spanish. We all should.

Mexicans were great fighters. Mexicans were great people. Mexicans were great fans.

He cited Mexican battles. He overpronounced names.

He coaxed his boys. Speak English, *por favor*.

Morales spoke. Barrera spoke. They spoke haltingly.

They pledged results. They showed their youth. They oozed dignity.

The gig broke up. Morales and Barrera mingled.

Reporters closed in. Interpreters assisted.

Standard stuff.

Nobody said, "You get my rocks off."

Nobody said, "You make me feel alive."

Nobody said, "Nationalism is all shuck-and-jive."

I thought about youth. I thought about glory. I wondered how brain cells dispersed.

I thought about middle age. I grooved on self-preserving circumspection.

Morales brought some guys. They vibed buddies. Barrera brought some guys. They vibed entourage.

They wore reflecting sweat suits. They waxed sullen. They looked like the Tonton Macoute.

They brought some girls. The girls brought babies.

One baby cried. Mom fed him Pepsi. Mom shut him up.

Bob Arum mingled.

He glowed. His cheeks glowed. His cheeks looked rouged and augmented.

TICKETS SOLD. Mexicans bought them.

They eschewed "Latino." They eschewed "Chicano." They were born here. They were born there. They were "Mexican."

Tickets sold fast. Tickets sold out.

I schmoozed PR flacks. They extolled the demographic.

Working folks. Mexicans. Cognoscenti.

I prowled the Mandalay Bay. I caught the weigh-in.

Barrera looked drained. Barrera looked scared. The Tonton looked apprehensive.

I prowled the casino. I surveilled the ticket booths. I cataloged rumors.

Morales hates Barrera. Barrera hates Morales.

Turf tiff. T.J. versus Mexico City. Class clash. Middle meets moneyed.

They had soccer teams. The Morales Marauders. The Barrera Banditos.

They played. They clashed. The hell-bent jefes almost hurled heat.

My wife flew in. Some friends drove up from L.A.

We viewed a friend's wedding. We ate in mock cantinas. We strolled mock-Mexican streets.

We polled personnel.

The cognoscenti said walk-through. The starstruck said war.

■

The fans arrived. Mariachis piped them in.

It got loud.

The walls boomed. The walls trapped noise. The walls echo-chambered.

The fans lugged posters.

Morales. Barrera. Exhortings *en español*.

Balloons tapped the ceiling. Tricolored all.

A sound system cranked. Mariachi shit exclusive.

The room filled. The room roared. The room vibed bullring.

Fans positioned. Fans waved signs. Fans slugged cerveza.

Factions mingled. Factions placed bets. Total strangers held money.

I sat with the press. I watched the prelims.

They went fast. They went loud. The Mexicans drew cheers. The non-Mexicans drew silence.

TKOs. One decision. One woman's fight.

I hit the john. I crashed a rehearsal.

A baritone. A prime gig. The Mexican anthem.

We talked fights.

He liked Morales. Barrera was shot.

I bopped back. The noise reignited. I sat with my wife and friends.

A Morales guy flanked me. He was expansive. He was loud.

He waved a roll. He peeled C-notes. He placed bets.

Barrera guys bet him. A neutral popped up. He held the *dinero*.

A band filed in. Thirteen musicians.

Sombreros. Embroidered threads.

They entered the ring. They played loud. HBO cameras turned.

Fans held signs up. Cameras panned. Signs eclipsed views.

The noise built.

The fighters filed in.

The noise built.

The ring announcer spieled.

He spieled bilingual. He rolled his *r*'s. He rolled rich and rapt.

The noise built.

That cat sang the Mexican anthem.

The noise built.

The announcer introed the officials. The announcer introed the men.

He ratched his *r*'s. MoRales extended. BaRReRa rolled long.

The noise built.

The men derobed. They'd added weight. They'd sapped and replenished.

The ref gave instructions. The men touched gloves.

The noise built.

They went to their corners. They knelt. They crossed themselves.

The noise built.

The bell rang.

The noise stratosphered.

They moved. They squared off. They hit center ring.

Morales pops a jab. Barrera hooks to the body. Morales moves back.

Barrera. Fast hands. A shock.

Barrera moves in. He lands a right. He left-hooks downstairs.

Morales moves back. Let's bait and counter.

Barrera moves in. Barrera cuts off. Barrera double-hooks low.

Fast hands. Shocker. "Shot" — bullshit.

Morales backs up. Morales moves in. They trade right hands.

Morales backs up Barrera. His rights sting.

They square off. They trade. Morales backs up Barrera.

They circle. They pause.

Morales backs up. Let's bait and counter.

He taps the ropes. Barrera's on him. They trade hooks at the bell.

The 122-pound showdown between Erik Morales and Marco Antonio Barrera for the junior featherweight title would become the fight of the year. *(Photo by Ben Watts)*

The noise built. The noise leveled. The noise leveled loud.

Round 2:

Barrera stalks. Morales jabs.

It's a range finder. It's a sizer-up. It's a reach enhancer.

He's dancing. He's on his toes. Barrera closes in.

He lands a left hook. He lands a left/right.

Morales stands firm. Morales steps inside. Morales lands an uppercut. Morales rocks Barrera.

They stand. They trade. They deliver.

Morales has right hands. Morales has uppercuts. Barrera has killer hooks.

They disengage. Barrera moves in. Barrera hooks low.

Morales jabs. Morales moves in. Morales lands lefts and rights. Morales eats hooks.

He's fighting Barrera's fight. He's standing in. He's taking to give.

He's fighting close range. He wants to. His work vibes abandon.

He's pausing. Barrera's on him. He's launching hooks.

The bell. Hard to hear. One mini-gong.

The noise built. The noise releveled. The noise releveled loud.

Round 3:

Morales circles. Morales jabs. Barrera lunges. Barrera hits his knees.

He gets up. The ref wipes his gloves. Morales comes on.

Morales jabs. Morales leaves a jab out. Barrera hooks low.

Morales moves back. Barrera stalks. Barrera lands hooks.

Morales moves in. He lands two-handed. He moves back. Barrera presses.

He misses hooks. He lands hooks.

Morales leans on the ropes. Morales blocks hooks. Morales eats hooks.

Morales spins off. Morales lands two-handed. Barrera spins off. Barrera moves in. Barrera repins Morales.

He lands. He misses.

Morales launches. Barrera launches. They trade fucking wild.

The bell. A beep in a cacophony.

The noise cranked. The noise releveled.

I yelled. My wife yelled. Words went undiscerned.

A sign bopped me. A guy apologized. The Morales fan yelled. I read his lips. He said, "Barrera!"

Round 4:

Barrera stalks. Morales jabs. Morales spins and falls.

He gets up. The ref wipes his gloves.

Breather.

In round 4, Barrera focused almost
exclusively on Morales's thin frame, investing
in punches to the ribs that would weaken him
later in the fight. *(Photo by Ben Watts)*

Barrera circles. Morales circles. They're rubber-band-tight.
Barrera works the body. Morales moves back.

He flurries. He moves. He flurries. His work rate's up.

They regroup. They're in sync. They're synced to stand and
deliver.

War. Collaborative. Mexican.

They fight off the ropes. They spin loose. They reverse posi-
tions.

It's wild.

It's war in sync.

Barrera flurries. Barrera rings the bell.

The crowd stood. The nose releveled. I got the gestalt.

Bipartisanship. National pride. Love inclusive.

It had it even. Morales: punch stats. Barrera: aggression.

I held a piss. My heart fluttered. The noise hurt my head.

Round 5:

They move. They meet. They trade jabs.

Barrera hooks to the body. Barrera plows Morales. Morales hits the ropes.

Morales flurries off. Morales pops Barrera. Morales dominates.

Morales lands rights. Morales staggers Barrera. Morales lands uppercuts.

Barrera wobbles.

I vibe turning point. I vibe wrong.

Morales fades. Morales wings arm shots.

They both weave. They both wing. They both miss.

Barrera comes on. Barrera backs up Morales. Morales taps the ropes.

Barrera fades. Morales wings arm shots. Morales extricates.

They square off. They weave. They circle and stalk.

Sync. Pre-attack mode.

Barrera sucks it up. Barrera pounds Morales. Morales taps the ropes.

Barrera flurries. He's got juice. Morales fires weak.

The bell. A peep. One heartbeat heard.

I watched the prompters. I got close-ups.

I saw welts. I saw bruises. I saw deadpan will.

Round 6:

Slow-mo now. Save it. Sync the breather.

Jabs. Center ring. Barrera's lead right.

It's weak. Morales taps the ropes. He's weak. He pushes off.

He jabs. He lands. His jab looks weak. His arms look heavy.

Barrera hooks to the body. Barrera hooks twice.

Morales hooks to the body. Morales hooks twice.

They separate. They pause. They *breathe*.

Barrera lands. A right. A left. Body rockets.

Morales measures. Morales jabs. Morales uppercuts.

Morales stuns Barrera. Morales pushes him back.

The bell. Loud now. Loud against held breath.

Six down. Six to go. My card: three rounds each.

The noise notched down. The noise went hoarse. The noise deleveled.

Round 7:

They meet. They square up tight.

They brush heads. They trade body shots.

They work. They rest. They breathe. They claw at momentum.

Barrera's stronger. Barrera lands a right.

Morales jerks back. Morales moves back. Morales hits the ropes.

Barrera's on him. His head's down. He's landing combinations.

Morales rests. Morales reaches. Morales rallies back.

He comes off the ropes. He lands a right. He rocks Barrera.

Barrera takes it.

Barrera reaches.

Barrera rallies back.

Barrera rocks Morales.

The crowd yells. The crowd stomps. The crowd outrings the bell.

It was Barrera's fight. Barrera made Morales fight it. Morales wanted to fight it. Barrera made him. Barrera stamped the ticket. Barrera defined their mutual will.

Round 8:

Barrera moves in. Morales moves back.

They jab. They exchange. Barrera lands a one/two. Barrera rocks Morales.

Morales moves back. Morales hits the ropes. Barrera works the body.

Four shots. Evil. Evil shots back.

Morales shoves off. Morales lands lead rights. Morales lands uppercuts.

Barrera eats shots. Barrera goes low. Barrera lands to the liver.

They stand.

They deliver.

They launch arm shots.

They land and miss.

The noise schizzed on me. The roar went normal. Time schizzed. Three-minute rounds took six seconds.

I checked the prompter. I caught the damage.

Barrera bruised light. Morales bruised dark.

Dark rings. Sharp cheekbones. A ghost effect.

Dark eyes. Both men. Will smashed insensate.

Round 9:

Center ring. Exchanges. Barrera's advantage.

Morales hits the ropes. Morales flurries. Morales rallies back.

Barrera rallies back. Morales hits the ropes. Morales rallies back.

He finds some snap. He dredged it. Barrera takes it.

Sync:

They're both fried. They circle. They buy some breath.

Barrera charges. Barrera knocks Morales back.

They both flurry. They both miss. They both land.

They rest. They regroup. They earn breath.

They're slack. They're arm-shot. They're on deficit.

Barrera comes back. Barrera lands. Barrera hurts Morales. Barrera pounds him to the ropes.

The bell rang.

Fans screamed.

Fans screamed "Morales!" Fans screamed "Barrera!"

The syllables blended. The names clashed. The names unified.

Round 10:

Center ring. Wide punches. Misses.

Exhaustion. Bilateral. Cumulative.

They come close. They lean close. They brush heads. They punch way wide.

They breathe. They dredge.

Morales gets air. Morales lands three rights. Morales hurts Barrera.

Barrera sways. Barrera wobbles. Morales loads up.

He's fried. His tank's dry. He stands still. He moves back.

They rest. They breathe. They dredge.

Barrera gets air. Barrera gets legs. Barrera drives Morales back.

Morales stands. Morales swings. Barrera swings back.

They're insensate. They're on Queer Street. They're the standing dead.

The bell. A peep in screams.

I checked the prompter. I caught close-ups.

Barrera bled. One sliced bruise. Morales wore black hollows.

Round 11:

They trade jabs. They trade rights. They plant and hold.

Barrera lands body shots. He's got more pop. Morales lands arm punches.

They lack pop. They hurt anyway. They push back Barrera.

He backpedals. He takes more. He sucks it up.

He shoves Morales. Morales lays back. Morales finds the ropes.

Barrera plows in. They tangle. The ref extricates.

Barrera lands a right. Barrera lands body shots. Morales slides left. Barrera shoves him back. Barrera taps the body.

The bell. Loud again. 360 sound.

I checked my card.

Even at 6. Barrera takes 7 to 9. Morales takes 10. Barrera takes 11.

Barrera—4 points up.

A sign sailed. I saw Morales upside down.

Round 12:

They touch gloves. The crowd stands. It's respect.

They swarm. They flurry. They catch big breaths.

Morales bounces. Morales moves in. Morales hooks downstairs. Morales backs up Barrera.

Barrera plants and stands. Barrera backs up Morales. Barrera
backs him into the ropes.

Barrera's fists left Morales's face bruised,
but he ended the bout with a large wound
under his own left eye. *(Photo by Ben Watts)*

Morales flurries off. Morales moves back. Morales looks shaky.

Barrera jumps. Barrera lands hooks. They're close. They tangle. Morales goes down.

It's a slip. It's not a knockdown.

Morales took no punch. Morales slid and fell.

The ref rules a knockdown. The round goes 10–8. Miscue and break to Barrera.

Morales gets up. Barrera goes in. Wild punches arc to the bell. It's over.

I sat down. My legs caved. My bladder said, "Run."

The Morales fan slapped my back. I dredged some high-school Spanish. Barrera's fight. 10–8 to clinch. Insurance past a 10–9.

The Morales fan smiled. Fuck it. Coin comes and goes.

The crowd breathed in. The crowd breathed out. The crowd stood still.

The bell rang. The announcer coaxed applause. The crowd delivered.

The announcer scanned his cards. The announcer delivered.

Judge Duane Ford: 114–113 — Barrera.

Judge Carol Castellano: 114–113 — Morales.

Judge Dalby Shirley: 115–112 — Morales.

The crowd booed. Signs sailed. I saw "Barrera" upside down.

The Morales fan shrugged. The neutral tried to pay him. The Morales fan blew off the money.

Heist.

Dry hump.

Fucking.

Misappropriation.

Consensus thinking.

The WBC.

"World of Bandits and Charlatans."

The fans reviled the verdict. The fans glowed through it. The fans yelled, "Barrera!"

■

The crowd walked out. I joined my friends. A chant built. The one word: "Barrera!"

I felt punch-drunk. I felt de-Protestantized.

My dad should have seen it. My dad had perspective. My dad had race and geography.

We walked out. We hit the HBO party. We ate some Mexican food.

The walls leaked sound. Chants crashed the party. The one word: "Barrera!"

We all felt punch-drunk. We ate and split. We roamed the casino.

Jackpot gongs went off. Whoops and red lights.

I peeled my ears. I heard echoes.

"Barrera!"

I saw the Tonton Macoute. They held coin cups. They wore reflecting sweat suits.

They brought their girls. Their girls brought babies.

A baby cried. A girl fed him Coca-Cola.

Where I Get My Weird Shit

It's a puzzle cube. Memories and conceits snap off inner gears. Images replace colored blocks and click to cohesion. Bar rows connect. Plumb lines appear. You take what you need and what you were and sift it through what you've become. You impose order. You lay on some moonshine. If you're skillful and honest and pure, it all works.

I'm from L.A. My folks hatched me in a cool locale. I checked in at the hospital Bobby Kennedy checked out of. My mother hated Catholics and dug ruthless men. Bobby K. would have rocked her *ambivalente*.

My birthright mandates a disclaimer:

I viewed L.A. as a native. I never saw it as a strange land chronicled by outside writers. I grew up there. I sifted data and transfigured it kid-style. It was diverse shit. The connecting threads were corruption and obsession. Kiddie noir was my metier. I lived in the film noir epicenter during the film noir era. I developed my own strain of weird shit. It was pure L.A. It was bravura L.A. for one reason: I denied the existence of non-L.A. shit.

Because I'm from there. Because I thought L.A. was everywhere. Because I was that xenophobic and self-absorbed. Because I *knew* my weird shit was the best weird shit alive. Because you don't smear your hometown with outside writers' perceptions. Because L.A.'s weird shit *is* the best weird shit on earth and I grew up where it flourished prosaic.

My dad worked for Rita Hayworth circa 1950. He told me he poured her the pork. My mom wet-nursed juicehead film stars. My dad was lazy. My mom was workaholic. My dad taught me to read at age four.

I gained access to scandal rags and the Bible. Profligacy and the stern rule of God hound me still. I got man's schizoid nature young. We lived in West Hollywood. My dad called it the "Swish Alps." We lived beside a Lutheran church. Proximity made me a Lutheran. Martin Luther torched the world in 1530. Martin Luther reviled the Catholic Church. He blasted its corruption. He disdained its celibate laws. He was horny and craved some fine trim.

Papists took their orders from Rome. My mom said so. I puzzled the logistics. I developed a theory: The Pope spoke through their TV sets.

The Bible featured sex and wall-to-wall carnage. Ditto the scandal rags. Martyrdom and trysts with Rubi Rubirosa. Sex and published smears. My narrative gift incubated. My imagination afire.

My folks split the sheets in '55. My mom got main custody. I shuttled between them. I studied their separate lives. I logged their separate cultural donations.

My mom drank bourbon highballs. I watched her shape-shift behind booze. She dated men who vibed the film noir psychopath. I caught her in flagrante twice. My dad lurked near the pad and spied on his ex. My mom fed me healthy meals and epic novels. My dad fed me Cheez Whiz and the fights. He taught me to root. I rooted for Mexican fighters over Negroes. I rooted for white fighters first and last.

Race: A '50s primer. Sex: the big deal above all. The '50s joke ne plus ultra: I want to find the guy who invented sex and ask him what he's working on now.

Both parents made me read. Both parents hauled me to flicks. My dad riffed on nympho movie stars. My mom spieled on actors she nursed. She took me to a Martin and Lewis show. A scene portrayed a dog driving a car. It cracked me up for days running. My mom found the reaction extreme. She was enlightened. She took me to a kid shrink.

The shrink was female. She gave me play blocks and probed my eight-year-old mind. She quizzed me per dogs and divorce. I said I liked to read. I said I liked the fights. I said I *loooooved* to tell myself stories and think.

My therapy lasted three sessions. I caught my mom hobnobbed with the shrink. The gist: I was imaginative and fucked up.

The two-parent shuttle continued. I bopped back and forth and picked up dirt. Rita Hayworth—nympho. Rock Hudson—fruit. Floyd Patterson—cheese champ. Mickey Rooney—satyr. ZaSu Pitts—a sweetheart and a pleasure to nurse.

June '58 hits the calendar. My Walpurgisnacht goes down. My mother is murdered. The scenario is SEX. The crime goes unsolved.

I went with my dad full-time. He exulted in my mother's death and tried not to gloat in my presence. My bereavement was complex. I hated and lusted for my mother. Bam—she's dead. Bam— my imagination finds CRIME.

The fixation sidestepped my mother's death and locked in on surrogate victims. The Black Dahlia became my murdered woman of choice. Her death-details were savage. They blitzed my mother's death-details in malign imagery. The Dahlia was my mother rendered hyperbolic and distanced enough to be fantasy-savored. She was my invitation to mourn once-removed and my beckoning to all-time obsession.

I studied Dahlia news clips. I rode my bike to the Dahlia's

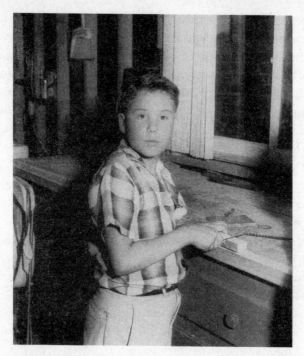

James Ellroy in 1958 at age ten. Just after cops told him his mother was murdered, a newspaper photographer took this photo. *(Photo courtesy of James Ellroy)*

dump site. I brain-spun savior stories. I rescued the Dahlia as the killer's blade arced.

I never posed her story as a novel. I brain-spun the tales for kicks. I did not equate my mother with the Dahlia then. I did not know that her death betrothed me to crime.

I read kids' crime books. I jumped to Mickey Spillane's Mike Hammer. The stories were vindictively anti-Commie. I dug Mike Hammer's fervor and rage. I was a childhood Red basher. I raged to punish some unseen other. I was stalking my mother's killer then. I didn't know it. I didn't know that I was dredging shit for my own future pages.

My dad let me read for thrills and ignore my homework. My dad let me hoard scandal rags and skin magazines. We watched crime TV shows. My dad knew a costar on *77 Sunset Strip*. He said the guy's wife "flashed her snatch" at him. My dad spoke in non sequiturs. He assumed my sex knowledge. He praised male homos. He said they expanded the pool of fuckable women. He saw groovy quail on the stroll. He always responded thus: "Somebody's screwing her, and it sure isn't us."

He let me learn life void of good-parent intrusion. I did poorly in school and educated myself. I read *From Here to Eternity* in 1960. Crime merged with social history. I gorged on a life-in-the-raw text. Institutional sadism/the adult laws of sex/young men reared as cannon fodder. Schofield Barracks/Hawaii/1941—a spritz on my All-L.A. World and the spark point of my grandiose kid ambition.

Dig it:

You can do this. *You* can write big stories. *You* can become a great writer.

Dig the subtext:

Fuck school. Fuck hard work. Fuck that bromide that you're french-fried fucked without a high-school diploma. Read, watch crime flicks, bop around L.A. Fantasize and pick your nose and tell yourself stories.

Dig the subtext decoded:

Be lazy. Be slothful. Disdain adult wisdom. Be inflamed with your fatuous new self-knowledge.

My life skills were substandard then. They declined from '60 on.

I lived to read and fantasize. I shoplifted books, food, and car models. I cruised L.A. on my tacoed-out bike. Dig the gooseneck handlebars and chrome fenders. Check the rhinestone-studded mud flaps. Orb the plastic saddlebags, *aaa-ooo-gah* horn, and toy tommy gun. Grok the speedometer—it tops out at 150 miles per hour.

I bike-stalked girls. I was a conspicuous stalker. I stalked rich Hancock Park girls and Jewish girls west in Kosher Kanyon. They spotted me by daylight. My taco wagon magnetized and drew yuks. I stalked better by nightfall. I parked and reconnoitered on foot. I peeked windows and glimpsed undies and skin.

I stalked through summer '61. I detoured to protest gigs and chucked eggs at ban-the-bomb fools. The Berlin Wall ascended. Uncle Sam and the Commos played chicken. A newsman ran a nightly warometer graph. The odds on nuke war soared to 90%. I knew it was curtains. America was fucked. Mike Hammer couldn't save us from this one. The crisis filled me with nihilistic glee. *I* was fucked. I would never become a great writer. I *could* brave fallout and steal books with impunity.

The crisis tapped out. The warometer lied. I grooved a theme—small lives set against big events. Summer '61 snapshots bipped off a screen in my head.

Bomb-shelter kits on sale in a Christmas-tree lot. The Larchmont Safeway picked clean. Our dipso neighbor stocking up on scotch and cigarettes. Those ban-the-bomb pinkos egged up.

It was history. It was dramatic infrastructure. Memory and conceits connected. I was seeing things. I was sensing things. I was living free and dreaming big. I was indexing big future pages.

Nobody called me bright. Nobody tagged me with bipolar disorder. I was a charmless mini-misanthrope with poor hygiene. I was an egomaniac with cystic acne. I was an acquired taste that no one ever acquired.

I squeaked through junior high and hit high school. Adult life loomed wicked large. Fairfax HS was almost all Jewish. I stood out only as a gentile and bad-skin exemplar. I craved attention. I lacked attention-getting skills. I was a poor student, worse athlete, worse social mover still. Stock losers and teenage lepers shunned me. My loserdom did not conform to adolescent rebellion laws. Stock martyrdom bored me. I disdained the canonized alienation of disaffected kids worldwide. I wanted to promote myself as strictly unique and attract commensurate notice. I was a rebel with self-aggrandizement as cause.

I pondered the dilemma. I hit on a solution. I joined the American Nazi Party. I debuted my führer act in the West L.A. shtetl.

It backfired—and worked.

It got me *some* attention. It got me recognized as a buffoon. I did not subvert the status quo at Fairfax High School. I did not derail the Jewish hegemony. I passed out hate tracts and "Boat Tickets to Africa." I anointed myself as the seed bearer of a new master race. I announced my intent to establish a Fourth Reich in Kosher Kanyon. I defamed jigaboos and dug the Protocols of the Learned Elders of Zion. I ragged Martin Luther Coon and hawked copies of "The Nigger's 23rd Psalm." I got sneered at, I got laughed at, I got pushed, I got shoved. I developed a sense of politics as vaudeville and got my ass kicked a few times. I learned how to spin narrative and elicit response. I knew that I didn't hate Negroes or Jews—as long as they comprised a rapt audience. I harbored a warped sense of the early-mid '60s. I nursed a writer's feel for timing. I honed my ability to stand tall and eat punches. I learned to front my crazy shit and revel in it as unique.

My Nazi act succeeded and tanked. It moved me, bored me, and vexed me in sync with my audience response. I lived to fantasize and assimilate storylines. Good books and TV fare subsumed my performance art. I flew with shit that clicked real in my gourd.

It's fall '63. My dad's health is fading. Poor nutrition and Lucky Strikes are playing catch-up. Bam—*The Fugitive* debuts on TV.

It's pure concept. There's a small-town doctor. His marriage is fucked up. His wife's an alcoholic shrew. A one-armed bum B&Es the doc's pad and snuffs her. The doc gets tagged with the snuff.

He's tried, convicted, and sentenced to fry. Prissy Lieutenant Gerard takes him to death row. Bam—the train derails. Bam—he's on the run forever. He's chasing the one-armed bum. The cop's chasing him.

The show grabbed me. The show obsessed me. The show messed up my sleep. Dr. Kimble ran. I ran along at warp speed.

There's Kimble. He's a slick cat. He's haunted and twitchy and doomed. He's isolated like me—but imbued with better looks and hygiene. The cop's hounding him. The cop's got some secret agenda. My dad thinks he's a fruit. He's a chicken-chasing Charlie at the Hollywood Gold Cup.

Kimble hits numerous towns. They all look like studio lots or L.A. He's a lightning rod. He attracts sexual discontent and ennui. The grooviest woman in town always finds him.

Real women. Women ripped by loneliness and hunger. Lois Nettleton, Patricia Crowley, Diana Van Der Vlis. Barbara Rush, Sandy Dennis, Madlyn Rhue, Shirley Knight. Suzanne Pleshette, Elizabeth Allen, the great June Harding—the most accomplished TV actresses of the era.

Ooooooh, Daddy-o!!!! They were tripping up my trouser trout triumphant!!!

Kimble was a heat-seeking missile. The women sizzled with longing. Nobody got laid. Exigent circumstances precluded it. Kimble's sprint was one long dry hump. It was my futile drive for selfhood refracted. The women were my mother transmogrified.

The Fugitive slammed my imagination. Mass-market noir—Tuesday nights at 10:00. Counterpoint to my nutty life and weird public life ascendant.

My dad had a stroke on 11/1/63. I came home from school. I found him weeping and babbling. He was streaked with his own feces and urine.

His condition horrified and repulsed me. I saw his death as my abandonment and my own death decades hence. I started prepping for life solo. I started shutting him out.

He spent three weeks at the VA Hospital. His condition and survival prospects improved. I ditched school every day. I bike-looped L.A. I swiped nudist magazines. I visited my dad. I watched episodes of *The Fugitive*. They ticked time to the JFK hit. I recall the plotlines and the guest-star women still.

My dad split the VA on hit day. Jack's death and the attendant hoo-ha bored him. Ditto for me. Fuck Jack. We were Republicans and Protestants. Jack took his orders from Rome. The fruit cop almost nabbed Kimble that Tuesday. Patricia Crowley's red hair beamed in black-and-white.

MY DAD RETRIEVED IT. My dad blew it anew. I distanced myself. I sabotaged out of his grasp.

He resumed smoking. He resurrected his high-salt/high-fat diet. I ditched school most days. I flunked the 11th grade. I bike-roamed. I watched *The Fugitive* and read crime novels. I brain-screened crime fantasies. I eyeballed rich girls and their fortyish moms throughout Hancock Park.

Obsession suited me. My *self*-obsession blinded me to extraneous social trends. America mourned Jack the K. It was fodder for my Nazi shtick and no more. LBJ goosed the Vietnam troop count. I stumped for nuclear war. A store cop detained me for shoplifting. My dad had a heart attack as I sweated custody. The Jack-hit aftermath metastasized. Conspiracy talk bubbled up. My feelers perked. I dug the inherent mystery. I brain-screened Dallas scenarios for Doc Kimble. Jackie Kennedy was June Harding for the poor.

The blur heightened. School became a nonendurable drag. I was seventeen. I was white. "Free" would make it the trifecta. I stepped up my Nazi antics. I got suspended from class for a week. My dad started calling me "you kraut cocksucker." I painted swastikas on the dog's dish. My dad wore a Jewish beanie to torment me.

I returned to school. I juiced the escape process. The Folk Song Club met. I regaled and disrupted with a pro-Nazi tune and a chorus of the "Horst Wessel Lied."

They expelled me. It was midweek in mid-March of 1965. I walked south on Fairfax. I've got the details memorized.

The smell outside Canter's Deli. School kids sneaking cigarettes. The old Jews headed for shul.

I hitched home on Beverly Boulevard. I felt airless and scared. I got a jolt of destiny. High-school dropouts were fucked. I'd better become a great writer fast.

THE NOTION HELD. I stalled the work. My wacked-out education continued.

Future writers hide inside books and snort up the craft by enjoyment. They read and learn structure and style. Their curiosity points them to subject matter. They read to titillate and edify. They scratch the itch to see life revealed. They swing on an I-can-do-this/I-can't-do-this tether. The novel form awes them. The soapbox aspect entices. A sense of potential accomplishment looms. The novel is autobiography mislabeled. The novel avenges sand kicked in the face and larger and more longstanding trauma. The novel enraptures career losers with justifying visions of self. The novel itemizes and encapsulates experience and contains it within a worldview. The novel takes abstraction and turns it to dramatic incident. The novel makes incident specific and loftily abstract. The novel explicates moral concerns to the novelist himself and reveals them through his dramaturgical choices. The novel bestows a huge ego on the novelist and jerks him to humility concurrent. The novel is a big fucking endeavor. The puzzle-cube aspect of the novelist's gift always stuns.

Novelists mold memories and conceits. Their images replace colored blocks and click to cohesion. Plumb lines appear. They take what they need and what they were and sift it through what they've become. Their voices build off a mute state often nurtured in recklessness and privation.

The novel is a daunting task. It takes some building up to. My prelude took fourteen years.

I dawdled post–high school. I nursed an urge to blow town. My dad let me join the Army. My dad had a second stroke my second day in. I exploited his condition. I faked a nervous breakdown.

The Army scared me shitless. I hated the discipline. I was a craven and seditious faux führer. I did not want to go to Vietnam.

I got an emergency leave. I visited my dad on his deathbed. His last words to me: "Try to pick up every waitress who serves you."

The Army cut me loose. I was parent- and draft-free at age 17. I got a jolt of destiny. Teenage orphans were fucked. I'd better become a great writer fast.

"Fast" is relative. Fourteen years runs relative against a lifetime. "Great" is relative. It's often a self-bestowed or posthumous tag.

Ellroy's father, Lee. *(Photo courtesy of James Ellroy)*

It was time to live and read. It was time to complete my pica-resque education.

I matriculated in L.A. I majored in booze and dope and minored in random desiccation. I read a shitload of crime novels and true-crime books and eschewed "mainstream" literature. I ate up plot, structural density and character development through implication. I judged books by their human content and authen-ticity. I made qualitative judgments and dropped further analysis. I possessed no gift to gauge abstraction. It was pure assimilation. I lived in a fictional criminal universe and brain-screened criminal fantasies. I committed petty crimes out of sloth and moral default. I shoplifted food, booze, and books. I stole empty pop bottles from reclamation bins. I broke into apartment-house laundry rooms and pried coins out of washers and dryers. I stalked Hancock Park girls, broke into their pads, and sniffed their underwear. I did county-jail time. I hobnobbed with other jejune jerkoffs and Mickey Mouse misdemeanants. We lied about our beaucoup bitches and criminal exploits. I honed my nascent narrative skills via jerry-rigged jailhouse jive.

That was narrative output. Bullshit sessions rife with brag. I spritzed to cellmates and my nonjail pals. I chose my words deftly. I put the art in bullshit artiste. My themes were crime and my indigenous lunacy. I knew what I vibed. I did not try to under-mine the perception. I knew that candor would hold my audi-ence. I knew that macho posturing would discredit me. I understood the rules of verisimilitude. I worked off my outré appearance. I was 6'3"/140–60 pounds of it zits, and always the ripe snout pustule.

Most kids riffed off machismo and politics. The era mandated topical discourse. Winning fistfights and Us-versus-Them — "the Establishment" as punching bag.

I detailed my *losing* fistfights. John "the Whale" Blackman falls on me at John Costa's pad. I enter a booze blackout. I wake up bruised in a Christmas-tree lot. There's the Mex drag queen Peaches at the "New" County Jail. Peaches gropes my knee. I pop him. Peaches has heavy hands like Alexis Arguello. Peaches pounds me.

"The Establishment"? Fuck that. Counterculture rage denotes a new conformity. Every puerile street punk hates the Establishment. Their critique is short on analytical rigor and long on personal pique. Street punk Ellroy knows this. He can't quite voice it epigrammatically. He's a neoconservative crashing in parks and Goodwill bins. He craves women like then-unknown Peggy Noonan. He's got a not-quite-acknowledged moral ace up his sheeve.

Goofball Ellroy rarely thinks in abstractions. Goofball Ellroy feels this:

He created his own shit. The Establishment did not fuck him. He made his own choices. He plumbed his own course. He *engaged* his own shit.

Weird shit. *Gooooood* shit. Painful shit compounding at a horrible cost. Righteous shit for future pages.

The '60s and '70s bopped forth. I bopped forth heedlessly. I got drunk. I got bombed. I ragged the counterculture and their candy-ass angst. I surfed their dope tide. I failed to note the contradiction.

I ate Benzedrex Inhaler wads. I drank Romilar CF cough syrup. I scored uppers off a fruitfly named Gene the Short Queen. I mainlined Methedrine. I grazed on grass. I lurked, loitered, listened, and *learned*. I nabbed the noxious *Nachtmusik* of my far-out fatherland. Crime crystallized crisp in my cranial cracks.

There's L.A. It's epidemically everywhere. It's a circumscribed circus and draconian dream. It's a lavish land of caveman cops, shakedown shills, and jungle-bred junkies. It's a hyperbolic whorehouse and a hip hermaphrodite hutch. It hops on its hind legs and howls. It's a blistering blur blowing its way right through me.

I *lurked*. I dug a preppy girl named Margaret Craig. I tooled by her two-story Tudor crib and love-looted it voyeur-style. I *loitered*. I stood stock-still and stared in wide windows. I *listened*. I vacuumed up verbal verities verbatim. I *learned*. My odious orbit offered up insinuating insight. It demystified and dedoctrinized.

Bam—there's the LAPD. I'm in their custody. I pass through drunk tanks and the "Glass House." My lie detector clicks in and climbs counterclockwise. I look. I *learn*. I know they're not evil. They've been media-mauled and damningly demonized.

Bam—I'm in jail again. I'm bored. I'm alert. I'm scared. I look. I *learn*. I listen to the language of lowlife lassitude. It's rancid rationalization. I could have been/I should have been/they *owe* me. *Society* made me corrupt.

Bam—I meet a duo named Solly and Joan. We toke Thai stick and talk. Solly's handsome and weak. Joanie's joined to him in gender-role jive and juvenile lust. She knows he's lost/she knows he won't change/she hangs on nonplussed. She's sunk by stuff outside her volition. Women always get fucked.

I learned. I retreated and read.

I read Dashiell Hammett at the downtown library. I read Ross Macdonald by flashlight in the parks. I read meretricious crime writers all over L.A. I read Jolting Joe Wambaugh in jail and out.

The New Centurions/The Blue Knight/The Onion Field/The Choirboys—visionary work by a cop. L.A. revised. Authoritarianism dissected. Authority sanely lauded over chaos. A *counter-*counterculture view of 1960 up. Absurdism sans leftist drill. A horrible compassion and indictment of moral default.

Wambaugh burned through me. Wambaugh made me dredge abstractions and spin epigrams. Wambaugh made me think what it all meant.

Wambaugh sang me a swan song. Wambaugh changed me forever. Here's how I know that:

He made me ashamed of my life.

NOT ENOUGH TO change it. Close, but not yet.

It took more lunacy and more bad behavior and a large pus sac on a lung. It took more books read, more books gauged, more books consciously assessed. It took more self-disgust and more destiny jolts and more ache to be someone.

I was Don DeLillo's Lee Harvey Oswald writ pit-faced and tall. I had a "far mean streak of independence brought on by neglect." It was self-neglect entirely. I merged with Bad Lee in desperate yearning and diverged with him in design. Smudge history or rewrite it to your own specifications? No contest at all. Lurk outside Margaret Craig's window or seek flesh-and-blood women? All bets are off.

I cleaned up in '77. I was 29. Chronology favored me. I survived my picaresque education. Survivable drugs and low street-crime stats stood on my side. Jail tiers were bereft of gangbangers and race cliques. Scared kids with poor survival skills could endure and learn.

Learning is a motherfucker. I learned the hard way. I don't recommend it. Outrageous circumstance nailed me. I cultivated the gift and curse of obsession. The gift finally won.

I changed my life. I credit Almighty God with the save. I disowned profligacy. I sought righteousness. I swooned to write books. Literature is a deep calling. I knew it at the depth of my shame.

It's been good—and it's nowhere near over. Now I learn from *my* words on the page. I dig the mystical aspect. My weird shit out in the *spiritus mundi*—particles popping in air.

There's a kid or some kids somewhere. I'll never know them. They're particle-puzzle-cubing right now. They might be mini-misanthropes from Moosefart, Montana. They might be demi-dystopians from Dogdick, Delaware. They dig my demonic dramas. The metaphysic maims them. They grasp at the gravity. They'll duke it out with their demons. They'll serve up a surfeit of survival skills. They won't be chronologically crucified.

They'll shore up my shit. They'll radically revise it. They'll pass it along.

Stephanie

Murder files hook you fast and drag you in slow. The crime-scene report wires shock. Read it for facts and milieu. Don't extrapolate. Don't expect clear explication. Big files fill ten boxes. Logic builds and fractures. Chronologies disperse. The act creates the disorder. It leads you to the victim slow.

Summary reports, Teletypes, mug shots. Non sequitur license-plate stats. Ding-farm runaways polygraphed and shipped to Camarillo. The polygrapher's negative stats.

FI cards. Street creeps braced and cut loose. Shredded APBs. Canvassing sheets. Wrong-case misfiles, mug-run cards, and rap sheets.

Family photos. The victim's address book. Her scent or your wish fulfillment of it many years old. Snapshots of her smiling, posed in out-of-date clothes.

Women only. They make me read and look. Old paper as perfume. Longing as perceptive tool.

Unsolved files only. Apply your mind male and rude. Reset fractures. Reroute narrative. Make data blips cohere.

I've read a dozen murder files. I started with my mother's file and moved on. I read unsolved/female/sex-murder files

*only. I'm not a detective. I'm not a cop wannabe. I've never
solved a crime. I come to know the women sometimes.*

*I study the death pictures. I always do it first. Take me back
and show me the horror. Make me feel your loss fresh and
new.*

DETECTIVE BUREAU/HOMICIDE DIVISION/LOS ANGELES POLICE
DEPARTMENT. DR# 65-538-991 [MURDER/187 PC]. VICTIM: STEPHANIE
LYNN GORMAN/WHITE FEMALE/AGE 16. DOB: 6-11-49. DOD: 8-5-65.
STATUS: UNSOLVED/REOPENED/LAPD UNSOLVED UNIT AT WORK.

The crime scene:

West L.A./"Beverlywood"/southeast of Beverly Hills. Upper-
middle-class Jewish/all residential/crime stats down around zilch.

A corner house. Hillsboro and Sawyer. Stucco/late-'40s
vintage/three bedrooms, pristine. A rear garage. Side-street access.
A cement backyard. A five-foot connecting wall. A street-access
wood door set in.

A backyard patio. Two chaise lounges. Sliding-glass doors that
lead in. A rumpus room. A patio view. A side hallway. Go to the
northeast bedroom.

It's by the front door. Windows look out. You see the front lawn
and street. You see the house next door.

A door leads to the master bedroom. A door leads to the hall.
Roll 37 years back. Pop the doors and LOOK.

It's a small room. It's a girl's room. It's the older sister's pad. A
west-wall dresser. A north-wall desk by the window. Daybeds line
the south and east walls. They hit perpendicular. An end table
separates them. A lamp and knickknacks sit upright. There's a
cold-cream jar lid in between. There's a matchbook on the floor.
There's a nightstand in the northeast corner. There's a knocked-
over lamp. There's an east-wall portrait. It's bright oil paint. It's the
older sister beaming. There's a stuffed turtle toy on the east bed.
Both bed covers are lime green.

Stephanie Lynn Gorman as seen in her Hamilton High School yearbook photo, freshman year, 1965. *(Los Angeles Times Collection, Department of Special Collections, Charles E. Young Research Library, UCLA)*

On the floor: two gray sweat socks. Close by: a lidless jar of cold cream. Gauge in. They're beside the south bed and matchbook.

A chair by the connecting doors. Clothes under it: panties, denim shorts, one tennis shoe. Gauge in. The matching shoe is on the floor. It's near the west-wall dresser.

There's a cord looped to one south-bed leg. It's white chalk line. It's mason's cord. The free end is frayed. There's a shell casing on the floor. It's between the wall and the south bed. By the east bed: three more shell casings.

Bloodstained carpet. It's near the east bed. It's between the outer edge and the shell casings.

The casings are small. The cord is loose-weaved and three-stranded. The bloodstain is red and bright pink.

There's Stephanie Gorman.

She's on the floor. She's on her knees. She lists against the east wall. She's by the east-bed foot.

She's half-nude. She's bottomless. She's wearing a knit top and bra. They're knife-slashed up the middle. The top hangs loose. The bra hangs off her neck and shoulders.

Drag burns on her right hip. Both wrists abraded. Cinched cord on her right wrist. Loose strands pressure-frayed.

Gunshot wounds:

Two in her chest. One in her neck. One in her forehead.

Her lower lip and left breast are bruised. Her inner lip is swollen. Her forehead sustained a contusion.

She's in a begging pose. She's against that wall. Bullet force bruised her back. The east wall got an indentation.

It happened in broad summer daylight.

HER FATHER and sister found her.

6:00 p.m., 8/5/65. Ed and Cheryl Gorman come home. Cheryl's bedroom door is shut. They open it. They enter the room. They see Stephanie.

Ed Gorman goes to her and lifts her. He puts her on the east bed. He covers her with a quilt and some clothing. He calls LAPD. West L.A. Division responds.

Stephanie's mother came home. Ed Gorman told her. The LAPD arrived.

Lieutenant Grover Armstrong. Detective Sergeants Robert Byron and William Koivu. SID men, latent print men, photo lab men, crime lab men. Ten LAPD men total.

The detectives talked to the family. The family said this:

Ed Gorman was a lawyer. He had an office downtown. Cheryl worked for him today. Julie Gorman was a housewife. She played tennis today. She came home at 3:00 p.m. She saw Cheryl's bedroom door shut. She paid no attention.

She went back out. She went to the beauty shop. She came home to *this.*

The tech men fanned out. The detectives studied the crime scene. The photo men took pictures. Ed Gorman said he disrupted the scene. He covered Stephanie. She's up on the east bed. Her head's brushing the toy turtle.

The cops walked the house. They saw no forced entry. They saw no ransacking. They found a cord strand near the front door. They walked the patio. They found two bloodstained towels. They were on a chaise lounge.

The detectives talked to the family. They rebuilt Stephanie's day.

She went to Hamilton High summer school. It was one mile away. She carpooled with two friends: Paul Bernstein and Ilene Jackman. They always left school at 12:30.

The detectives called Ilene Jackman. They told her. They calmed her down. They learned this:

Yes, they went to school. Yes, they drove home. They dropped Paul off first. She dropped Stephanie at 12:45. Stephanie walked through the back gate.

She's in the house now. She's there *alone*.

An ambulance arrived. Attendants took Stephanie to the L.A. County Morgue.

They scheduled an autopsy. Print men dusted the crime scene.

They turned up latent prints. They elimination-printed the Gormans and all the cops. The Gormans slept under sedation. The investigation kicked in: Friday, 8/6/65.

Cops canvassed the neighborhood. The next-door lady said this:

She heard screams yesterday. It was 3:30 to 4:30. They came from the Gorman house. They came from the northeast corner. She thought it was the Gorman girls playing. The lady lived one house north. The property lines were tight in. Her gardener was cutting the lawn yesterday. He worked 1:30 to 2:30.

Neighbors reported a candy-selling crew. They were Negro kids. They were door-to-door knocking. There was a whole slew.

A kid called West L.A. station. His name was Dave S. He said he parked outside the Gorman pad yesterday. He was looking for this guy Bob Gelff. Gelff lived there maybe two years ago.

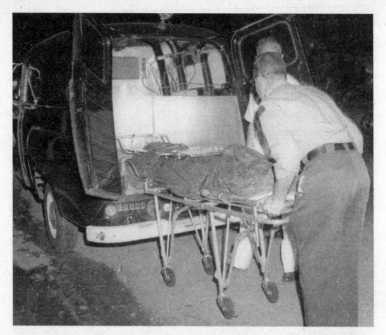

Stephanie Gorman's body is removed from her home and taken to the morgue. *(Los Angeles Times Collection, Department of Special Collections, Charles E. Young Research Library, UCLA)*

The tip got shined on. The tip got misplaced. The Gorman job made the papers and TV. They had tips up the wazoo.

A neighbor woman called in. She found the Gormans' pet loose. It was 4:00 p.m. yesterday. She put the dog in the Gormans' yard. She called out to Stephanie. She got no answer.

A neighbor kid called in. He was a Hami Hi student. He saw two Negroes cruise the Gorman house. It was yesterday. It was 12:50 p.m. They drove a '55 Ford.

A neighbor woman called in. She saw a '53 or '54 Olds parked at Durango and Sawyer. It was this morning. A man got out. He walked to a trashcan. He removed a pink blouse.

More tips came in. Neighbors called in. They snitched off the Negro candy crew. They snitched off a Negro church-solicitation crew. A parole officer called in. He snitched off two local rape-os. A neighbor man called in. He saw two male Negroes in a '55 Ford. They were distributing handbills.

Neighbors snitched off Negro workmen. Said Negroes bugged off work yesterday. Said Negroes aroused suspicion. A neighbor woman called in. A male Negro stood on her porch yesterday. It was 11:30 to noon. She lived on Hillsboro. She lived near the Gormans.

The canvassing cops braced local parolees. The geeks ran the gamut: GTA, weapons beefs, burglary, escape. They all checked out alibi-clean.

A bartender called in. He reported weird shit at the Red Rouge

August 5, 1965: Friends and neighbors gather outside the Gorman home the day of Stephanie's murder. *(Los Angeles Times Collection, Department of Special Collections, Charles E. Young Research Library, UCLA)*

Bar. The Red Rouge was way east on Melrose. The bartender said this:

A guy came in last night. He stayed from 10:00 to midnight. He was white/50/6'/200. He wore "old-type" clothes. He said, "They don't know what's happening. It will be headlines. They'll read about it in the papers tomorrow. It's tough to be a clown."

More canvassers came on. Metro Division supplied them. They house-to-housed. They questioned residents. They worked fifteen car-plan sectors. They worked north to the L.A. Country Club. They worked south to the Santa Monica Freeway. They worked east to La Cienega. They worked west to Hillcrest Country Club. They logged nontips and nonsense tips. They logged suspicious Negro sightings.

Byron and Koivu interviewed the neighbor's gardener. His name was George Iwasaki. He told them this:

He worked 8/5/65. He worked between 1:00 and 2:00. He parked near the Gorman house. He saw a man peeping the house. The peeper stood between the house and the neighbor's house. The peeper peeped the northeast bedroom window.

Iwasaki described him:

White male, Latin type, 43–45 years old. 5'7", 140 pounds. Sallow cheeks, unshaved, unkempt hair.

Attire: cotton twill shirt and pants. Matching "uniform type." Fresh-starched, light blue.

The man looked suspicious. Ditto his standing place. Iwasaki knew judo. The man gave him a bad look. Iwasaki smelled scuffle. He prepared to go.

Their eyeball duel ended. Iwasaki did yard work. He did not see the peeper again.

Dr. Harold Kade performed the autopsy. Stephanie Lynn Gorman/Coroner's File #19597.

She was 5'3"/100 pounds/brown hair, brown eyes. She was healthy. Gunshot wound #1 perforated her heart and left lung. The result: Massive hemorrhage. Gunshot wound #2 perforated her right lung. The result: massive hemorrhage. Gunshot wound #3 penetrated her trachea, esophagus, and vertebral column. The result: massive hemorrhage. Gunshot wound #4 fractured her skull and penetrated her brain. The result: massive hemorrhage.

Kade checked her reproductive system. The uterus, fallopian tubes, and ovaries: *Grossly normal. No lacerations of the vagina, rectum, or perineum.*

The Gorman job continued. Homicide Division jumped in. Sergeants J. R. Buckles and W. R. Munkres clocked on.

They found the Negro candy sellers. They cleared them. They questioned the Gorman family. They learned this:

Stephanie was a good girl. She did not flirt or provoke boys. She got top grades. She held class office. She excelled at Palms Junior High and Hami. She had no enemies. She did not truck with bad kids.

SID kicked back ballistics. The weapon: a .25-caliber auto. The millimeter equivalent: .635. Right-hand twist/six lands and grooves/Colt brand autos excluded. In evidence: 4 "Western" brand shell casings, 4 .25-caliber bullets. In progress: crime report cross-checks for the same type gun and MO.

The detectives worked. They debunked hysterical tips. They cleared suspicious Negroes. They read recent crime reports. Two nuts-at-large stood out.

Nut #1: "The Shoe-Tree Rapist." At large since 2/4/62. A West Valley habitué. A unique MO.

He cruises residential blocks. He spots housewives outside. He enters their pads through rear doors. He finds neckties or electric cords. He finds vaginal jellies or cold cream. The ties and cords act as restraints. The jellies and creams lubricate.

He wears gloves and masks. He grabs the women and binds them. He stuck a shoe-tree in his first victim's vagina. His next five victims fought him off. He ran out their back doors. He never speaks. He may be a mute. He may drive a '48 or '52 Chevy. He's good for 13 burglaries and 7 attempt rapes. Witness descriptions vary. He *is* a white male. He *may* be 19 to 23. He *may* be 30 to 40. Sometimes he appears unshaven.

Nut #2: "The Remorseful Rapist."

He's a white male "Latin type." He's about 26. He's 5'11"/185. He's got a crew cut and a neat appearance. He hits apartment pads in Wilshire and Central Division. He hits pads near bus lines.

He targets lone women. He cons his way in. He shows a small revolver and subdues them. He tapes their eyes and mouth. He rapes them. He apologizes post-rape. He shows them the gun is a toy.

The detectives worked. They found the Negro church crew. They cleared them. They checked out three local meter men. They cleared them. They went to Stephanie's funeral. The crowd ran 1,000 strong.

Hillside Memorial Park. Rabbi Michael Albagli presiding. Relatives, friends, and neighbors. Ed Gorman's clients and Hami Hi kids. Tears and soliloquy. Ed and Julie Gorman distraught.

The detectives worked. They skimmed old crime reports. They read ballistics reports. They read FI cards. They checked out loiterers detained and released. They fielded crank calls. A kid called in. He said Stephanie was a hooker. She nixed a Hami football player. He shot her for it. A crank note came in. It snitched off actor Richard Burton. More neighbors called in. They snitched off suspicious Negroes. A Hami girl called in. She said Stephanie dated Paul Bernstein and Steve Spiegelman.

SID retained the slugs and shells. Techs ran comparison tests. The slugs and shells matched no slugs and shells from prior confiscations. The print men studied the elimination prints. They found four prints remaining. They photographed them. The photo lab made blow-ups.

A sketch artist worked with George Iwasaki. They created a peeper sketch. The detectives talked to Dr. Kade. He offered this opinion: Stephanie Gorman was not a virgin at her time of death.

The detectives talked to Ed and Julie Gorman. They questioned them per Stephanie and sex. The Gormans deemed her a virgin. She had a checkup on 4/3/65. Talk to Dr. Fred Pobirs.

Buckles and Munkres saw Dr. Pobirs. He confirmed the checkup. He consulted his records. He saw no pelvic exam notes. He said she was 15 then. If she wasn't a virgin, I would have told the family.

The detectives questioned Stephanie's friends and classmates. They confirmed Stephanie's good-girl status. They talked to boys she dated. They had 8/5 alibis. They denied sex with Stephanie. They were credible. They vouched Stephanie's chastity. The detectives figured this:

Doc Kade might be right. Doc Kade might be wrong. Natural function or accidents cause vaginal rupture.

The detectives braced registered sex offenders. They ran RSO mug shots by George Iwasaki. He nixed them all. They were not the northeast-bedroom peeper.

It was 8/11/65. L.A. was wicked hot. The Watts Riot broke out. LAPD responded. A manpower call blared. LAPD men answered en masse. The riot featured arson, sniping, and looting. It was Suspicious Negro Armageddon. The National Guard arrived. A curfew was imposed. L.A. shut down. L.A. stayed indoors. L.A. watched the riot on TV. LAPD got swamped. The riot impeded travel. The riot fucked up communications. Normal LAPD service got suspended. Hot investigations lost time.

The riot de-conflagrated. Order got restored. South L.A. got singed to Cinder City. LAPD service resumed *slooooow.*

The Gorman job: stymied, quicksand, sludge.

Buckles and Munkres wrote a progress report. Lieutenant Pierce Brooks approved it. The report ran hypothetical reconstructions.

12:45. Stephanie gets home. She goes to her bedroom. She drops her schoolbooks and purse. She goes to the kitchen. She has a snack.

Stephanie has dry-skin problems. She goes to the master bathroom. It adjoins Cheryl's room. She creams her rough skin. Maybe the suspect grabs her there. He's already in the house. The skin-cream bottle—found in the bathtub—not normal there.

But:

No forced entry. That cord by the front door. Maybe he knocks. Stephanie answers. Maybe he just barges in.

He hits her. He subdues her. It explains her torn lip. The bruise on her forehead—call it blow two. Maybe it's a fall-down bump from blow one.

He carries Stephanie. He *drags* Stephanie. Her right-hip brush burns suggest this. Cheryl's bedroom is close. Stephanie is helpless or unconscious. He pulls the south bed out. He throws her on it. He binds her wrists to the east-bed legs. He spread-eagles her. He strips her lower body. He throws her clothes on the floor. He cuts her top and bra up the middle. He goes to the master bedroom. He finds a Jergens jar. He returns to the bedroom. He lubricates Stephanie's rectum and vagina. He tosses the jar and lid. Remember—the jar on the floor/the lid on the nightstand.

Doc Kade's opinion: sodomy and rape. *Tests for residues or foreign fluids inside the body not yet conducted.*

The killer assaults Stephanie. Stephanie regains consciousness. Say she struggles then. Say it's like this. Say she struggles throughout the whole thing.

Her wrists break free. Remember—the right-wrist cord still on her arm/the cord strands loose on the bed leg.

She gets off the bed. The killer corners her. He blocks the doors. Stephanie stumbles. She hits the east wall. She kneels— horror/shock/exhaustion. He shoots her four times. His gun's an automatic. The spent shells eject left to right. He's bloody now. He goes to the master bedroom. He grabs two towels. He wipes himself off. He goes out the back door. He hits the patio. He drops the towels on a chaise lounge. He goes out the back gate. He's on Sawyer Street. He's gone.

And—feature this:

Stephanie dies in Cheryl's bedroom. A sibling resemblance exists. Was *she* the intended vic?

The Gorman job faded out newswise. Postriot shit upstaged it. Stephanie got brief coverage. It played up her good-girl status. She was young, bright, lovely. She got straight A's. She was Hami Hi "in" crowd. She was movie-mad. She got extra gigs in *Pollyanna* and *Bye Bye Birdie*.

The detectives slogged. They issued a bulletin. It featured a crime summary and the peeper sketch. It went out 8/24/65. It went to the Feds and PDs nationwide. LAPD got kickbacks: similar MOs/divergent MOs/MOs off the beam. Rape-os, rape-o killers, bondage rape-os. Burglar rape-os, knife rape-os, gun rape-os, child rape-os, girl rape-os, woman rape-os, old lady rape-os.

Some freaks resembled the sketch. Most freaks didn't. George Iwasaki viewed nationwide mug shots and nixed them. They got no print matches. They got no ballistic matches. They got more phone tips and more letters. They cleared three hundred suspects. They issued bulletin #2. They sent slug and shell samples to the FBI and CII. Bulletin #2 begged for comparison slugs and shells. It featured the four-print blow-up. It begged for kickbacks: All suspects known or in stir.

No matches. Straight kickback zeros.

The Feds had a slug and shell. Ditto CII. LAPD retained two. The bulletin hit Canada and Mexico. Shit: no matches, more zeros.

The detectives slogged. They reinterviewed Stephanie's classmates. They reconfirmed her good-girl status. They interviewed Cheryl's male friends. They cleared them. They checked West L.A. FI cards. They braced Beverlywood freaks. They torqued wienie waggers, jailbait johnnies, glue sniffers, hopheads, and public jackoff freaks. They cleared them. They cleared local deliverymen. They cleared Ed Gorman's Negro ex-gardener. They cleared suspicious Negroes. They cleared rape-jacket Negroes citywide.

The Gormans were fine people. Ed was a fine lawyer. He had no enemies. His reputation gleamed. He served his synagogue selflessly. Julie's rep gleamed. The "good-girl" Gorman sisters were unassailably thus. They did not provoke or dick-tease. They did not backyard-sunbathe provocatively. Stephanie frequented the Standard Club. She wore demure outfits. She never wore revealing bikinis.

The Shoe-Tree Rapist—still at large. The Remorseful Rapist— likewise. Likewise *très* many sick humps.

THE GORMAN JOB slogged on. The Gorman job slogged on full-speed.

It was proactive. It was reactive. It ran tangential. It ran straight ahead. It was footwork and filework and gruntwork. It was a full-fledged freak symphony.

They got call-ins. A local girl ratted off a local "wino type." She said he resembled the sketch. George Iwasaki saw him and nixed him. No print match/no viable gun stats. The Green Bay, Wisconsin, PD called. They had a local freak. *He* resembled the sketch. Iwasaki nixed a mug shot. No print match—*adieu.*

Doc Kade called. He had late test results. *The vaginal and rectal semen tests: inconclusive. Plus: no other foreign fluids present/no sperm isolate.*

They cleared a Crest Drive wienie wagger. He flashed his shvantz from his balcony. Crest Drive adjoined Hillsboro and Sawyer. They cleared a freak nicknamed "Wino." He forged prescriptions. He popped goofballs. He habituated the Mar Vista Bowl. He pushed mary jane to kids. They checked out a 6/4/64 case. A freak kidnapped a Hami Hi girl. It was bold and streetside.

He flashed a knife. He made her get in his car. He made her disrobe. He kissed her breasts. He let her go.

That one went nowhere. One still-at-large freak.

They checked out a 3/12/65 gig. It was a parked-car caper. It featured a Hami girl and a boy. The girl was topless. Her name was in Stephanie's address book. The caper was Mickey Mouse. They cleared the boy.

"Harvey the Confessor" confessed. Harvey was habitual. He showed up at West L.A. Station. He copped to the Gorman job. The cops heard his jive confession. The cops cut him loose.

Fall '65 dragged on. They checked out the Standard Club. It was in Cheviot Hills. It was mid-upscale Jewish. The Gormans partied there. Maybe some freak saw Stephanie there. Maybe his hard-on commenced there. Maybe Stephanie flipped his freak switch.

They did 122 interviews. They ran gun checks concurrent. They checked 8/5/65 time cards. They logged rumors. They logged more good-girl rebop. They found some freak employees. They found some ex-cons. They looked at them close.

They read rap sheets. They charted work histories. They charted work absences on 8/5/65. They leaned on the freaks.

One Negro had two DUIs. Fuck him—he's a lush. One Negro had multiple busts: burglary/ADW/check-bounce tsuris. One Negro had a stat rape bust.

They leaned on them. They gun-checked them. They print-checked them. They cleared them both.

They checked out snack-bar guys, pool guys, lifeguards, tennis pros. They braced a potential rape-o. He picked a girl up at the club. He invited her to a movie. He drove her to the Hollywood Hills. He tried to promote a fuck. She said no fuck. He drove her home then.

The Standard Club washed out. They ran gun checks, print checks, and show-ups with George Iwasaki. They got bupkes. They punted. They tracked obscene-phone-call reports.

They waded in. They slid through slime. They tracked back four years. They tracked freaks who called young girls and freaks who bugged women about their daughters.

It was ugly. Bondage themes and straight fuck themes ran equal. The callers: all male. The victim-complainants: all female.

"Baby, let's fuck." "I want to eat your pussy." "I heard your sister works at Kentucky Fried Chicken on Pico. Do you and your sister fuck?"

"If you don't come across, I'll hurt your children." "I know you got a 19-year-old daughter. Meet me on Ventura. Wear a skirt, blouse, and no nylons, or something will happen to her."

This freak was typical. He calls a young girl. He says he's a school official. He asks embarrassing questions. He tells her to take her measurements. Ditto *this* freak. He calls a Valley woman. He tells her to wear high heels and eschew underwear. He tells her to meet him at the Akron store on Sunset. The cops show. He doesn't.

The detectives tracked reports. They grilled known phone freaks. They cleared them. Phone freaks were tough to catch. More freaks at large.

They dumped the phone shit—12/29/65. Cheryl Gorman got a late Christmas card. It mentioned a meeting in 7/65. The family had gone down to Coronado. Ed and Julie played bridge. Stephanie and Cheryl hit the beach.

They met two boys. Cheryl said she was reading *The Collector.* It's about a freak. He kidnaps a woman. He holds her hostage. She dies in captivity.

The kids played a game. The boys tied up and untied the girls. It was brief chuckles. That was all of it.

That was July. Cut to late December. One boy sends a Christmas card. It mentions the rope trick.

The detectives studied the card. The detectives drove to San Diego. They found the boys. They grilled them. They polygraphed them. They cleared them.

Adios, 1965—1966 struts in.

1/5/66: The lab tests the south and east bedspreads for semen. The *east* bed hits positive. There's no sperm isolate. There's a blood-type A reaction. The result: inconclusive. The stain is near the foot of the bed. It's near Stephanie's death pose. The rest of the bedspread tests positive: A-type blood reaction. That marks the *specific* stain inconclusive. That means the semen could match A or O blood. Stephanie was type O. There were no foreign fluid types in her rectum or vagina.

1/7/66: The lab tests the bloody towels. They get a type-O reaction. It's probably Stephanie's blood. Stephanie *might* have wounded the killer.

The detectives worked. The lab confiscated new crime-scene guns. They examined them. They test-fired them. They got nil results.

2/22/66: SID tests the Gorman hair samples. Most test out to Stephanie and Cheryl. One doesn't. This hair is coarser. It's not a Negro, Mexican, or Oriental hair. It's assuredly Caucasian.

2/22/66: The lab tests Stephanie's fingernail clippings. They find no scraped flesh. They find blood traces. They're too small to type. They can't tell if she scratched her assailant.

2/28/66: LAPD pops the Remorseful Rapist.

It's a traffic stop—2nd and Serrano. It's a male Mexican. His name: Edward David Apodaca.

He's packing tape and a toy gun. He stands in a show-up. Thirty-eight victims ID him. The Gorman cops grill him. He's gun-checked, print-checked, poly'd, and cleared.

3/8/66: A neighbor lady rats off a loiterer. He's standing at Pico and Roxbury. He matches the police sketch. Patrolmen haul him in. The detectives grill him.

His name is Mr. K. He's an alien. He hails from Gyula, Hungary. He's a schizo and a nut-bin habitué. He's got a nationwide rap sheet: vag/disorderly conduct/wienie wagger beefs.

He won't cooperate. He won't take a poly. They book him for Murder One. They put him in a show-up. George Iwasaki views him. He says maybe, maybe not.

Mr. K. talked a little. He said he escaped Patton State Hospital.

The detectives called Patton. They learned: Mr. K. escaped 8/5/65 — the Gorman snuff date.

But:

Mr. K. split late in the day. The time glitch cleared him.

Mr. K. got unbooked. Murder One — *nyet*. Patton sent a crew down to shag him.

3/24/66–3/31/66: Two Metro cops hit Georgia Street Juvenile.

They run record checks. They check current and recent Hami kids. They check the boys for juvie beefs. They check the girls as sex-beef complainants. The girls shoplift clothes and cosmetics. The girls run from titty pinchers and whip-out men. The boys run the fucking alphabet.

Lots of sex shit. 288PC — forced oral cop. 288 — voluntary. 288 — mutual suck. Voyeur busts, malicious mischief. Some kid molests a prepubescent girl. The cops pop him. Said kid gets popped at a fruit bar later. A 14-year-old boy attacks two 11-year-old girls. He slides on it. He gets popped for Peeping Tom later. Lots of GTA, some grand-theft merch, some parked-car sodomy. Wienie waggers galore. Glue sniffers, grasshoppers, juiceheads galore. Fruit rollers, fruit teasers, high-school fruitettes. Firebugs, chronic runaways. A doozie right after the Gorman job — 8/13/65. Venice Boulevard and Ocean Front Walk. There's a public restroom. There's a Mex kid pulling his pud. The kid states: "I was thinking of a Hami Hi girl."

They went through 5000-plus names. They turned up 201 rap sheets. They weeded out unlikelies. They grilled the pure freaks. They print-checked them and gun-checked them. They got diddly-shit.

4/4/66: The L.A. Police Commission gets a mailed note and poem. Said note and poem read thus:

> Did they ever find who snuffed out Stephanie Gorman? Was he of Lago Vista Dr., Beverly Hills? Used to frequent the pool hall in Westwood?

And her name was Stephanie.
She came from Hills Beverly.
A quick roach was he around the house.
I declare, look here, you may find out
(An idea to a mystery)

The detectives worked it. Lago Vista Drive/men named "Roach"/Westwood poolhalls. It wasted man hours. It went nowhere. A cryptographer read the poem. She said it was gobbledygook.

6/20/66: LAPD gets hip to Dave S. Remember—he called West L.A. Station. It was 8/6/65. He said he went by the Gorman pad on 8/5. He looked for Bob Gelff. Bob used to live there.

Dave S. was 21. Dave S. went to Hami. Dave S. got popped for 288 once. Dave S. had a bad-check warrant: extant in Orange County.

6/21/66: Metro cops grill Dave S. He tells his Bob Gelff story. He parked in the Gormans' driveway. He thought he saw someone peek out a window. No one came out. He split.

The story made no sense. Gelff *didn't* live there. Dave S. nixed a polygraph. Dave S. split the interview. Dave S. called back. He said he'd take the poly now.

They set up the test: 7:00 p.m., 6/21/66. Dave S. called up and cancelled. The detectives talked to Bob Gelff.

Shit, we sold the house. The Gormans bought it in '61. The Gormans had it in '65. Shit, Dave *knew* where I lived.

The cops rebraced Dave S. They requested a formal statement. He refused. They arrested him.

They got him a public defender. He refused to talk. They booked him for Murder One.

He spent two days in the shitter. He agreed to a poly. He took the test. He came up clean.

His prints didn't match. He owned no guns. George Iwasaki viewed him. George Iwasaki said nix.

They released Dave S. Orange County grabbed him. Bam—
bad-check warrant extant.

The Gorman job was 11 months old. It was dead-stalled and
fucked.

RICK JACKSON TOLD me about Stephanie. My neck
hairs stood up.

Rick works LAPD Homicide. He's a superb detective and one
of my best friends. We talk long-distance. We prowl crime-
historical L.A. We talk CRIME. We dig the horror. We transmit
chills. We rap logic and moral perspective. We dig crime as social
barometer and buffoonish diversion. My wife says we cackle like
schoolgirls.

Stephanie Lynn Gorman. DR 65-538-991. DOD: 8/5/65.

Rick gave me a synopsis. Details nudged me. A pinprick memory blipped.

It's summer '65. I'm 17. There's a Hollywood newsstand.
There's a girl's picture. It straddles a newspaper fold.

Blip—no more, no less.

Rick said the case went active. It was a fluke. It happened like
this:

It's 2000 now. The older sister's middle-aged. She attends a
party. She meets an LAPD man. She mentions her sister's case.
She *wonders*. She requests a status update.

The man calls Robbery-Homicide. Detective Dave Lambkin
picks up. He works the Rape Special Section. He's a 20-year officer. He doesn't know the Gorman case.

The man shoots the sister's request. Lambkin responds. He
reads the Gorman file. He notes the unknown prints. He sends
them to the FBI.

The Feds run them through the CODUS computer. They get
a single-print match.

The kickback supplies a name. The man was young *then* and
old *now*. He's now a suspect.

That blip. That picture. A slight expansion—her pageboy hairdo.

Rick's synopsis. The horror. The Watts Riot bit. *My* L.A. '65 summer. Stone's throw to *her*.

Show me the file. I need to *see*.

I FLEW OUT. It was December 2000. I booked a room in Beverly Hills. Beverlywood adjoined it. Stone's throw to Hillsboro and Sawyer.

It was cool. L.A. smelled like fresh rain. I ignored it. I conjured up the hot summer of 1965.

I rented a car. I drove to Parker Center. Rick introduced me to Dave Lambkin. He was mid-40s, bald, and fucking bug-eyed intense. He talked fast and articulate. His thoughts scattergunned and coalesced precisely. He said the file ran fourteen boxes. He gave me the suspect update.

Call him Mr. X. Mr. X is sixty-nine *now*. Mr. X was thirty-four *then*. He had a minor rap sheet. *Très* that—one receiving stolen goods bounce, à la '71.

Hence: prints on file. Hence: the CODUS match. Hence: major suspect status.

No Gorman link. That's good. It jukes the random-sex factor. Ed Gorman's dead now. The mother and sister don't know X-Man. They've wracked their memories.

So:

We're running background checks. We're feeling positive. We've placed him in West L.A. then. We've surveilled him. We've got his prints on a coffee cup. We snatched it at a diner.

We need more facts. They're armament. They'll fuel the search warrant. They'll define the approach.

Show me the file. Show me the pictures first.

We walked to the Rape Special cubicle. I saw the boxes and binders. I saw a taped-on wall tableau. That memory blip blew out full.

The *L.A. Times.* The pic on the fold. The pageboy girl.

Lambkin passed me the pictures. They were faded Koda-chrome. The colors looked sun-bleached. Shades beamed surreal.

There's the patio. There's the bloody towels. The south bed's askew. There's one spent shell.

I clenched up. I knew she'd be next. I wanted to see it. I trusted my motive. I know my eyes would violate.

There—

I couldn't peel her beauty back from the horror. I felt immodest and clinically focused. Her softness merged with the blood.

I CALLED IT quits early. The file boded vast and too detailed. The pictures held me for now.

Dead women own you. Call it blunt and simple. She's Geneva Hilliker Ellroy redux.

I went back to the hotel. I time-traveled. I placed myself in context with that blip.

It was "Freedom Summer." I was seventeen. I was a year and three months older than Stephanie. I lived five miles northeast. I attended Fairfax High School up to mid-March. Fairfax was largely Jewish. I was gentile and fucked up. I craved attention, love, and sex. I did nothing constructive to earn it. I lusted for Jewish girls. I stalked them by bicycle. I pulled anti-Semitic stunts in school. I got my ass kicked. Fairfax kicked me out.

My dad was old and frail. He let me join the army. I hated the army. It scared me shitless. My dad had a second stroke. I faked a nervous breakdown. An army shrink bought it. My dad died 6/4/65. The army kicked me loose.

I bopped back to L.A. I was seventeen and draft-exempt. The army gave me go-home pay. I forged my dad's last three Social Security checks. I had a roll. I got a cheap pad. I got a handbill-passing job. I shoplifted food and booze. I popped pills and smoked weed. I ran 6'3" and 140. Everything frightened me. I read crime books, fantasized, and jacked off. I was a teenage-misanthrope/hybrid-scaredy cat.

I stalked girls. My mode was the all-unilateral monogamous crush. My anti-Jewish stance was a shuck. It was kid iconoclasm. It was a love scrounger's yelp for help. Fairfax High was snotty and rigidly stratified. The Fairfax district bordered Hami Hi's. Hami was equally Jewish. Hami was allegedly more snotty and more stratified. Hami kids were hip, Hami kids disdained geeks, Hami kids rode the cool zeitgeist.

Proximity.

Stephanie was lovely. I did not doubt her good-girl status or sound character. She would have beckoned. I would have stalked her. I would have harbored tender thoughts. Booze might fuel a real approach—T-Bird chased by Clorets. She might reject me flat. She might reject me gently. She might hear me out. I was tall, I had my own pad, I had a murder-vic mom—sometimes the desperate impress.

Not likely. Lovely girls scare desperate boys. Ed Gorman would nab my shit quicksville. He'd kick my goy ass off his porch.

Yeah, I would have stalked her. No, I'd never harm a hair on her head.

THE HOUSE WAS INNOCUOUS. The northeast bed-room light was on. Rick and I staked it out.

Daytime crime, nighttime surveillance. We both loved crime locations. They spoke to us. They inspired time travel. They juked our talk.

We sat in Rick's car. Holiday lights beamed—Christmas sprays and menorahs. I mentioned a book. I read it circa '65. It was a thriller called *Warrant for X.*

Rick said X-Man looked good. He was at the crime scene. They didn't know when. They *did* know he *did not* know the Gormans. He matched the peeper sketch. He was a Latin-type Caucasian. I speculated. Stephanie fought him. He panicked and shot her. Rick quoted Dave Lambkin. Dave was a sex-crime expert. Dave had this factors-in-place riff.

Would-be killers harbor fantasies. They rarely act them out. Most would-bes never kill. Sometimes factors converge. The right victim appears. The opportunity hits. Stress factors goose the would-be. Family grief, sex abstinence, booze or dope impairment. His switch flips. He acts.

I said that might apply to my mother's case. It's the victim-killer nexus. Specific men kill specific women and kill no more. They bring fantasies to the act. They juxtapose their rage and lust against a female image. Maybe my mother vibed loose prowess. Maybe Stephanie vibed kindness to plunder. The killer killed my mother. He probably hit her and raped her unconscious. Stephanie screamed and fought. She got off the south bed. She disrupted her killer's fantasy.

He killed her. The act traumatized him. He never killed again.

Rick said maybe, maybe not. It didn't vibe intentional snuff. It vibed rape panic and rape escalation. The fuck brought the cord and gun. The gun for threat, the cord for suppression. Most rapes went unreported. Rape as social stigma—1965. Stephanie might be vic 16 or 60. The nexus, the alchemy—something made him kill her. I said her beauty and softness. Bam—his switch drops. He sees outtakes from his shitty life. His stress context implodes. A happy kid dies.

Women as one-way mirrors. Women as Etch-a-Sketch boards. The killer snags one real image and starts to revise. His revisions tap signals. It's sex semaphore. Details get distorted and magnified. It's a funhouse mirror now. It's all in his head. The woman loses proportion. She gains bizarre shapes. She gets dehumanized.

We shitcanned the analysis. We rapped rude and wrathful. We ran a righteous right-wing reverie. The Gorman job was individual forfeit. The Gorman job was moral default. Nothing justified

it. The killer had to pay. His childhood trauma and attendant jus-
tifications bought him no mercy chits. Fuck the cocksucker
dead —

I DUG INTO the file. I met Dave Lambkin's partner, Tim
Marcia. He complemented Lambkin. He was big and athletic.
He walked with a roll. He talked less than Lambkin. He weighed
his words and zoomed to the point.

We dug binders out. I read the autopsy report and first summary report. I rechecked the crime-scene shots. I theorized. I
indulged possible wishful thinking.

No vaginal or rectal hurt. No foreign fluid types. Virgin and
nonvirgin assessments. No semen or Jergens cream inside her.
Vaginal rupture by natural cause.

Doc Kade was dead. Koivu was dead. Ditto Munkres and
Buckles. Byron was in a rest home. He was senescent. There was
no one to clarify.

My sense: no penetration. The killer didn't rape Stephanie.

Tim Marcia agreed. She was young and tight internally. She
was struggling. Her legs were unbound. There's no Jergens on
bedspreads/no Jergens floor drip. There's the east-bed semen
stain. Maybe it's a forced oral cop. Maybe the killer jerked off.

I asked about vault evidence. I mentioned bedspread DNA.
Marcia said a cop tossed it. It was an outrage. Some cop on a
spring-cleaning kick.

I read reports. I skimmed mug shots. I checked the peeper
sketch. Dave Lambkin did a cutout trick. He took a side-view mug
shot of Mr. X. He placed it against the side-view sketch. They
dovetailed exact.

Mr. X looked good for it. They couldn't brace him yet. They
ached for it. Vengeance beckoned. Knock, knock — come here,
motherfucker.

I read the file. I hobnobbed with the Shoe-Tree and Remorse-

September 2002: Detectives Dave Lambkin, Tim Marcia, and Rick Jackson stand in front of the old Gorman home. *(Todd Hido/Edge)*

ful Rapists. I read the obscene-phone-call log. I remembered *my* calls to strange girls. I tried to come off as a kool kat. The girls laughed and made me hang up.

I found the San Diego notes. I found the boy's Christmas card. I read *The Collector* that summer. It turned me on. The captive woman was a redhead. My mother was a redhead. Samantha

Eggar was a redhead. She played the captive in the film. I saw it during the Watts Riot. It played in Beverly Hills—stone's throw to Hillsboro and Sawyer.

Tim Marcia and I discussed a wild card. The Gorman job—consensual sex goes blooey.

Pros and cons. Coronado/the rope trick/the *Collector* connection. A secret boyfriend unnamed. The gun and rope as book-movie props. The boy's shaky psyche. Chaste kicks and Stephanie's imposed limits.

It flew for ten seconds. It flew apart then.

Why use the sister's bedroom? Stephanie's room was out back. Mom and Dad parked in the rear. They're home—oops—let's split.

And:

The torn lip/the punch there/the head bump/the drag burns/ the cord by the front door.

Dave ran the file by a Fed profiler. He posited a front-door approach. The killer knocks. Stephanie answers. It's her last look at daylight.

I skimmed the file. I read the Georgia Street Juvie reports. *I* spent a night at Georgia Street. It was August '65. I shoplifted some ice cream. LAPD popped me.

It was scary. Tough kids made fun of me. A friend's dad got me out. He took me to County Probation. I was too old to adopt. Somebody signed a paper. It made me an "emancipated juvenile."

The reports detailed a world wild and wimpy. It's all middle-class Jewish freaks. Two names jumped out. I knew one guy at John Burroughs Junior High School. I smoked weed with another guy. He knew my pal Craig Minear. Craig crashed his 2-seater plane. He died November '70.

I read the file backwards and forwards. I became friends with Dave and Tim. We yukked at phone-call outtakes and picaresque sex freaks. We discussed the rape and no-rape angles. We lauded and mourned Stephanie.

Tim and I drove to Hami. We checked old yearbooks and found Stephanie. She's sleek in her Phi Delt sweater. Her page-boy's down and swept by barrettes. Her expression shifts picture to picture. She's a pensive kid. She tries to show happiness. She doesn't always succeed.

I told Tim that I loved her to death. He said he did, too.

THE INVESTIGATION BUILT. Dave and Tim built that warrant for X.

They had his CII#, FBI#, LAPD arrest stats. The Auto-Track computer system shot them ten prior addresses. They had his wife's and ex-wife's stats. He married the ex in '62. *He lived in West L.A. in '65.* They had stats on his kids and kid brother. The "Family Index" ran 100 pages. It tallied prior addresses and driving records. It listed other people living at old addresses. Mr. X had a son and a daughter. The son was clean. The daughter had busts: dope/theft/prostitution.

The case hinged on the print. The case would build off X-Man's denial. No, I wasn't in that house. Bullshit, you *were*.

LAPD print-solved a '63 case. It went to court four years back. Hollywood Division/fall '63. Male killer/female vic.

They ran unknown prints. They utilized CODUS. They got a match. The man lived in Minnesota. He denied his presence in the pad. He claimed navy duty then. Navy records disproved it. A jury convicted him.

The print was *it*. The confrontation would goose a reaction. We'll make sure his wife is gone. We'll brace him alone. We'll hook him in slow. We'll bring a search warrant.

Dave was writing the warrant now. It was detailed and legalistic. They were looking for this:

Personal records. Vehicle records—late '50s to late '60s. Firearms and ammo. Docs describing X-Man's size on 8/5/65. Photos of X-Man in a blue uniform. Mason cord or photos of X-Man with same. Docs establishing X-Man's whereabouts on

8/5/65. Docs establishing connections to the Gorman family. Photos, film, or video depicting violence against women. Pornography depicting women posed in restraints.

The approach ran tripartite. The print/the warrant search/ X-Man's reaction and/or denial. George Iwasaki was dead. Age would alter X-Man's looks. Eyeball wits were out.

Dave and Tim were swamped. Breaking jobs swarmed their Gorman commitment. Dave worked the warrant part-time. Other work diverted him. He buzzed through Rape Special. He passed the wall tableau. He always said, "Sorry, Stephanie."

I STUCK AROUND L.A. I cruised the Gorman house a.m. and p.m. I read the file. I explored Dave S.'s jive story and exemption. I thought about Stephanie. I brought flowers to her grave. I pondered the "Laura" syndrome.

The book and movie define it. Homicide cops dig the gestalt. The title woman is lovely and perplexing. She's a murder vic. A cop works her case. Laura's portrait seduces him. She turns up alive. The vic is someone else. Laura and the cop fall in love.

It's ridiculous wish fulfillment. It negates the hold of the dead. They inhabit your blank spaces. They work magic there. They freeze time. They render our short time spans boldly precious. They build alternative memory. Their public history becomes your private reserve. They induce a mix of vindictiveness and compassion. They enforce moral resolve. They teach you to love with a softer touch and fear and revere your obsessions.

My obsessions were born in 1958. "Son, your mother's been killed" and the upshot. She was my first untouchable crush. Stephanie was a daughter or a prom date. She's dancing out of a shroud. I don't know her. *I can feel her.* She's twirling. She's showing off her prom gown. I can smell her corsage.

DAVE AND TIM built the warrant. They planned their questions and signals. They brought Orange County cops in. Two agencies conferred. A judge signed the warrant. X-Man's ex lived in Riverside County. They planned a dual approach. Dave and Tim would brace X-Man. Two cops would brace the ex. She was with X-Man in '65. She might know some stuff.

The date was set: 1/23/01.

I went home. My wife and I talked about Stephanie and digressed ourselves hoarse. I reveled in Helen's brilliance and flesh-and-blood *life*.

We rented *Bye Bye Birdie*. We scanned the crowd scenes. We couldn't spot Stephanie. Rick and I talked long-distance. Rick was happy. LAPD was forming a Cold Case Squad. It was all oldies/24-7. Rick, Dave, and Tim were set to start.

Fuck happy. Rick was thrilled. Time travel unlimited.

I rented *Pollyanna*. I saw Stephanie.

She was ten or eleven. She stood on a bandstand stage right. Hayley Mills sang "America the Beautiful." A line of girls flanked her. They all wore the Stars and Stripes.

There's Stephanie—alive and in color. She's a child on the safe side of sex. Her eyes dart. The moment flusters her. Her hair was lighter then. She's got hazel-brown eyes like me.

I hit Rewind and Fast Forward. I did it *x*-dozen times. I watched her. I caught every breath. I filled some blank spaces up.

THE BRACE WENT DOWN. It clicked like clockwork.

Two units in place. Bam—X-Man's wife leaves early. Dave and Tim walk up.

They're nervous. They've got butterflies like Godzilla. They've got badges and IDs out. They knock on the door. X-Man opens up.

He's friendly. He's not flustered. They mention an old murder. He doesn't clench up.

He invites them in. They all sit down. He appears befuddled—old murder, huh?

Dave and Tim start to explain. X-Man cuts them off.

That 16-year-old girl, right? I remember that. I was across the street. I was at a friend's house.

The sister ran over. My friend was a doctor. He wasn't in then. I ran over to help. I saw the body. The cops came. The cops shooed me out.

Oh, fuck—

He came off credible. He came off true. He smiled. He betrayed no nerves. The boom didn't drop.

Dave quizzed him. X-Man responded. The doc and wife— alive and well. Yeah, we're still in touch.

There's the boom. It fell on *you*. Oh shit, we're fuck—

They schmoozed up X-Man. His credibility held. They said good-bye and walked out.

They found the doctor. They braced him. They braced his wife concurrent. They backed X-Man up.

Heartbreaker/square one again/fluke fingerprint/months trashed and fucked.

Dave called and told me. He described "the worst day of my life." I reran *Pollyanna*. I cued Stephanie up.

It's over. It's not over. It's been a year plus. Closure is nonsense. Nothing this bad ever ends. The killer is crucial and irrelevant. He knew Stephanie for ten minutes. He never loved her. His memories are brutal and suspect.

Baby, who were you? How would you grow and who would you love? Did you know you'd touch driven men and teach them?

You've got torchbearers. Three detectives and one chronicler. We want to know you. It's a pursuit. It's a likelier outcome than justice.

We're spinning our wheels. It doesn't matter. We get glimpses. You're twirling in your prom gown. Color us devoted. Color you gone.

Grave Doubt

1.

HOUSTON PD/DISTRICT 6/BEAT 6870.

DATE: 5/13/81.

TIME: 9:30 P.M.

LOCATION: 8935 NORTH FREEWAY.

PREMISES: SAFEWAY PARKING LOT.

CRIME: CAPITAL MURDER.

VICTIM: BOBBY GRANT LAMBERT/WHITE MALE/53.

SUSPECT: GARY GRAHAM/BLACK MALE/17.

INCIDENT # 035207084.

The crime scene:

The Safeway lot. Rectangular. Sixty yards deep.

Night lights. Parking lanes and slots.

A fence behind the store. Small homes adjacent. Strip malls moving north.

A frontage road. Parking-lot access. A freeway adjacent.

The beat: low-shelf. Urban blight ascendant.

Motels. Gas stations. A low-end black demographic.

Eyewits state:

The victim enters the store. The victim walks the aisles. The victim grabs items.

Three packs of lunch meat, bread, cheese, milk, cookies, Ritz crackers, onions, gloves, garbage bags, a carton of Raleigh cigarettes, a six-pack of V-8.

A cashier totals the items. The victim pays with a C-note.

The victim exits the store.

He walks twenty feet. A black male walks up behind him.

Witness Bernadine Skillern observes.

She sits in her car. Two kids sit with her. Her daughter's in the store.

The black male accosts the victim.

He grabs his back pockets. The victim reacts.

He pulls away. He turns.

The black male grabs his collar. The black male puts a gun to his head.

Witness Skillern observes.

She fears a shooting. She tries to deter it. She leans on her horn.

The black male turns. Witness Skillern sees his face. The victim breaks free.

Witness Skillern hears a "pop" noise. The victim drops his grocery bag. The black male walks away.

Other wits observe. Their names:

Daniel Grady/white male/age 35. Wilma Amos/black female/age 32. Sherian Etuk/black female/age 29.

The victim staggers. The victim weaves to the store.

Witness Skillern starts her car. The victim falls in the doorway.

Witness Skillern tails the black male. He's in her headlights. He starts to run.

He runs around the store. Witness Skillern's kids scream. Witness Skillern turns back.

Store employees call the cops. An ambulance shows. Paramedics examine the victim.

He's DOA.

PATROL UNITS SHOWED. Homicide showed.

For Houston PD: Detectives W. W. Owen and J. W. Ellis.

They checked the grocery bag. They checked the gunshot wound.

Small caliber. The entry point: near the sternal notch.

They check the victim's clothes. They found:

One comb. Two pencils. A lighter. Best Western motel matches. A key for room 208.

The vic's driver's license. Issued for Oregon State.

Coins: $2.07. Sixty hundred-dollar bills.

A botched heist. The killer got chump change. The killer missed six grand.

A tech crew arrived.

Techs shot the body. Techs shot the crime scene. Morgue men removed the body.

Patrol cops checked the lot. They found the vic's van. They impounded it.

Owen and Ellis braced the wits.

Witness Skillern described the incident. Witness Skillern described the killer:

A black male. 18 to 20. 5'9" to 6'.

Slim build. Slim face, clean-shaven. Close-cut Afro. White jacket/black slacks.

Witness Grady described the incident. Witness Grady described the killer:

A black male. Tall, slim, young. White sport coat. Small-caliber pistol.

Witness Amos went home. Witness Amos phoned Homicide.

She described the incident. She described the killer:

A black male. In his twenties. Short dark hair, clean-shaven. Black slacks/white coat.

Witness Etuk described the incident.

She's working a check stand. She hears a "pop!" outside.

She looks out the window. She sees a black male.

He wears a white blazer. He wears black slacks. The window glass blurs his face.

He backs off from the victim. He backs out of sight.

Owen and Ellis hit the Best Western.

They talked to a desk clerk. They talked to a barmaid. They talked to a guard.

Room 208: registered to Ronald M. Allen.

He was from Burbank, California. He checked out at 9:05 p.m.

Owen and Ellis checked the room. They found:

Paper slips. Names and phone numbers. Cleaning receipts for Bobby G. Lambert.

One ashtray. Cigarette butts.

Two brands. Raleigh, one other.

Owen and Ellis checked the switchboard. "Allen" made 16 toll calls.

They wrote down the numbers. They drove to the morgue. They gave the numbers to a coroner's detective.

The detective called them. He called five area codes. He hit Mrs. Ron Allen.

She said Ron split Houston. He was in Vegas now. Bobby Lambert shared his Houston motel room.

Bobby had Houston business. She didn't know what. Bobby left his wife recently.

The detective called around. The detective traced Bobby's van. The detective snagged a cop in Pima County, Arizona.

The cop said he couldn't talk now. The cop said he'd call Homicide.

Owen and Ellis drove to Homicide. The cop called them.

He said he checked Lambert out. He queried a dope line. He hit positive. Lambert was dirty.

Ellis requested more data. The cop said he'd call back.

Another cop called back. He said:

Lambert was dealing. He got popped on 8/14/80.

Oklahoma City.

Lambert flies dope in. Lambert gets nabbed. Lambert's under indictment.

Some coke. 20,000 Quaaludes.

Owen and Ellis worked all night. Detective D. W. Autrey assisted.

He drove to the impound. He checked Lambert's van.

He found:

Marijuana.

Three shotguns.

One New Mexico driver's license. One Canadian driver's license. One radio operator's license. One insurance card. One draft card.

Made out to:

Billy Francis Smith — DOB 3/1/30.

Plus:

Court docket papers. Oklahoma District Court. A bail receipt for Bobby G. Lambert.

THE AUTOPSY RAN pro forma. Ditto the forensics.

The vic died from gunshot trauma. He ate one .22 slug.

The DEA called Owen and Ellis. They laid out Bobby G.

Bobby was a dealer. Bobby was an ex–carny man.

Bobby was a con man. Bobby was a sleaze.

Bobby loved to gamble. Bobby loved Vegas. Bobby hung with a cat named Ron Allen.

Ron was a gambler. Ron was a pool shark. Ron and Bobby meant grief.

Owen and Ellis hit the Safeway. They found another eyewit.

His name was Ronald Hubbard. He worked at Safeway. He offered this story:

He was shagging carts. He saw a man outside. The man hid his face.

Hubbard walked toward the store. Hubbard heard a shot. Hubbard saw the man holding a gun.

Hubbard described the man:

Black. Early 20s. 5'5", 120–130. Short Afro, clean-shaven. White blazer, black slacks.

Owen and Ellis called Witness Skillern. Ms. Skillern came to Homicide. Ms. Skillern worked up a composite.

Autrey and Detective Rascoe assisted.

Ms. Skillern chose feature strips. Ms. Skillern built a face.

Facial tone: F-1-1. Nose: N-9-2. Lips: L-3-1. Eyes: E-58-2. Chin: C-26-2. Hair: H-131-2.

Autrey worked the composite. Owens and Ellis worked Lambert.

They braced the wife. They braced the DEA. They braced the Pima County cops.

They got bland shit.

Lambert was a hustler. Lambert was a sleaze. Lambert shot pool in Houston.

It vibed inconsequential. The murder vibed heist.

Autrey got a call.

The caller's name was Wilma Mukes. She offered this story:

Her sister's name was Florence McDonald. Ms. McDonald went to Safeway. Their sons tagged along.

Said sons:

James Mukes/black male/age 7. Alfonzo McDonald/black male/age 10. Leodis Wilkerson/black male/age 12.

Ms. McDonald goes in the store. The boys sit in the car. The boys see the shooting.

They know the shooter. They've seen him before. He hangs near their pad.

Autrey braced Ms. McDonald. She offered this story:

The boys saw the shooting. The boys saw the shooter. The boys saw him one day later.

He stood across the street. He stood by Judy Brown's pad.

James Mukes saw him. James yelled at Leodis and Alfonzo. James yelled, "There's the man that did the shooting."

The man ran off. The boys told Ms. McDonald.

Autrey braced Judy Brown. She offered this story:

The man sounds like Curly Scott. Curly knocked up her daughter.

She had her baby. Curly came around less.

Curly was tall and skinny. Curly was clean-shaven. Curly lived at 7339 Phillips.

Autrey checked Curly out. Detective D. W. Cook assisted.

They learned:

Curly had priors. Curly had bond forfeits. Curly had warrants extant.

Curly had four recent addresses. The Phillips pad plus three.

Autrey and Cook looked for Curly. Autrey and Cook tapped out.

Owen and Ellis rigged a photo spread.

They laid in a Curly Scott mug shot. They laid in four random males.

Witness Hubbard viewed the spread. He did not see the shooter. Witness Hubbard viewed Witness Skillern's composite. He said it resembled the dude.

Witness Amos viewed the spread. She did not see the shooter.

Witness Skillern viewed the spread. She did not see the shooter.

Witness Etuk viewed the spread. She did not see the shooter.

Owen and Ellis looked for Witness Grady. Owen and Ellis tapped out.

The Lambert job was one week old. The Lambert job was dead.

Owen and Ellis got a call. A wrecker-driver offered this story:

It's 5/13. It's 10:00 p.m. He's out in his truck.

He passes Stuebner Air Line and Gulf Bank. He's close to Safeway. He spots two black males in a Plymouth.

They look "suspicious." He tails them. He nails their license plate.

The black males see the truck. The black males speed up. The black males vanish.

Owen and Ellis traced the Plymouth. The owner: one Linda Ann Thomas.

Owen and Ellis braced Ms. Thomas. She offered this story:

Her son drove the car. She never did. She supplied her son's stats.

Reginald Thomas/black male/DOB 4/6/63.

Reginald Thomas called Homicide. He offered this story:

He shopped at Safeway. His girlfriend lived close. He bought their babies' diapers there.

Owen and Ellis braced Thomas. Owen and Ellis rebraced Ms. Thomas.

Thomas stated:

He went out that night. He picked up his girlfriend. He arrived at 7:30 or 8:00.

They split. They parked off Stuebner Air Line. A truck pulled up. The driver killed his lights.

Thomas freaked. Thomas drove his girlfriend home. They arrived around 10:00.

Thomas viewed the composite. Thomas did not know the man.

Ms. Thomas said she had two more sons. Their names: Earnest and Melvin.

Melvin was in jail. The charge was Murder.

OWEN AND ELLIS made calls. Cook and Autrey ran point.

Melvin Thomas: Case 24251061.

A gunshot murder. A .22 pistol. No weapon received.

"Another suspect" tossed it. Location unknown.

Cook and Autrey called the lab. The lab ran tests.

The Thomas slug. The Lambert slug. Let's compare.

No go.

The Thomas slug was scarred. The comparison failed.

Owen and Autrey called Juvie Probation. They learned:

Melvin Thomas was popped on 5/12. Melvin Thomas did not kill Bobby Lambert.

Cook and Autrey rehit Safeway. The manager viewed the composite.

He stated:

It looked like a shoplifter. He popped him some months back. He was about 19. He was 5'10" to 6'. He was very thin.

The manager checked his records. The manager tapped out.

No file notes. No complaint report.

Cook and Autrey ran computer checks. Cook and Autrey tapped out.

No complaint listing. No numbers extant.

The Lambert job was twelve days old. The Lambert job was dead.

ROBBERY CALLED HOMICIDE. Detective J. W. Whiteley called Autrey.

Whiteley popped a kid. He resembled the composite. He packed a .22.

He was seventeen. His name was Gary Graham.

Graham was a heist guy. Graham went on a heist spree. Graham used various weapons.

His spree dates: 5/14 to 5/20.

They popped Graham on 5/20. They ran lineups. The heist vics ID'd Graham.

Graham was a heist guy. Graham was a rape-o. They popped him this way:

Gary Graham in 2002. He asked his supporters to show up at his prison "with rifles, shotguns, AK-47s, and whatever else is necessary to protect our rights." *(Copyright © Houston Chronicle)*

5/20/81. About 3:00 a.m. A cabbie stops for gas.

She's female. She's in her cab. She's 57 years old.

She pumps gas. Gary Graham walks up.

He says his car died. He needs a ride. The woman says okay.

Graham gets in the cab. They drive to the Tidwell exit.

Graham redirects her. They drive to an empty apartment complex.

Graham pulls a gun. Graham robs the woman. Graham gets fifteen dollars.

He's pissed. He needs six yards. He tells her he's "going to make it" with her.

She says she's too old. Graham hits her. Graham tells her not to lie.

They enter the complex. They enter a vacant unit. Graham makes the woman disrobe.

He tells her he's going to "fuck her in the ears and the eyes and everyplace else."

Graham brandishes the gun.

Graham rapes the woman.

Graham attempts anal rape. Graham fails to penetrate.

The woman fears death. The complex is empty. Her body will rot unfound.

She talks to Graham. She describes her apartment.

It's comfortable. It's warm. She might find more money.

Graham buys it. They drive to her pad.

They enter. Graham says he's got nothing to lose. He don't plan to get caught. He'll burn if he does.

Graham grabs jewelry. Graham grabs other items. His movement and balance are off.

He tells the woman to disrobe. The woman tells him to go first.

Graham disrobes. Graham gets in bed.

Graham has the gun. Graham tells the woman to "suck him."

The woman starts to disrobe. Graham starts to fall asleep.

The woman waits. Graham falls asleep. The woman grabs his gun, his clothes, and her money.

She weighs killing Graham. She decides not to. She locks Graham in her pad.

She walks to the manager's pad. The manager calls Houston PD.

Graham pulled twelve known heists. His spree ran seven days. He used partners sometimes.

His partners: at large. His .22: in the property room.

Autrey retrieved it. The lab ran tests.

The lab concluded:

It was NOT the Lambert weapon.

The Homicide team braced Graham. He denied the Lambert snuff.

He offered no alibi. He said he might have been with a woman.

He didn't know her name. He couldn't peg a location.

Owen and Ellis rigged a photo spread.

They laid in Gary Graham's photo. They laid in four other black males.

Witness Skillern viewed the spread. She said the Graham pic resembled the shooter.

But:

The shooter was darker. The shooter's face was thinner.

Inconclusive. A nonbinding ID.

Owen and Ellis propose a lineup. Ms. Skillern agrees.

9:00 P.M. 5/27/81.

The show-up room/Houston PD.

Five black males. Jail whites. Gary Graham in slot 3.

One-way glass. Wits and cops behind it. The black males under lights.

Witness Amos is sick. Witness Amos is absent.

Witness Hubbard views the lineup. Witness Hubbard declines to ID.

He stresses:

He never saw the shooter's face. The shooter hid his face.

Witness Skillern views the lineup. Witness Skillern ID's Gary Graham.

Owen drives Ms. Skillern home. Ms. Skillern states:

She recognized Graham from his photo. The photo looked like the shooter.

But:

The man's skin was too light.

But:

She saw the live lineup. She saw the live man.

NOW she was sure.

OWEN AND ELLIS braced an assistant D.A. The D.A.'s Office filed.

ARRESTED AND CHARGED: CAPITAL MURDER/182ND DISTRICT COURT/CAUSE 3353780.

GARY GRAHAM/HPD # 337682.

2.

The trial. Judge Rick Trevathan presiding.

Carl Hobbs for Harris County. Ron Mock and Chester Thornton for Graham.

The County had no confession. The County had no evidence. The County had a one-witness case.

The judge appointed Mock. Mock was a two-year lawyer. Thornton was three.

Thornton asked for the job. Thornton knew Graham. Thornton handled a previous beef.

Mock was first-chair counsel. Thornton was backup. Both men were black.

The County gave Mock a budget. For "investigation and research."

$500.

Mock hired a PI. Merv West charged $30 an hour.

Mock talked to Graham. Graham copped to the heist spree.

Graham copped to booze and dope habits. Graham offered an alibi: "I was high somewhere."

Thornton knew Graham. Thornton knew his story.

Graham had six siblings. Six kids cross-hatched. Different parent combos.

Graham's folks split up. Graham's dad did heist time. Graham split the 7th grade.

Graham roamed Houston. Graham caused trouble. Graham bunked with relatives. Graham fathered kids at thirteen and fifteen.

Mock thought Graham was guilty. Thornton wasn't sure.

They got the heist-spree stats. The spree stats resembled the snuff stats.

Mock issued orders. Mock told Thornton to work the family end.

Get some character wits. Lube the penalty phase.

Graham gave Mock some names. Potential alibi wits. Mock gave the names to Merv West.

West did not contact them. West sniffed the vibe: Mock thinks Graham did it.

West talked to some cops. They thought Graham did it. West assimilated their vibe.

He's guilty.

West braced Sherian Etuk. West braced Daniel Grady. They did not ID Graham.

West checked the Safeway lot. West checked the night lights. West concluded:

Witness Skillern would be hard-pressed to see the shooter's face. The distance and lighting would impinge on her.

West checked out the victim. A cop supplied rumors.

Lambert was a con man. Lambert might have been queer.

West called some Graham family members. West glommed some anecdotes. West checked Graham's juvie record.

West rode the gestalt. He's guilty.

West worked with Mock before. West knew Mock's style.

Mock had clients presumed pure. Mock had clients presumed bad. Mock did not waste PI time on the bads.

Mock strategized. Mock consulted Thornton. They concurred:

The spree stats screwed Graham. Exclude them at the guilt phase. Eschew an alibi defense.

The judge might balk. The judge might allow spree data.

Exclude Graham's gun. Exclude the negative test.

It would bring in the heists. It would prejudice jurors.

Mock thought he could win.

Graham was a juvie. The case lacked death-penalty intent.

The trial ran a week.

Mock got the heists excluded.

Wilma Amos testified. She said she saw the victim inside the store.

They spoke. They discussed gloves.

Ms. Amos saw another man. The man wore dark pants and a white jacket. The man looked at the victim.

Ms. Amos stood in a check-stand line. The "other man" left the store.

Ms. Amos paid for her items. Ms. Amos walked out.

She heard a horn. She saw the victim and the "other man" "tusseling."

The "other man" shot the victim. The "other man" walked away.

The night lights were good.

But:

She could not ID the "other man."

Daniel Grady testified. He said his wife went shopping. He sat in his car.

The victim left the store. A black male approached him. The black male grabbed the victim's back pockets.

The victim dropped his groceries. The victim pulled away. The black male pulled a gun. The black male shot him.

Grady saw the black male's face. Grady could not ID him.

Bernadine Skillern testified. She said she sat in her car. Two kids were with her.

The lot lights were good. She could see people. She could recognize them.

A black male approached the victim. The black male was Gary Graham.

A tussle occurred.

Ms. Skillern honked her horn.

Graham turned. Graham looked straight at her.

Graham shot the victim. Graham fast-walked away.

Ms. Skillern kicked her engine. Ms. Skillern kicked her lights. Ms. Skillern tailed Graham.

Graham turned. Graham looked back. Graham started to run.

The kids started to scream. Ms. Skillern stopped her pursuit.

Mock did not challenge Amos and Grady. Mock did not impugn their non-IDs. Mock did not want to risk equivocal answers.

Mock cross-examined Skillern. Mock did not impugn her. Mock referred to Gary Graham as the killer.

Trial pages 360–361. Mock to Skillern:

"According to your testimony, Mr. Lambert would have been to the defendant's left at the time they first had an encounter?"

Trial page 375. Mock to Skillern:

"All right, so you had seen the defendant's right side when you first approached him?"

Trial page 378. Mock to Skillern:

"I think your testimony was that as you blew your horn, he turned his head toward you for a split second?"

Skillern to Mock: "Meaning Mr. Graham?"

Mock to Skillern: "Yes, ma'am."

The trial wound down. Two alibi wits volunteered.

Loraine Johnson. Jo Carolyn Johnson. Graham's cousins.

They knew Gary got popped. They knew in May. They offered alibis in October.

They went to the courthouse. They found Ron Mock. They offered this story:

Gary was innocent. Gary went to a party on 5/13.

The party occurred in an alley. Loraine had a toothache. Cousin William's birthday was 5/15. That's why they knew the date.

The party was informal. The party went late. William was there. Five women showed.

Gary arrived before 6:00. Gary stayed through 1:00 a.m.

Gary left one time only. Gary and William walked to a liquor store.

It was six blocks away. They bought some liquor. They walked back.

Mock disdained the story. Mock shined on the wits.

Mock said Gary would be found guilty. Mock said Gary *was* guilty. Mock said he'd try to save Gary's life.

Mock wanted penalty wits. Mock wanted to build mitigation.

The trial ended. The jury adjourned. The verdict was GUILTY.

THE PENALTY PHASE. Pro–Gary Graham:

Graham's stepfather testifies. He states:

Gary was nice to him. Gary visits his mother. Gary mows the yard. Gary cleans and helps his mother.

Gary cares for his mother. Gary is not violent. Gary tries to provide for his kids.

Graham's grandmother testifies. She states:

Gary stays with her sometimes. Gary's mother has a nervous condition.

Gary never gives her trouble. Gary loves the Lord. Gary has never been violent.

The County presents its case. The heist spree explicates.

Robbery. Thirteen counts. Eyewit IDs.

The dates: 5/14–5/20/81.

5:30 p.m. 5/14/81:

Graham robs a man. Graham employs an accomplice. Graham employs a Magnum revolver.

Graham steals the man's briefcase. Graham steals the man's car.

9:00 p.m. 5/14/81:

Graham hits a car wash. Graham displays a revolver. Graham robs two women.

He calls them "bitch." He steals their Cadillac. He leaves the car he drove up.

10:00 p.m. 5/14/81:

Graham employs the Cadillac. Graham employs an accomplice.

They hit a Stop & Go lot. They jump in a van. They accost two men. They demand their watches and money.

Graham pulls a gun. Graham fires it. Graham nails a man in the neck.

The bullet hits the man's larynx. The man survives.

Graham steals the van. The accomplice escapes in the Cadillac.

4:30 p.m. 5/15/81:

Graham hits a Woolco parking lot. Graham approaches a man. Graham asks for a ride.

The man agrees. The man drives him to a Jack in the Box. Graham says it's the wrong one.

The man pulls out. Graham pulls a shotgun. Graham steals the man's van.

6:30 p.m. 5/15/81:

Graham hits a parking lot. Graham sees a man in a Cadillac. Graham asks him to jump-start his van.

The man agrees. The man prepares his battery.

Graham pulls a shotgun. Graham herds him into the van. Graham calls him a "motherfucker." Graham threatens to blow him away.

Graham steals his money and checkbook. Graham steals his Cadillac.

8:30 p.m. 5/15/81:

Graham drives the Cadillac to a nightclub. Graham approaches a man outside.

Graham pulls a shotgun. Graham steals the man's toolbox and keys.

The man reports the heist. The man enters the club. The man exits at midnight. He's with a woman.

12:00 midnight. 5/16/81:

Graham enters the parking lot. Graham has an accomplice.

They attempt a heist. Graham pulls a shotgun.

The man has no swag. Graham and the accomplice disperse.

1:00 a.m. 5/16/81:

The Caddy runs out of gas. Graham pushes it. An accomplice assists.

They push it to a gas station. A man and woman assist.

The accomplice pulls a shotgun. Graham and the accomplice try to steal the man's van.

The man resists. The accomplice shoots him in the leg. Graham and the accomplice steal the van. The man is dragged 50 feet.

5/16/81:

A family's car breaks down. They stand out on a highway.

Graham pulls up. He has an accomplice.

They offer help. They give the father a ride.

Graham pulls a shotgun. Graham tells the man he's going to kill him. Graham aims the shotgun and fires.

The man knocks the barrel down. Graham shoots him in the leg.

Graham steals his necklace, watch, and money. Graham tells him they're going back to kill his family. Graham throws him out of the car.

11:00 p.m. 5/18/81:

Graham hits a parking lot. He employs an accomplice. They accost a man in a parked car.

Graham pulls a pistol. Graham opens the passenger door. The accomplice opens the driver's-side door.

They rob the man. They steal his billfold and watch. They steal his car.

12:00 midnight. 5/19/81:

Graham hits a parking lot. Graham employs an accomplice.

Three people flank two cars. Two men, one woman. Graham and the accomplice approach.

Graham has a pistol. The accomplice has a shotgun.

They search the people.

Graham says, "You son of a bitch, motherfucker, give me your shit."

Graham hits a man with his gun. Graham cocks the gun. Graham puts the gun to the man's mouth. Graham demands his watch, ring, and wallet.

Graham touches the woman's breasts. Graham steals her wedding ring.

Evening. 5/19/81:

Graham hits a parking garage. Graham asks a man for directions.

Graham pulls a revolver. Graham steals the man's wallet.

Graham gets in the man's car. Graham makes the man drive around the garage. Graham tells the man that he's killed six people.

5/19/81:

Graham hits a parking lot. Graham approaches a woman. Graham offers to buy her car.

The woman says no. Graham says he's got a gun. Graham demands her car keys. Graham steals her car.

Nine victims testified. Nine wits described Graham's actions.

A Youth Council worker testified. She said she knew Graham. She knew his reputation.

His reputation was bad.

The penalty phase concluded. The jury voted Death.

GRAHAM WENT TO death row. Graham copped to ten heist counts. Graham got twenty years per.

Judge Trevathan appoints appellate counsel. He files Graham's automatic appeal.

Rejected/Court of Criminal Appeals/6-12-84.

7/13/87: Graham's lawyers file State Habeas Corpus. Rejected/2-19-88.

2/23/88: Graham's lawyers file Federal Habeas. Rejected/2-24-88.

8/31/88: The Fifth Circuit Court of Appeals affirms the rejec-

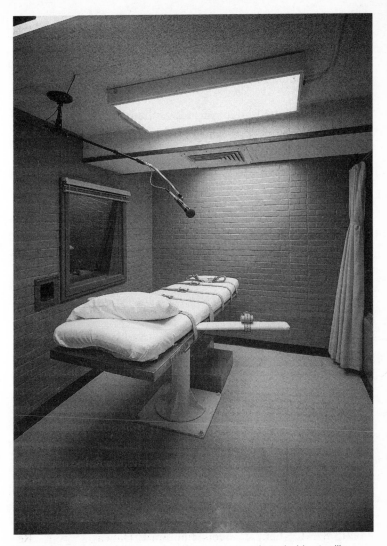

The lethal injection room at the Texas state prison in Huntsville.
(Copyright © Guy Koppenburg, 2003)

tion. Said court issues a stay of execution pending two Supreme Court decisions.

7/3/89: The Supreme Court vacates the Fifth Circuit's judgment. It remands Graham's case to the Fifth Circuit Court of Appeals.

3/7/90: The Fifth Circuit vacates Graham's death sentence.

1/3/92: The Fifth Circuit reverses the previous decision. It affirms the denial of Habeas relief. The Supreme Court affirms the judgment—1/25/93.

4/20/93: Graham refiles State Habeas.

4/27/93: The Court of Criminal Appeals denies relief.

4/28/93: Governor Richards grants a stay of execution. The State District Court resets the date: 6/2/93.

4/28/93: Graham's lawyers file a Writ of Certiorari.

5/24/93: The Supreme Court denies said writ.

6/2/93: The Court of Criminal Appeals stays Graham's execution pending a Supreme Court decision.

Said decision goes down. The Trial Court sets a new date: 8/17/93.

7/21/93: Graham files a civil suit. The suit requests a Board of Pardons hearing. The hearing is scheduled for 8/10/93.

The hearing occurs. The Board of Pardons files an appeal notice. Graham's execution is stayed.

4/20/94: The Court of Criminal Appeals voids said stay.

The process continued. The process attenuated.

Graham got new lawyers. They filed new writs.

They stressed the alleged incompetence of Graham's trial counsel. They stressed the sole eyewit. They stressed the contradicting eyewits. They stressed the alibi wits.

Briefs/writs/motions/hearings/appeals.

Lethal injections scheduled and postponed.

Publicity. Graham—pro and con. The Lambert snuff as justice cause célèbre.

Defense committees. Hollywood endorsements. Amnesty International. A twenty-minute agitprop film.

A schmaltzy soundtrack. Gary Graham—Nelson Mandela West.

The process dragged. Graham stayed on death row. Graham changed his name to Shaka Sankofa.

The process dragged into 2000.

3.

Houston was the shits.

I caught it coming in. I caught it off a high freeway.

Some strip malls were new. Some strip malls were old. Future strip malls stood half-completed.

The floor plan jarred. The color scheme clashed.

Jerry-rigged suburbs. Southwest pastels. Too much white on beige.

It was humid. It was hot in November.

I flew in with my friend Rick Jackson. We brought our paperwork. Graham's appellate lawyer supplied it.

Rick was a PI. He was ex-LAPD. He worked murders in Hollywood. He worked major crimes at Robbery-Homicide. He sandwiched in a USC master's.

Rick loved crime. Rick loved crime past his vocation. Rick loved the riddle of motive and lives in duress. Rick loved crime as social history. Rick loved crime with the guilelessness of a kid discovering sex.

Rick cosigned the death penalty. Rick sent two men to death row. One man fried. One man killed himself.

I cosigned the death penalty. I dismissed the inherent inequities based on class and race. I believed in punishment and the ultimate censure of vicious and wanton acts. I knew the death penalty did not deter murder. I believed that the death penalty unified and set a tone of intolerance for murder. I countered all rebuttals steeped in mitigation. Poverty did not move me. The cumulative effect of historical racism did not move me. I weighed systemic injustices against the necessity for judiciously applied vengeance and viewed the abrogation of individual rights as a palatable trade. My bottom line—thoroughly reasoned and in no way disingenuous:

If you have to know why we need the death penalty, you're never going to know.

One counterthought torqued me. One quasi-rebuttal lurked.

I dismissed most mercy pleas based on mitigation. I dismissed the unequal levy of death decrees against people of color. I could not condone the execution of innocent men and women.

Hence Gary Graham.

I read the paperwork. Rick read it. We discussed it.

The details played ambiguous. The details contradicted and counterweighted. The details lacked the cohesive logic of innocence or guilt.

Graham's spree follows the Lambert snuff. Some snuff details and spree details cohere. Graham says he's killed people. Graham tells a victim: If I'm caught, I'll burn.

Witness Skillern's ID. Variant IDs. The alibi wits.

Rick's bottom line:

He wouldn't file a case off a single-wit ID.

We checked into our hotel. We prepared to roll.

We had a phone list. Rick made calls. We arranged interviews.

Rick called Detective Owen. Owen worked for the DEA now.

Owen was brusque. Owen said he was vague on the Graham case.

Rick called Detective Ellis. Ellis lived in San Diego. Ellis said he was vague on the Graham case.

Witness Grady was dead. We tried to locate Witness Amos. We tapped out.

Rick called Witness Skillern. Rick left a message. Rick asked her to call the hotel.

Rick called Witness Etuk. Rick called Chester Thornton and Ron Mock. They agreed to interviews.

Rick called Florence McDonald. She promised to find her son and James Mukes. Leodis Wilkerson was long gone.

Rick called the D.A.'s Office. An assistant pledged more paperwork.

Rick called Witness Hubbard. Rick left a message. Rick asked him to call the hotel.

Rick called the Terrell Unit. Rick confirmed our meet with Gary Graham.

We studied our papers. We gleaned new details.

Per photo spread #2:

Witness Skillern views mug shots. Graham is clean-shaven. Graham has short hair.

Four men have longer hair. Four men have facial hair.

Ms. Skillern said the shooter was clean-shaven. Ms. Skillern said he had short hair.

Four shots bear dates. Four shots bear booking numbers. Graham's numbers are obscured.

Ms. Skillern says Graham looks like the shooter.

But:

The shooter had darker skin.

Ms. Skillern views a live lineup. Ms. Skillern ID's Graham.

Graham was in the lineup. Graham was in photo spread #2.

Graham was the only man in both displays.

Ms. Skillern knows this. She tells Detective Owen. She recalled Graham from spread #2.

From the defense brief. A known expert comments.

Dr. Elizabeth Loftus:

There is an enhanced likelihood that a witness will identify the person in the lineup whom she has seen in the photo spread, whether or not the person is actually the one whose crime she witnessed.

. . . This familiarity may be mistakenly related back to the
crime rather than back to the photograph where it may properly belong.

Rick found the logic credible. I agreed.

From the defense brief. Two wits volunteer.

4/93:

Malcolm Stephens sees news spots on Gary Graham. He
relates them to an event.

It's 5/13/81. Stephens approaches the Safeway. His wife is with
him.

A black male runs in front of their car.

He's "about 5'5" . . . compact, but not big, short hair, no beard
or anything like that."

They approach the store. They get close. They see the victim
prone.

Cut to:

1982.

Mr. Stephens sees the black male again.

He's by some apartments. He's familiar.

They talk. Mr. Stephens tries to place him.

He puts it together. He's the parking-lot dude.

Mr. Stephens sees him "several more times." Mr. Stephens
"learned more about him."

Cut to:

4/93. Gary Graham on TV.

He's *not* the Safeway killer. He's not the parking-lot dude.

Mr. Stephens comes forth. Mr. Stephens views the Skillern
composite.

It looks like the parking-lot dude. It does not look like Gary
Graham.

I thought it was bullshit. Street jive triumphant. Rick agreed.

I called my friend Bill Stoner. Bill worked Sheriff's Homicide.
He worked it fifteen years.

I asked him if he'd file on a one-wit ID.

Bill said, "No way."

HOUSTON WAS BIG. Freeway grids crosshatched it. Dive neighborhoods stretched wide.

Rick dug the grid aspect. Heist men loved freeways. On-ramps greased quick escapes.

Graham stayed mobile. His spree turf stretched wide. He dodged hot-car bulletins. He spreed for seven days.

I drove. Rick navigated. We toured black Houston.

The strip malls were old. The houses were shabby. Triple locks and window bars reigned.

The color scheme held. Southwest shades abundant. The bars and steel doors clashed.

Witness Skillern didn't call. We left a card in her mailbox. Witness Hubbard didn't call. We left a card on his door.

It was hot. Pedestrians walked slow. Houston was heat-warped.

We drove by the alibi alley. We drove to the Safeway. We logged six miles between.

The Safeway was defunct. The building was a new-car showroom.

We toured the parking lot. We toured in daylight.

I turned off the sun. I turned on the night lights. I added vintage cars.

I added flustered witnesses. I saw what they saw.

Witness Skillern sees Gary Graham. Graham's 5′9″. Graham is thin.

Witness Grady sees a man. He's "tall and slim." He wears a white sport coat.

Witness Amos sees a man. He's "in his twenties."

Witness Etuk sees a man. He wears black slacks and a white blazer. Windows blur his face.

Witness Hubbard sees a man. He's 5′5″, 130. He's "in his early twenties." He hides his face.

Three boys see a local dude. They recognize him. They provide no other description.

The initial statements cohere on clothing. The initial statements diverge on height.

Subsequent affidavits recohere.

Witness Etuk—'93 affidavit—less than 5′6″. Witness Amos—'93 affidavit—5′4″. Witness Stephens—'93 affidavit—5′5″. Witness Wilkerson—'93 affidavit—shorter than the 5′6″ victim.

Ambiguous. A partial consensus in 1981. A greater retrospective consensus.

I said it was all fucked up.

Rick praised indoor murders.

We braced Alfonzo McDonald. We braced him at his pad.

His family watched. They ran the TV concurrent.

Rich charmed them. He played up his white beard. He said he was Saint Nick in disguise.

We questioned McDonald. He offered this story:

He's eight years old. He's in his mother's wagon.

He's with Leodis and James. He sees a tussle. The white guy's shorter and heavier than the black guy.

He hears shots. The white man runs in the store. The black man runs away.

The cops quizzed Leodis mostly. Leodis was twelve. Some cops came around. Some cops displayed pictures.

That's all he knew. He was a kid then.

WE BRACED SHERIAN ETUK. She offered this story:

She was a fast checker. She worked the express line. She got bored. She watched people for fun.

5/13/81:

She's checking. She's got downtime. She looks out the window.

She sees a man. She thinks he's cute. She studies him.

He's black. He's short. He's muscular. He's dark complected. He's wearing a turtleneck. He's wearing dark pants and a tan jacket. It might be vice versa.

He's late 20s/early 30s. He's got a low-cut Afro.

She's inside. He's outside. He's leaning on a column.

She's checking. He's loitering. She peeks at him. She peeks ten to thirty minutes.

Their eyes meet. He's good-looking. He's well-dressed.

She's checking. She's bored. An old girl's counting coins.

She looks outside. She hears a "pop!" She sees muzzle light.

A white man staggers up.

He makes the store. He collapses. The cute man walks off.

She transfers to another store. She fears reprisals. The killer might be a "hit man."

Her account contradicted her initial account. She said she never saw the man's face.

I said it was all fucked up.

Rick said hit men were out. Serial killers were in.

RON MOCK HAD a suite downtown. His office was Black History Month.

Wall paintings. Photos. Malcolm X and Dr. King. Muhammad Ali.

Mock was gracious. Mock was feisty. Mock was blunt.

Mock said, "Gary Graham's a dumb-ass son of a bitch."

Mock said, "His lawyers educated him to be articulate."

Mock said, "He's full of born-again bullshit."

Rick said, "Do you think Graham did it?"

Mock said, "Yes."

I said, "Did he admit the crime to you?"

Mock said, "No."

I stretched out. Rick stretched out. We sensed a monologue.

Mock delivered.

He talked. He fucked with an unlit cigar.

Bernadine Skillern was gooood. He didn't impugn her. She was "strong as an acre of garlic."

Two women showed up. Alibi wits. He didn't use them. They weren't credible.

The case was all strategy. His budget impinged. He got $500.

He excluded the heists at the guilt phase. He looked for character wits. He tapped out cold.

Rick cited Merv West's affidavit. West claimed you sandbagged Graham.

Mock denied it. Mock stressed his strategy call. Mock said he'd try Graham the same way today.

I cited the other eyewits. I cited their descriptions.

Mock cited strategy.

He didn't press them. He didn't want to risk equivocation.

I shut my eyes. I screened pictures.

I conjured eyewits. I conjured spatial perspectives. Mock described Graham's heist spree. Mock described his rape.

My pictures blurred. Mock presumed guilt. I leaned toward his assessment.

WE DINED WITH Chester Thornton. We let him expound.

Thornton was gracious. Thornton was perceptive. Thornton was blunt.

He wasn't sure Graham did it. He wasn't sure he did not. He knew Graham. He handled his juvie case. Juvie records were sealed. He refused to divulge data.

I stretched out. Rick stretched out. We sensed a monologue.

Thornton delivered.

He knew Graham already. He had more bench time. He should have run the show.

Ron Mock was an insider. He secured court appointments. He played the game well.

Judges sided with prosecutors routinely. Judges assigned defense counsel in capital cases routinely. Judges looked for adequate and noncombative lawyers.

Competent lawyers. No inspired defenses. No reversals on appeal.

Thornton spoke abstractly. He did not condemn Ron Mock flat-out.

He cited poor strategy. He cited Merv West's affidavit. He cited West's early presumption of guilt. He cited West's lackluster job.

He found one alibi wit compelling. Jo Carolyn Johnson made sense.

He questioned Graham's overall counsel. He assumed partial blame.

He critiqued the Texas court-appointment system. He critiqued the death penalty.

Play-ball lawyers got capital cases. They notched big paydays. They contributed to judges' reelection campaigns.

Texas law ran exclusionary. Death-penalty opponents could not serve on capital juries. Their opposition meant they could "not discharge the law."

The prosecution trumped Graham's lawyers. It occurred at voir dire.

They got their jury. They got their consensus.

We'll "discharge the law." We'll condemn off one ID.

Dinner wound down. Thornton and Rick had dessert.

I screened witness perspectives.

THE TERRELL UNIT:

Gun huts. Reinforced fences. Barbed-wire balls.

One-story cell blocks. White-glazed brick. High guard-to-con numbers.

Terrell was new. Terrell was adjunct death row. The State executed at Huntsville.

A guard boss escorted us. A PR man tagged along.

Terrell sparkled. Inmates passed by. They wore white jump-suits.

We hit a hallway. We saw the interview slots.

There's Gary Graham—aka Shaka Sankofa.

He's mid-sized. He's lean. He's sweating.

A glass wall enclosed him. It bisected two cubicles.

His. Ours. Wall phones for conversation.

We settled in. Graham had his phone. Rick and I shared ours.

We explained our purpose. We stated our credentials.

Rick said he was ex-LAPD. Rick said he'd never file a one-wit case.

We schmoozed Graham. We lubed him. Rick called him "Shaka." I called him "Mr. Sankofa."

Rick asked him when he went Muslim. Graham bristled. He said "Sankofa" was an African name.

We shitcanned the pap. Graham consulted a defense summary.

He spieled.

His epic raw deal. His fucked-up trial. The Hollywood cats out to spring him.

He spoke precisely. He spoke grammatically.

I diverted his spiel. I wanted to contextualize 5/13/81.

Will he see the date as a demarcation line? Will he know which events pre- and postdated it—because he killed a man that night? Will he reveal his guilt through this chronology?

I asked questions. Rick asked questions. We passed our phone back and forth.

Graham revealed shit.

He said he pulled his spree bombed.

He boozed. He sniffed coke. He smoked weed. He popped black mollys.

He consulted his summary. He said he copped to ten heists. He could not recall dates. He could not recall his accomplices.

I mentioned weapons. Graham stressed his .22. The cops exonerated it.

Rick mentioned other weapons.

Graham said he used a shotgun. Graham said he used a ".45 Mag." Graham said he bought them on the street.

Graham admitted that he used other weapons. Graham undermined his seized-gun logic.

He could have had another .22. He could have shot Lambert with it.

Graham got pissed. He had a canned pitch. He wanted to revive it.

Rick mentioned his shotgun assault. Graham lied. Graham said the guy grabbed the gun. The gun popped accidental.

I mentioned the rape. Graham lied. Graham said it was consensual sex.

The woman claimed she was raped. He didn't contest it. The D.A. never filed.

I explained why.

They had you for murder. They had you for ten heists.

Graham protested. Graham offered this story:

A friend drove him to a club. He met the woman. They drove to her pad.

They got drunk. They had consensual sex. They got in a beef.

He fell asleep. He woke up. The cops were there.

The woman said he stole her money. It was bullshit. *His* money was gone.

Rick took over. Rick let Graham talk.

I stared at him. Rick and I shared the receiver.

Graham said he stayed at his grandma's house. He had a '65 Mustang. The engine was out.

Graham described his trial. Graham described his appeals. Graham described his "community support."

His syntax lapsed. He malapropped. He reverted to street jive.

I sat back. I let Rick talk and listen.

I studied Graham. I watched his lips. I waived guilt versus innocence. I waived his arguably unjust ordeal.

He was a thieving, raping, misanthropic sack of shit. He was meretricious appetite and cunningly justified self-pity. He was conscienceless and remorseless. He was monstrously empty.

The PR man showed. Our time was up.

RICK HAD FRIENDS near Houston. We detoured for dinner.

We discussed Gary Graham. Rick shared my assessment.

We discussed guilt versus innocence. We both leaned toward guilt. We both had doubts.

Rick's friends were great. We laughed and bullshitted. We rehashed historical crimes.

We dined at a golf club. I phased in and out of the talk.

Culture shock grabbed me. The fairway view and death row.

I said, "Fuck the death penalty."

4.

Witness Skillern dodged us.

We traced her to her daughter's house. We left a card.

Rick called the daughter. The daughter ran point.

No. She won't see you.

The press burned her. The activists burned her. Call her lawyer.

We bagged it.

Rick flew home. I flew home.

We flew home sans indictment. We flew home sans exoneration.

I flew home apostatized.

I didn't thank or blame Gary Graham. I thanked and blamed spatial perspectives. I thanked and blamed skewed memories and height variance.

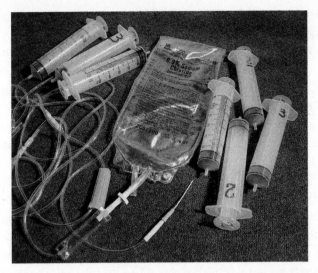

It takes two minutes and $86.08 worth of sodium thiopental, pancuronium bromide, and potassium chloride to execute a prisoner. *(Copyright © Guy Koppenburg, 2003)*

I thanked Chester Thornton. I perched that grave man near my heart.

He taught. He explicated. He worked in ellipsis.

He ran anti-blues riffs. No rhetoric on racism. No vote for reparation. No glorified black victimhood à la Jesse Jackson.

He didn't know if Graham did it. He shared blame for Graham's plight. He indicted the systemic corruption he worked in. He set his polemic in Harris County, Texas.

He layered in statistics. He let me extrapolate.

The full house on Huntsville death row. The Harris County Wing. DNA reversals. Sixty-odd convicts released nationwide.

Joe Stalin said it:

"One death is a tragedy. A thousand deaths is a statistic."

I extrapolated. It was easy. My bottom-line resistance dissolved.

A flawed system. A proven nondeterrent. A proven vouchsafe of judicial error. The empirically based evidence that some innocent fry.

A mass-market palliative. A sop to the fatuous notion of "closure." A dialogue diverted and subsumed by details of wantonly afflicted murder. The institutional catharsis of human sacrifice.

Thornton lectured well. Thornton sermonized interactively. He withheld Sacco and Vanzetti. He placed me under night lights and let me develop conclusions.

I labored with the prosaics. A prosecutor's appellate brief helped.

A woman named Roe Wilson wrote it. The brief rebutted the defense summary with stern force.

It dissected the contradicting eyewits. It buttressed Witness Skillern's account. It trashed the alibi wits' affidavits. It portrayed them as jerry-rigged and possibly collusive. It logically rebutted the defense critique of the photo-spread procedure.

Ms. Wilson thought Graham did it. His appellate defense disagreed.

Ron Mock thought Graham did it. The cops agreed. Rick Jackson leaned that way.

I leaned that way. Logic took me there. Legal doubts detoured me. The solo ID constrained my full vote.

From the Holy Bible. Deuteronomy 17:6:

"On the evidence of two witnesses or of three witnesses, he that is to die shall be put to death; a person shall not be put to death on the evidence of one witness."

Gary Graham might die this year. This piece is my petition to spare his wretched life.

Postscript: Gary Graham was executed on 6/22/2000.

My Life as a Creep

Sex almost killed me. I managed this without human contact.

It was a stretch. I worked at it. The process consumed nine years. It was a self-willed immolation.

I won't indict the era. The '60s and '70s did not sanction me. I disavowed the counterculture ethos and disdained the wild history I lived through. I won't condemn my country and its alleged puritan code. That code does not exist as verifiable fact. Snotty Europeans invented it and obscured its origins. They love and hate America. They worship our culture and wonder how it got so big, bad, and brilliant. They are vexed by the notion that America fucks more than the rest of the world combined and continues to challenge the urge.

I'm an American. I've got horns and a challenging nature. I've got Calvinist instincts. They balance my profligate side. I came to get laid and explore my own soul.

That balance kicked in late. It did not exist in the '60s and '70s. The balance then was booze versus dope and which woman to jump in my dreams.

This memoir is a three-count indictment. Count one: I lied

and stole and spawned bad juju. Count two: I did it in a
cravenly circumspect manner. Count three: I creeped out the
whole female race.

   The indictment is self-proffered. That gives it some oomph.
This memoir is my jury brief and mitigation plea.

   Sex made me do it.

1.

A hippie fuckhead did my horoscope. We shared some T-Bird and
discussed it. He said my chart was a bummer.

Pisces meant passive. My Scorpio moon meant sex and hot
passion. He saw potential conflict. I was born under a baaad sign.

It was 1967. I was 19. I stood 6'3" and weighed 140. My father
had a 16" shlong. I labored under this Oedipal trauma. I had
severe acne. Pizza-pit pustules on my back and forehead. I had
short hair in the Summer of Love.

I lived in L.A. My parents were dead. I was a draft-exempt
dropout. I was kicked out of school in '65. My father let me join
the Army. I bopped to Fort Polk, Louisiana.

I hated the Army. It scared me. I regretted my enlistment and
plotted my escape. My father had two strokes. I exploited his ill-
ness and faked a nervous breakdown.

My psycho act worked. The Army shitcanned me. I was free,
white, and seventeen. I returned to L.A. I forged my father's last
three Social Security checks and cashed them. I found a cheap
pad at Beverly and Wilton.

The old man was profane and sex-obsessed to the end. I
watched him die. His last discernable words were: "Try to pick up
every waitress who serves you."

I did not fulfill his last wish. I freaked out on sex in my own
unique manner.

Beverly and Wilton was downscale and wholly prosaic. It
adjoined Hancock Park. Hancock Park was high swank and allur-
ing. It was full of well-scrubbed girls in pleated skirts and cash-

mere sweaters. They lived in big Spanish and Tudor houses. I wanted in.

I worked busboy and dishwasher gigs. I got a C-note a month off my mother's insurance. My aunt in Wisconsin sent me the money.

I read crime novels and went to crime movies. I shoplifted food, books, and liquor. I got popped once. I was six months short of eighteen. I was too old to adopt and too young to live solo. I did two days at Georgia Street Juvie. The court declared me an "emancipated juvenile."

The decree included formal probation. I met my PO once a month and snow-jobbed him. I had three pals named Lloyd,

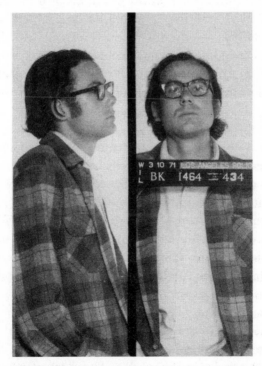

James Ellroy's mug shot, from a 3/10/71 drunk-driving bust. *(Photo courtesy of the LAPD)*

Fritz, and Daryl. I was their stooge. They lived with their parents.
I was parent-free and had my own pad. They dug me for that reason. We boozed and smoked weed at my crib. They teased me.
They ragged on my zits and sad-sack demeanor. I ignored them
and popped off to a fantasy cloud.

The cloud was SRO. Hancock Park girls joined me. The white
wisps billowed.

I turned 18. It was March '66. I was a street-legal adult with no
stated agenda. I got off probation. I drank and smoked weed and
took time shares on that cloud. The cloud was a motel/love shack.
It housed the Sexcapades of 1966.

My time shares passed too quickly. Masturbation took 3.4 minutes. Booze and weed sparked and hindered my fantasies. I could
not sustain narrative lines. I could not give myself to all the
women I craved.

Women and girls scared me. I could not address them drunk,
stoned, or sober. I torched for Fritz's sister Heidi. She did not
reciprocate. I torched for her friend Kay. She did not reciprocate.
I torched for girls named Missy, Julie, and Kathy. I torched Hancock Park to the ground.

Hancock Park was a magnet. The pull was affluence and sex. I
grew up poor and enticingly adjacent. My father worked intermittently. Our pad stunk. Our dog shat on the floors. Women were
pictures in magazines and silhouettes in windows. I saw my
mother nude. I saw her in bed with men. I caught my father in
bed with a classmate's mother and framed a close-up of the
mechanics. Hancock Park was a paint-by-numbers work in
progress. I had some colors and instincts. My brushstrokes were
too broad for the compartments.

Fritz was in college. The grind wore him thin. He found some
Dr. Feelgoods and copped amphetamine scripts. The shit jacked
him up for long cram sessions.

He gave me his excess stash. I found my narrative voice.

Uppers gored my gonads and scaled my skull and cleared my climb to Cloud 9.

The high lasted 12-plus hours. It allowed me to brain-screen epic fantasies. I courted and captured my crush objects and worked in some sleazy scenes. Uppers torqued my imagination. Euphoric narratives resulted. Uppers dried up my zits and gave me my father's shlong.

I jacked off for twelve hours a pop. Climax was not an option or a possibility. My dope-depleted dick shriveled and flopped in my hand.

My fantasies conformed to set lines. Love and sex got equal play. I laid on the tenderness. I etched explicit details softly.

I lusted for a murder victim named Elizabeth Short. She was known as the Black Dahlia. I discovered her in the wake of my mother's murder. Betty was my mother transposed. I knew it on a pop-psych level. I traveled back to '46 and rescued her. We coupled at the Biltmore Hotel. Betty showed me the nude pics she allegedly posed for. I got off on them as I condemned them.

I loved a TV actress named June Harding. She was a high-end ingenue. She had a steady gig on *The Richard Boone Show*. She did a few guest shots on *The Fugitive* and costarred in some lox about nuns.

June Harding was tallish and slender. She had dark hair and eyes. She vibed brainpower and self-knowledge. She was wholesome. She was a dare. She was young. She didn't know what she wanted.

She secretly wanted Yours Truly. Dexedrine and Dexamyl convinced me. I gave her access to the secret thoughts I withheld from God and my buddies. She dug the whole quilt. Crime books, dogs, and classical music. Sports cars. Victory in 'Nam. The Lutheran Church wasn't that bad. Don't you pray when you get scared?

We got married. We made love a great deal. We got a big pad in

Hancock Park. June starred in TV shows. I chased the Dahlia killer full-time.

I had my Hancock Park harem. Soul mates on a cloud. Kathy and Kay rated marriage. Julie and Missy rated dates at the Swinger Motel.

I was picking up pop-culture vibes. Experimentation was in. The swinger ethos transcended class strictures. It had to be true. Hugh Hefner said so.

Hancock Park was rife with fortyish women. I observed them obsessively. They lounged by backyard pools and abused their Latin domestics. They were upper-class moms with teenaged daughters and time on their hands. They were bored, vexed, and horny—sirens from the pens of my favorite "mainstream" authors, Harold Robbins and Irving Wallace.

I watched them shop on Larchmont. Their skirts hiked and stretched. I memorized their faces and gave them my mother's body. I gave them a yen for young flesh.

Mine. Julie's and Missy's.

Hancock Park rocked to our fervor. Three-ways reigned. It was a sordid and joyous ode to inclusion. Sex was divine and dirty concurrent. It was everything. It was a freakish glandular disposition. I reveled in God's joke. I shared it with my body.

Comedowns ended my stories. The dope morphed out of my system. I became a widower and libertine bereft.

Fly, crash and burn. Dehydration. Sleeplessness and exhaustion. Mental fatigue. Itchy skin. The Hancock Park Eviction Blues. The punch line to God's Big Joke.

I drank my way out of it. I screened women's faces until the screen went black.

Fritz lost his upper script. I lost Hancock Park.

I tried to score my own prescriptions. I went to some Dr. Feelgoods and said I had to lose weight. They didn't buy it. They said I should *gain* weight. I put out bad vibes. I couldn't con the collusively inclined.

The widower bereft. The libertine shackled.

Fritz took pity. He got me a date with his sister. Heidi drove. I squirmed and chewed Clorets to kill my booze breath.

Heidi cut me off at date one. She set me up with her loser friend Cathy. She billed me as a tall guy with his own apartment.

Cathy was still in high school. She was dowdy and plump. She dragged me to *The Sound of Music*.

I killed a short dog of T-Bird at intermission. Cathy asked me if I drank to forget. Her parents were drunks. She knew the drill and knew my story. My mother was murdered. My father was dead. She was hot to mother me and cosign my shit.

We went out six or seven times. I described my shoplifting exploits. Cathy scolded me. We parked and kissed sans tongue.

Cathy held the line there. She refused to escalate. I tried everything short of brute force. My theatrics exhausted her. She put up roadblocks. She dragged me to her friends' pads for little soirees. She knew she could muzzle me in their presence.

Her plan backfired.

I met some new Hancock Park girls. I coopted Cathy's pedigree and acted like Hancock Park was my birthright. I saw some Hancock Park interiors. I dug the wood-paneled walls and arched doorways. I met some fortyish mothers. They smiled and glowed and showed me their bodies in motion. I memorized some fresh fantasy backdrops.

I visited bathrooms and checked out medicine chests. I saw pills galore. I memorized labels. I started to get An Idea.

I called one of Cathy's friends and promoted a date. We saw the flick *Harper* and necked in Fern Dell Park. The girl shot me some tongue.

I dumped Cathy. The tongue girl dumped me. I called Heidi. She blew me off. I called her friend Kay. She told me to get bent and die.

I was a teenage leper. I was an acquired taste that no one ever acquired. I acted on That Idea.

Christmas '66.

I broke into Fritz and Heidi's house. The family was gone. I entered through the kitchen door. I reached into the pet-access hole and tripped the inside latch.

I prowled in the dark. I knew the floor plan. I hit the upstairs bathrooms and tapped the medicine chests. I stole two painkillers and bopped downstairs for a chaser. I hit the liquor tray and poured a stiff scotch.

I hit Heidi's bedroom. I stretched out on her bed and picked up her scent. I stole a pair of white panties.

The downers and booze kicked in. I got scared. I didn't want to weave and bump things. I left the house in sloooow motion.

I BROKE INTO Kay's house and Kathy's house. I established a simple procedure.

I walk by first. I pack a flashlight. I look for cars in the driveway and lights on inside. Lights and cars mean ABORT. Their absence means GO TO PHASE TWO.

I walk to a pay phone and call my targets. It's '66 and '67. Phone machines don't exist. People shag all their calls.

Someone picks up. I disguise my voice and fake a wrong number. No answer means GO.

I walk back. I check the downstairs windows for loose screens and half-open panes. I bend back nails, remove screens, and vault up and in. I find unscreened windows and climb in unfettered.

I hit Kay's house and Kathy's house just like that. I got in the first times I tried.

Kay's folks were abstemious. I couldn't find any liquor or pills. I hit the icebox and snarfed some cold cuts and fruit. I explored Kay's bedroom. I stole a panty-and-bra set.

Kathy's house confused me. I couldn't determine her bedroom. I guzzled out of all the jugs on a sideboard. I stretched out on all the upstairs beds and screened some fantasies. I picked up the smells and textures of high-end life in repose. I hit a chest of drawers and an armoire. I stole two sets of panties and bras. I had to make sure I had hers.

They smelled intimate. Detergent as an aphrodisiac. Fabrics that touched *her*.

I scored some downs. I popped them with a sweet liqueur. I staggered home and passed out in a heartbeat.

'67 WAS A RUSH. I was the Hancock Park Phantom.

I hit my targets at odd intervals. I stuck to my entry plan and stole things that wouldn't be missed. Underwear and cold cuts. Shots from the jug. I deployed exit plans and stopped stealing pills. I employed restraint. I didn't want to blow future prowls. I hit Julie's house and Missy's house. I hit Kathy's house and Kay's house repeatedly.

The thrill was sex and secret knowledge. Small details accreted and filled my image bank. Schoolgirl bedrooms. Unmade beds. Panties discarded and kicked under the sheets.

I never questioned my right to steal, break and enter. I never justified or rationalized it with the rhetoric of rebellion. My buddies tried to hip me to the wild winds of change. I ignored their broadsides on peace, love, and revolt. It was feckless horseshit and piffle for a coddled generation. I never told my buddies that I broke into houses. They would have tagged the act as hippie aggression. They would point to my poor-ass origins and conclude that I coveted Hancock Park from an aggrieved perspective. They wouldn't get it. I plundered private worlds with no rancor. Scents. Tactile pleasures. Soiled panties as perfume. My own country clubs—in and out windows.

My unspoken credo was MORE. My appetite fed off that word. My mandate was sexual excitement. My major course of study was women. My focus was faces read and assessed for signs of my own hunger. My release was the maternal bond corrupted. Women, girls, and me. Reconstructed families abed in Hancock Park. A warm hearth and a plaque inscribed MORE.

Pinup next door: Kaya Christian, in the November 1967 issue of *Playboy. (Reproduced by Special Permission of* Playboy *Magazine © 1967 by* Playboy*)*

2.

I stole the November *Playboy.* The Playmate pulverized me.

Her name was Kaya Christian. Her name fit. Her lithe loins lashed my Lutheran libido. She was the blonde that redefined all blondes and rendered all other blondes obsolescent. She vibed divine intervention.

Her smile mocked the magazine she posed for. *Playboy* was a stroke rag for horny dipshits. This dipshit knew that at 19. I was a longstanding *Playboy* plebeian. Nothing prepared me for Kaya.

She floored me. I stole six more issues and spread her all over my walls. She followed me to bed and the bathroom.

Standard jackoffs undermined our love. I wanted MORE. I broke into Julie's house and hit the medicine chest. I wanted ups. I got Band-Aids and bullshit.

Lloyd had dope pals in Hollywood. I tagged along on some runs. We tapped out on uppers. I quaffed T-Bird and Seconal cocktails as a consolation prize. I blacked out and woke up in Christmas-tree lots. I brushed off sawdust and pine needles and kept going.

I went on a bender. I blew my rent roll and got kicked out of my pad. I stole some blankets from a Goodwill box and moved into Robert Burns Park.

The ground was hard. The grass tickled. The automatic sprinklers doused me at odd times.

I got some job referrals. A racist psychic hired me to pass out handbills. She preyed on blacks and Mexicans and "healed" them. I dispensed flyers all over East and South-Central L.A. I put a wad together and reclaimed my pad.

Sex fate knocked on my door. It was divine *and* demonic intervention.

I ran into a high-school buddy. He had a woman in tow. She was 29. She had a free-spirit rap down. She had wild charm and a hard-ass nature. She needed a place to stay. She sized me up as a virgin doormat and said she'd fuck me for a roof.

I agreed. She moved in and fucked me four times. It was bad. *I* was bad. She informed me four times. She informed me during and after the acts.

I dug her anyway. I let her stay. I lived in hope of fuck #5.

It never occurred. She lived with me for three months and announced that she was a dyke. She moved in with a hot young woman.

I went on a bender. I blew my rent roll. My landlord kicked me out. I moved back to Robert Burns Park and found a dry spot by the toolshed.

I developed a routine. I stashed my clothes at Lloyd's place and bathed there twice a week. I shaved in public restrooms. I shoplifted cold cuts and liquor. I prowled Hancock Park and B&E'd at whim.

I frequented the Hollywood Library. They stocked the Irving Wallace oeuvre. *The Chapman Report* featured a nympho named Naomi Shields. Claire Bloom played her in the movie. I synced her face to Wallace's prose and slammed the ham in the stacks.

It was exhilarating and scary. Risk City all the way. I recalled the best Naomi parts and got off in .08 minutes.

Riffraff passed through the library. Hippies lugged smelly sleeping bags and grimed up the washrooms. I met a freak named Harvey. We discussed drugs. I described my frustration. I loved amphetamines—but lacked the social skills to procure them. Harvey told me about Benzedrex Inhalers.

They were nasal decongestants lodged in plastic tubes. Cotton wads were soaked in a chemical substance. You broke the tube and swallowed the wad. You got a righteous speed high.

Benzedrex Inhalers were legal. Drugstores sold them over-the-counter.

I bopped straight to a drugstore. I stole three inhalers and broke the plastic. The wads were two inches long. They were cigarette circumference. They smelled putrid. I gagged them down with a root beer.

They worked. They brought me Kaya and June. They sent me home to Burns Park. They gave me twelve hours of love under a blanket.

I LOVED WILLFULLY. I stole inhalers and flew every third or fourth day. I loved, crashed, boozed, and slept.

Rains disrupted me. I prowled for dry shelter. I found an empty house two miles southeast.

No inside lights and no running water. One piece of furniture. A moldy couch. My launch pad and bed.

I moved in. I stashed my blankets and spare clothes in a closet. I loved, crashed, boozed, and slept for two weeks. I came and went by night. I thought I was coooool.

11/30/68:
Four cops kicked my door in. They packed shotguns. They proned me out and cuffed me and popped me for Burglary.

THEY BROKE IT DOWN to Trespassing. I saw a judge and pled guilty. She thought I was a draft dodger. She ordered a probation report and imposed a no-bail decree. I spent three weeks at the Hall of Justice Jail.

It was spooky and instructive. I picked up B&E tips. I learned about Romilar CF—the cough syrup supreme. The other inmates laughed at me and called me "the Nutty Professor." I jived with some renaissance lowlifes. Armed robbers and career junkies. I said I shacked up with June Harding. Kaya Christian craved my ass.

Nobody believed me.

The judge released me two days before Christmas. My sentence: three years formal probation.

I walked back to Burns Park. I stole inhalers en route. Jail taught me jackshit. I was the Energizer Battery Bunny writ tall. I kept banging that drum. You couldn't touch my ruthless and impotent heart.

3.

The Versailles Apartments. A 6th floor room for 80 a month. Women abundant.

Lloyd got me the pad. My aunt shot me the coin. She warned me: My insurance dole was dwindling.

I liked the pad. Chipped moulding and a north view. My new PO liked me. Short hair and a wholesome demeanor.

He told me to avoid drugs and keep my snout clean. I said I would. He pegged me as low-maintenance and cut me a long lead. I signed up with a temp agency. They got me some office gigs.

The Versailles was a block off Wilshire and due east of Han-

cock Park. Wilshire was white-collar central. I walked to my gigs.
I killed a half-pint of scotch for breakfast and tailed women from
the Versailles.

They walked to work. I bird-dogged them. I screened
impromptu fantasies and expanded them on inhaler trips. I
honed my sex aesthetic.

I grooved on solitary women. Solitary meant lonely. Lonely
meant hungry. Hungry meant horny and estranged and thus
accessible. I grooved on outdated hairstyles and clothes. Styleless-
ness meant psychic weight. Heedlessness to current trends meant
spirit. Their fashion statement enhanced my creed: Fuck the
mass-market revolt of this era.

I stole a supply of Romilar CF. I drank whole bottles on con-
secutive nights and went on a B&E run.

The shit turned things psychedelic. I hit Kathy's house, Kay's
house, and Missy's house. I hit the bathrooms and popped pills
with abandon. I blacked out and came to on my bed two shots out
of three.

Shot #3 was killer. I hit Missy's pad *boooold.*

I entered just after dusk. I picked the latch on the service-porch
door and crawled through the kitchen window. Romilar made
things surreal. The house looked all new. Missy's bedroom was
wild. Weird colors blipped out of the darkness.

I found a soiled bra in the upstairs hamper. It was sweated up
from tennis or badminton. I brain-screened some pictures. Missy
and her freckles. Freckled breasts and chafed nipples.

I stole some speckled capsules. I didn't know how they'd mix
with the Romilar. I popped them anyway.

Goodnight, Sweet Prince.

I hit a work slump. I rented a cheap flop in Hollywood and got
a gig at KCOP-TV. The mailroom was a gold mine.

The station advertised record albums. Stupes sent cash in. I slit
incoming envelopes and stole it. I raked in lots of extra bread and
moved to a better crib.

6th and Cloverdale. Wilshire meets Kosher Kanyon. Old Jews and office slaves. Women abundant.

My insurance dole ran out. My mailroom scam covered the loss. I smashed up the company van and got fired. I got some short-term gigs and lived cheap. I broke into Missy's house and stole all the cash in a purse.

The act blew my shot at reentry. I burned that bridge deliberately. I felt the odds narrowing down. Some night I'd get caught. They caught me in the empty house. They broke the charge down. That wouldn't happen again. All my instincts said STOP IT.

August '69.

The Tate-LaBianca snuffs rock L.A. They ramify in Hancock Park. Magnetic window tape. Rent-a-cop patrols.

I stopped it. I never did it again. I held my memories close and sniffed the winds of change.

Porno bookstores were popping up citywide. I figured some law was struck down. Smut was street-legal.

Fuck-suck books. Beaver books. Glossy color pix. Unretouched detail. Low-rent backdrops. Less-than-perfect women with their legs spread wide.

Hippie girls sans hippie trappings. No tie-dye threads to mark fatuous statements. No love beads or peace signs. Guileless smiles. This is not degrading.

I understood the aesthetic. It dovetailed with my own. I understood the bottom line.

Exploitation sold as freedom. Inclusion for desperate men.

The books were pricey and hard to steal. I sidestepped the dilemma and got a job at a bookstore. I worked midnight to 8:00 a.m.

I worked alone. I rang up sales and stocked merchandise. You paid to browse. Fifty-cent tokens applied to your purchase. Horndogs browsed all night. It was cheap entertainment.

The store sold beaver books, fuck-suck books, homo books, novels, films, slides, playing cards, dildoes, cock rings, S&M gear, and French ticklers. Strategically placed mirrors deterred same-sex assignations. The clientele was all male and all loser. Bombed-out hippies, drag queens, and the great male unwashed.

Middle-aged closet queens with wedding rings and sheepish expressions. Devotees of *Cock It to Me* and *For Those Who Think Hung*. The underhung devotees of the Donkey Dan Dick Extender. The Beaver Patrol—USC frat boys fresh from late keggers.

The store was a waste spill. I belonged there.

I unpacked beaver books. I excised the most compelling women. We shared inhaler trips. I prayed for them. I played both ends against the moral middle.

Their debasement and potential redemption. No center ground. A faulty dilemma. My brief prayers and extended exploitation.

You thrill me. I love you. Don't do this anymore. I'm sure glad you went this far.

I tore out pictures and stole books. I tapped the till. I went to a beaver bar and watched beaver flicks. I zorched out on 50-cent drinks.

The bar sold beaver T-shirts and beaver caps with mock-beaver tails. I demurred. I had my mock-Christian agenda. I beaver-patrolled the bar and the store. A revelation hit: You're looking for one special woman.

I found her. She adorned a page of *Beaveroo* or *Beaverama*.

She was thirty-one or -two. She had pale skin and brown eyes. Long hair—straight and center-parted. Early gray throughout.

A long nose. A bump on the bridge. A pointed chin and under-arm stubble. Long legs. Wide hips. A starkly untoned stomach. The biggest hands and feet I'd ever seen on a woman.

She claimed me. She felt like something wondrous and all new. I pledged monogamy. I sustained it. My inhaler trips followed that line.

She did not look cheap, shallow, or in any way worthy of pity or censure. She didn't smile. She didn't mock her blunt pose. Her intent baffled me. I ruled out titillation and financial poverty. She looked forthright and altogether kind.

I prayed for insight and answers. I talked to her at the store. Customers heard me. They rolled their eyes and snickered.

The owner wised up to my thefts. He canned me and withheld my last paycheck. I got some temp gigs and built up a roll. I went on a two-month bender.

It was epic. I stockpiled food, booze, and inhalers and went at it hard. I holed up for two weeks at a clip. I popped inhalers and stared at her picture and jacked off monogamously. I drank and puked up cotton wads. I lost weight. I gorged on steaks and gained it back. I slept and woke up dry-mouthed and dizzy. I lost track of time.

I blew my rent allotment. The landlord started talking eviction. I had the coin to nail a cheap pad outside Kosher Kanyon. I knew a place by the Paramount Studios. The Green Gables Apartments—flats for $60 a month.

Lloyd moved me out and in. We pulled the dodge on the Q.T. The bender left me weak and frazzled. I slept for two days.

The Green Gables sucked. It was full of hypes and elderly rumdums. I squared myself away and looked for a job.

I was fried. I was cumulatively exhausted. I wanted to find a cushy gig and decompress. I wanted to stabilize during the week and FLY on weekends.

I tanked. The no-skill market was soft. I gave up and went on a mission.

Beaver Patrol as redemption.

I hit a dozen bookstores and prowled the beaver racks. I had to find more pics of that woman. She eluded me. I made do with my mind and one photo.

I went on a run. Inhalers and her picture. I started hearing Voices.

They hissed outside my window. They said "Ellroy" and "Pervert." They raged commensurate with the dope in my system.

I diagnosed the Voices. They had to be a dope side effect. It was a fleeting assessment. I popped wads and more wads and diagnosed them as real.

Police sirens hissed at me. The Voices hid in the *wheeeee*. I heard them. The man next door heard them. He smirked at me in the hallway. He knew my sex dreams. He screened them on his TV set. He knew I killed my mother. He totaled up my thefts. He read my mind. I blared my radio and jacked off in the dark to deceive him.

I popped wads and heard the Voices. I drank and banished them. I laughed them off and sucked down more cotton. They returned. They cut through all the sweet words I told Her.

I ran.

The Voices evicted me. It was mid-trip and peremptory. I stuffed cotton in my ears and left my things behind. I walked three miles east in record time. I saw a For Rent sign in Silver Lake.

A convenience room. $39 a month. A bed, a sink, and one communal shower.

I moved in. The building was full of rowdy wetbacks. My room was half the size of a jail cell. It felt like jail. The wetbacks scared me. The pad vibed Hideout or Psych Ward. I drank myself to sleep and popped inhalers the next morning.

The Voices returned. I covered my ears and hid on the bed. The heat coils in my blanket felt like microphones. I ripped them out and threw them at the wall.

The floor was mined and covered with bear traps. I hid on the bed and pissed all over the sheets. The Voices persisted. I ripped up my pillow and stuffed foam rubber in my ears.

I ran.

Straight to Robert Burns Park. Straight to my spot by the toolshed.

I passed out on wet grass. Water seeped through my pants and wiped out Her picture.

4.

She resurrected. She assumed a startling form.

My new probation officer.

Her name was Elizabeth Heath. We met late in '70. The resemblance staggered me.

Her face matched point by point. Her body diverged. She wore loose clothing—her contours eluded me.

I lost and regained a vision. God was responsible. I promised not to plunder Liz in my dreams.

Liz Heath was 30. She hailed from New York State. I saw her once a month and prolonged our visits.

Liz was gracious, intelligent, stern-willed, and funny. I groomed and prepared for our confabs. Liz was an occasion. I rose to it. I didn't know if I was a chameleon or a tight-assed square in waiting.

I knew that I loved her. My restraint proved it. I excluded her from my sex stories. This fueled more than hindered my love and allowed me to listen.

Liz told a good tale. She gave commonplace events a pop and a punch line. She gauged my basic weakness against my will and disregard for the world. She understood hollow boys on missions. They rock impervious. They mistake movement for substance.

Liz figured me out fast. She interceded with a distanced affection. She assessed me as a threat to myself and no great threat to the world. She caught outtakes from the next two years of my slide.

I lived in parks and empty houses. I shoplifted food and booze and dined-and-dashed at restaurants. I broke into apartment-house laundry rooms and jimmied the coins out of washers and dryers. I slept in Goodwill bins. I sold my blood and blood plasma. I got day-labor gigs and read in libraries. Lloyd assisted. I crashed in his yard and his mother's car. The LAPD assisted. They popped me for Petty Theft, Drunk, and DUI. I did jail jolts and purged my toxified system. I stole empty pop bottles from reclamation bins and re-reclaimed them for chump change. I snuck into theaters and watched movies.

I stole inhalers. I popped them. I did not masturbate. The Voices started every time I reached for my dick. They chased me out of parks and empty houses. I stuffed paper in my ears and walked.

I walked and screened stories. Out Wilshire to the beach. Back again. Obsessive movement. Twenty miles per trip. Kaya, June, and a wide cast of faces.

I saw them. I couldn't address them. The Voices drowned out my endearments.

I walked and trembled. People stepped out of my way. Women cringed and grabbed at their purses.

Inhalers sparked the Voices. Abstinence muffled them. The Voices punished me for the faces.

Liz left L.A. in '73. We said good-bye on the phone. She was warm. I was glib. I willed myself to ride out the hurt.

Lloyd's mother kicked him out of the house. He got a cheap hotel room. I rented floor space.

I had a fixed address. The thought encouraged me. I could do things and say things with impunity. The roof and walls would shut out the Voices.

Every floor had a bathtub and shower. I popped six inhalers and locked myself in the 3rd floor tub room.

I stripped and ran a bath. I got in and jacked off to a long line of faces. I ran the water to stay warm and cover the Voices.

I saw my mother's face. I *made* myself see it. I saw her naked. I said, "I love you." We made love in the last house we lived in.

The Voices swirled out of the water. I ignored them. I stayed with her all the way up to the crash.

IT WAS THE most impassioned and loving story I'd ever conceived. It shamed and horrified me.

It thrilled me. I wanted to screen deeper variations. I couldn't do it. The Voices said, You fucked your mother and killed her.

I stiffed Lloyd on my rent cut. The manager evicted me. I moved back to Burns Park.

The Voices followed me.

For two more years.

Inhaler trips. Trembling walks. A fantasy loop everlasting.

T-Bird. Jail for brief health retreats. Hot meals. No Voices. Good exercise.

I built up a dope tolerance. I gagged down more and more wads to achieve the same effect. Ten or twelve wads per trip. Three trips a week.

It fucked up my lungs. I caught pneumonia twice. The County Hospital cured it.

I trucked on undeterred. I followed my appetites. I missed Liz. I started watching men and women together.

Sweethearts in movie lines. Kids in parks. Who's that geek staring at us?

I read books and shagged epigrams and insights. T.S. Eliot. Highbrow shit. "We only live, only suspire, consumed by either fire or fire." A classy fuck flick: *The Private Afternoons of Pamela Mann.*

Barbara Bourbon in the lead role. A boss blond with a cool overbite. A cut-rate Kaya Christian.

Pam Mann's a horndog. She's a passive punchboard and a seductress. She's a nympho Candide. She's the poster girl for '70s excess. She fucks half of New York City in one day and comes home to fuck her husband. He's the best. She *really* loves him. Her day was satire and a goof on inclusion. Sex is everything and nothing.

I dug Barb and the message in equal measure. I picked up a subtext:

Sex was a lock for the cute and the glib. Love took balls.

Insight did not equal power or a will to change. My slide continued.

Lloyd had a pad in West L.A. I camped out on the roof. I went on a looooong T-Bird run and got the DTs in his bathroom.

Fluorescent blobs attacked me. Spiders crawled up my legs. The blobs tried to eat my eyes. Monsters jumped out of the toilet.

It was 100% real.

I batted at the bugs. I closed the toilet seat on the monsters. They oozed straight through the lid.

I drank them away. I passed out and woke up on the roof.

I was dead fucking scared. I *knew* the next drink or cotton wad would kill me.

I hitchhiked to the County Hospital and checked in to the drunk ward. I shared bed space with a dozen winos. A nurse fed me tranks. A doctor signed me up for a kick program.

Long Beach Hospital. Three hots and a cot. Antabuse—a deterrent drug that made you sick if you drank.

I spent two days in the drunk ward. I tried to sleep through it. The tranks helped. Other drunks suffered DTs. They saw things and heard things and hit things that weren't there. I wedged pillows around my head and cut off their jabbers.

I was young. The winos were old. They were my prophecy foretold.

A nurse drove me down to Long Beach. I donned khakis and a plastic wristband. I stayed scared.

I took Antabuse and went to therapy groups. I made up sex stories and directed them to the female drunks. I shacked up with June Harding and Kaya Christian. Barbara Bourbon wanted me for her next flick.

Nobody believed me.

My fear subsided. I rationalized it away. The DTs were a non sequitur. That was then. This is now. I could beat booze and dope my way. I was resourceful. I knew I could work out an angle.

I developed a bad cough. A nurse noticed it. I told her I'd had two pneumonias. She called in a doctor. He sedated me. He stuck a tube with a light attached down my throat and checked out my lungs. He didn't spot anything wrong.

I "graduated" the program and stayed on Antabuse. My cough persisted. I bopped back to L.A.—booze and dope free. My fear escalated. I tried to think up an angle. I tapped out. My imagination and will to scheme were shot to fucking shit.

I camped out on Lloyd's roof. My nerves were shot. My cough got worse. My attention span diminished. I felt body- and brain-snatched. It was an all-new sensation. Foreign cells invaded me. They crosswired my circuits and made me someone else. The wires were loose and schizzing me into a shutdown.

It happened.

I woke up on the roof. I thought: I need some cigarettes. A mental fuse blew. My mind went dead. I could not retrieve the thought I just expressed.

I reached for it. I failed. I grabbed at four simple words for an hour. I tried to think and say my name. I failed. I willed myself to think who and where I was. I hit a synaptic black wall.

I screamed myself hoarse. Lloyd heard me. He ran up to the roof. I couldn't think or say his name.

He called an ambulance. Some paramedics ran me to the County Hospital. They left me strapped to a gurney.

I heard voices. Nurses moved their lips and screamed silently. I screamed back. I saw a nurse prep a needle.

I CAME OUT of it.

I woke up strapped to a cot. My teeth were loose. My jaw hurt. Somebody whipped on me. My knuckles were cut and abraded. I fought back.

I remembered my name and those four simple words. God gave me my mind back.

A doctor diagnosed my mental condition. He called it a "post-alcohol brain syndrome." It was a rare occurrence indigenous to

sober drunks. It was physiological. It derived from tenuous absten-
tion. It rarely recurred.

He heard my cough and x-rayed me. He said I had a big lung
abscess. Proper care would cure me. Booze and dope would kill
me in a week's time.

Live or die. An easy choice once it confronts you.

I spent thirty days on an IV drip. I coughed up jars full of dark
sputum. A male nurse pounded my back and brought up more
shit.

I began to recover. I was twenty-seven. I had strong genes. God
commuted my sentence. He punished me for the thoughts of my
mother and rewired my circuits in mercy.

I believed it. My offense was just that transgressive.

I spent thirty days in bed. I charted my life back to day one and
up to the present. I plotted my survival and thought about women.

5.

Purgatory—a noun. My revised Protestant definition.

A desert of demonic deprivation. Cloyingly close to the Inhaler
Institute and Masturbation Mountain. Limbo for lascivious losers. A rigorous reminder of rapacious appetites and the precious
price they extract.

I went there. The main drags were Stay Straight Street and
Abstinence Avenue. I lived on Terrified Terrace. My brain wires
might broil and brown out any moment. God grants and revokes.
He knows me. I only seek Him when I'm scared.

I stayed scared. All day, every day. I tossed my Antabuse. I
didn't steal, drink, or pop inhalers. I left the hospital—cured. I
slept on Lloyd's roof and lived off plasma money. I read in
libraries and stared at women.

I banished June, Kaya, Barbara, and the whole cast of faces.
Their love would lure me back to the lung ward. Love was the
linchpin of my live-or-die dilemma. I put myself there. I was priapically proactive. Nobody victimized me.

I lucked onto a job. A guy in Lloyd's building worked at Hillcrest Country Club. He got me a caddy gig.

I dug the fresh air and swank atmosphere. I turned some nice coin and got a hotel room. My fear subsided. I sweated it out on the golf course. I dulled it with my semblance of decent behavior.

I stayed off booze and inhalers. I smoked weed and screened potential crime novels. Romantic stories. Dark and obsessive. Women abundant.

I followed women around Westwood Village. I tried to talk to them. I spooked them. They brushed me off. I batted zero.

I kept going. I kept banging that drum. I was headed for an epiphany.

Lloyd knew a bohemian couple. Solly played the flute and the sitar. Joan paid the rent and played muse. They had a crib in West Hollywood.

I spent some time there. Joan was kind to me. I liked her dark hair and blue eyes and nose that hooked off center.

I've got the moment memorized. It's on file as a permanent freeze frame. It was sex and love writ large in an instant.

Joan reaches for a cigarette. Her blouse gaps at the third button. I see her right breast in profile.

You must change your life.

That was '77. It's '99 now. I'm 51. Joan's the same age. June and Kaya are several years older. Barb Bourbon and Liz Heath are pushing 60.

They taught me. They presaged the brilliant and courageous woman I married.

I followed the Clinton-Lewinsky mess. I developed a well-reasoned and morally sane hatred of Bill Clinton.

He should have known better. He stole a woman's dignity. She's the worldwide synonym for blow job. It's a life sentence. Men will spot her in restaurants and bulge out one cheek. Her media fees won't cover the cost.

Some friends disdain this assessment. They point to my wild ride and imply hypocrisy. I would have done the same thing if I'd had the chance.

No, I wouldn't.

My past taught me better than that. My survival taught me the wisdom of stern judgment.

It's an exclusionist stance. It acknowledges the ride and honors the lessons I learned.

The retort is: It's only sex. Sex is nothing.

No, it's everything.

I attribute my survival to the seldom-sought presence of Almighty God. Skeptics and inclusionists might scoff at this. They can kiss my fucking ass.

The D.A.

There's the view.

Eighteen floors up/big window/east exposure. His ritual: Gawk and sip coffee. His daily memo: The view meant the climb.

Twenty-eight years. One bureaucracy. Schmuck kid to D.A. They tag their D.A.s like presidents. Its L.A. County ego. He's #40. His campaign dumped D.A. 39. He's ten months in. His office is still too big. He still loves the view.

Look south—there's City Hall. It's a film noir update. Look straight ahead—there's court buildings beaucoup. Look north—there's the "Twin Towers." It's County Jail overflow. They've got freeway views.

It's downtown L.A. It's all crime all the time. Courtrooms and lockups. O.J.'s Oasis/the Punishment Palace/the Misdemeanant's Motel 6.

It's Steve Cooley's world. Dig it dystopian. Check out his desk. It's orgy-size. It came with the job.

It's morning. He's thinking. His brainwaves are broiling bravura.

With Blake. With Rampart. With Olson-Soliah.

The Blake job—six months old/indictmentless/classic. One,

short time frame. Two, no guilt proof. Three, no alternative suspects. Rampart—a lurid labyrinth. The loony linchpin: a bent cop named Rafael Perez.

Perez admits his shit. Said shit includes dope ripoffs and frameups. Perez rats out Rampart Division. It's a testosterone-torqued Tijuana. It's the macho-maimed microcosm for the LAPD. There's a lawsuit lynch mob lurking. They're licking their lips. They'd love to loot LAPD. The mess is metastasizing.

Perez tattles tainted testimony. Court costs crescendo. Innocence invaded. Insignificant indictments incurred. Weigh the cost. It might be pull-the-plug time.

It started pre-Cooley. His predecessor caught it hot-hot. Cooley got in. Cooley formed the JSID—Justice System Integrity Division.

Protocols. Procedures to gauge cop misconduct. Rampart on *his* watch?—the scandal dies stillborn.

Olson-Soliah was hot. It was 10/29. Her plea date is 10/31. She might plead not guilty. She might go to trial. She might plead guilty and cop out. She tried to torch two cop cars. Her fuses fizzled. Ten years per car—predictable and wholly just.

Olson-Soliah went *back*. It's '74 now. Sara Jane Olson's righteous tag is Kathleen Soliah. Soliah's in the SLA. They're loony left-wing losers. They kidnap Patty Hearst. They extort her old man. They rob some banks and spew specious rhetoric. Cut to 5/17/74. Cut to East 54th Street. LAPD SWAT swats an SLA safe house. Six Commies catch tear gas. They cough and combust. The house ignites. Six crispy critters snap, crackle, and pop.

The stiffs are ID'd. There's no Patty Hearst and no Kathleen Soliah. Six notable new-left nudniks lay dead. Other SLA *Untermenschen* survive. They undulate underground.

Cut to 4/21/75. Cut to Carmichael, California. We're in Sacramento County. A baaaaad heist goes down. It's a "Righteous 211" in cop-speak.

The Crocker National Bank. Eight suspected SLA-ers. Four

inside. A four-fiend outside crew. A fifteen-grand take. A woman named Myrna Opsahl shotgunned for kicks.

Cut to 1982. Patty Hearst:

Caught/convicted/jailed/pardoned/released. She writes a memoir. She names the Carmichael crew.

Kathy Soliah worked inside. Kathy Soliah dumped cash drawers. Emily Harris killed Myrna Opsahl. Soliah quizzed Harris per Opsahl. Harris called Opsahl "a bourgeois pig."

Time trucks. There's Emily Harris and hubby Bill. They get popped for adjunct crimes. Time trucks anew. They go to prison. They get paroled. Patty Hearst's book appears. The Sacramento D.A. stays gun-shy.

Cut back to '76. The Feds try Kathy's bro Steve Soliah. Hearst says he's a getaway man. A jury acquits him. Double jeopardy saves him. Myrna Opsahl goes unavenged.

Cut to 6/16/99. The Feds nail "Sara Jane Olson." She lives in Minnesota. She's a housewife. She's got three kids. Her husband's a M.D.

She's extradited. She hits L.A. She bails out. Her pretrial process attenuates.

Steve Cooley perks up. Steve Cooley reviews Carmichael. Steve Cooley smells murder beefs.

Myrna Opsahl had a son. His name was Jon. He was a M.D. Cooley briefed some D.A.'s cops. They called Jon Opsahl. They updated him.

Kathy Soliah—popped for the car-bomb caper. The Carmichael job—primed for prosecution now.

Cooley kept calling Jon Opsahl. Opsahl bugged the Sacramento D.A. Opsahl got the gist. Opsahl vibed this:

Sacramento's reluctant—once bitten/twice shy. Cooley's running for D.A. Cooley leads the polls. Say he gets elected. Say he goes bold. Say he tries the case non-jurisdictionally.

Cooley got elected. Cooley took over. A local judge scoped the car-bomb evidence. Said judge said this:

"The history of the SLA, including Carmichael, could be introduced in the bombing case here, because it was part of an ongoing criminal conspiracy."

Cooley smiled. Cooley tapped his desk. Cooley checked the view.

Time trucked backwards. It's 5/74 again. It's yesterday once more.

He was a kid prosecutor. He was a kid LAPD reserve. The "SLA Shootout" ran live on TV.

He watched it. He *dug* it. It played live from his own beat.

Some show. Order triumphant. Adjudication circumvented—a tragedy. He almost grabbed his uniform. He almost went over.

He deferred his help. Time trucked forward. His Carmichael ploy might work. Sacramento might prosecute.

What a ride. What a fucking view.

■

The office was huge. Newcomers needed maps. Floors and floors/rooms and rooms/mazelike cubbyholes.

The Criminal Courts Building—Temple and Broadway.

Cooley knew every wall crack. He worked headquarters. He detoured. He worked Siberian outposts. He returned as top dog.

He toured the halls. He touched the walls. It was turf-marking time. You're *el perro primo/il cane supremo/chien numero un.*

Pinch me—I'm the D.A.

Cooley walked to his 10:00 a.m. meeting. Subordinates said hi. It was "Steve" and "Boss" mostly. The timid deployed "sir." Cooley looked embarrassed.

He cut through the squadroom. It was packed. Good cops all—prime PD transfers. They investigated cases. They guarded witnesses. They watchdogged him.

Pinch me. I've got bodyguards and drivers. Headwaiters kiss my ass.

Busting Robert Blake earned Steve Cooley
headlines, but reshaping the largest
prosecutor's office in the country—and one
of the most maligned—is the challenge of a
lifetime. *(Photo courtesy of the Los Angeles County
District Attorney's Office)*

Cooley walked. Cooley touched wall cracks. Cooley made his
10:00 a.m. meet.

The crew was there. The room was big. The desk was orgy-size.
The topic: the *new* Cold Case Unit.

It's Cooley's scheme. It's four DDAs plus LAPD detectives.
Let's solve old murders. Let's deploy DNA. There's a big state
grant—fifty million cold. Let's utilize our share. Local crime labs
are swamped. Let's blast through our agenda.

For LAPD:

Lieutenant Debbie McCarthy, Detective Rick Jackson, Detective Dave Lambkin, Detective Tim Marcia, et al. One supervisor. Three file-prowling/street-pounding/case-clearing dicks.

For the D.A.:

Lisa Kahn—deputy-in-charge. The widely known DNA "Goddess." John Lewin—stoic prosecutor. Nifty suit and slick haircut. Ellen Aragon—seasoned litigator. Piercing eyes chilled by large glasses. Vesna Maras—prosecutor/recent transfer/quiet-raucous wit. Dead ringer: the Eastern-bloc ingenue in Andrzej Waida flicks. Joe Scott—Cooley's media boss. A young 71. Deep L.A. roots. His dad was a judge. His dad slammed Big Bill Tilden for honking young boys.

Bagels and coffee sit warm. Packaged cream cheese melts. The crew shags coffee. Cooley shags a bagel. Lisa Kahn takes charge. She's the Goddess DIC.

We've got high-volume unsolveds. We've got evidence extant. We've got evidence destroyed. We've got jobs with no suspects, jobs with prime suspects, and whodunit jobs. We've got grant funding. We get one DNA sample-test per case. Our priority: nail suspects in hardcore sex snuffs.

Everyone agrees. It's charged and vocal. Cooley's noshing a bagel. He nods assent.

The cops take over. It goes orderly. We go McCarthy to Jackson/Lambkin to Marcia on down.

Subtext runs strong. We work *the* worst murders. Female victims/male suspects. Penetration/ejaculation/mutilation. Lust-now-pay-later crimes.

The cops riff prosaics. We read files, we ID victims, we locate or confirm evidence lost. We locate suspects free or in custody.

Lisa Kahn speaks. Remember—DNA convicts *and* exonerates. Cooley speaks. Remember—DNA is fully precise. It cannot distort or dissemble. We can serve justice both ways.

The subtext shifts. It goes telepathic quick. It's a mass

O.J. injection. Probative certainty—one thing. Shit-slick defense lawyers—another.

More cop talk. More D.A. talk. The ball bops beatific.

Rape kits/freezers/property rooms. The comb-old-cartons/computer run/field-new-calls essentials. Resentment sizzles. They're new. They're pumped and poised. They'll buck longstanding sloth.

Lab backlog. Lab incompetence. DNA as hot topic and Kafkaesque theme. Idle cons in Quentin and Folsom. Let's try a DNA scam! We might get lucky! It worked for O.J.!!!

More talk. Deft passes—cops to D.A.s.

Rape-kit tests. The consensual sex factor. Outside labs—can we employ them? Let's buy that new fingerprint computer.

Cooley mops up bagel crumbs. Cooley shifts his chair. It's his prelude to coda.

Cooley speaks. His chair's a pulpit. The orgy desk's a pew.

Murder solving—the detectives' stern duty. Sound teamwork as device. The prosecutor's duty: Win honestly in court. Usurp the autonomy of killers. Protect society on that basis ad hoc.

The pitch worked. The sermon on the orgy desk. Nonsectarian prayer.

The meeting adjourned. Cooley grabbed a bagel for the road.

THERE'S THE LIFE.

"The Life"—noun. Convict-derived. Denotes inclusiveness and sealed borders. You're in or out. You commit crimes. You run inherent risks. That's your membership card.

"The Life"—noun. Applied to whores and their high-risk existence. Applied to all sealed societies. Risk remains the membership card.

The L.A. D.A.'s Office—ditto.

Deep roots. 152 years. *Deeeeep* history.

Wild West days. Chinatown tong wars. Race riots. Lynchings.

Police scandals. Bent cops running prosties. Bent cops bombing cars. Bent cop homicides.

Scandal without. Scandal within. It's 1928. Asa "Ace" Keyes is D.A. Ace is convicted of bribery. Ace goes down. Ace gets two years in Big Q.

D.A. Buron Fitts—deep shit in 1930.

There's a whore ring. It feeds young cooze to high rollers. Allegations arise. Fitts allegedly quashes them. Suspicions arise. The grand jury indicts. Fitts endures. Fitts wins at trial.

Deputy D.A. Jack Kirschke—'60s swinging dick. Jack's wife is straying. She's fucking this clown Orville Drankhan. Jack finds them in bed. Jack whacks them. Jack does ten years.

Hot crimes. Perpetrated *within*. Statistical rarities. Emblematic? Sure.

You're in the Life. You make the law. You fight lawlessness without. You breathe the stink. You de-inoculate. You know the law. Your knowledge engenders recklessness. You crash the law without.

History. Dig it as picaresque. Load on that lore large.

La vida, la vie—Cooley fucking loved it.

The old days. The old D.A.'s cops—phone book-thumping goons deluxe. The rubber-stamp grand jury—Indictments R Us.

History lost. History least. The Office got hip and cleaned up. Credit time and trends without.

Racial roots rocked. The Spanish land grants and up. Mexican rule early. White rule ascendant—per population flux. The Office flew with the flux. The Office grokked that melting pot/Pacific Rim rebop. The Life was rigidly restricted and inimically inclusive. It lived by the law and flowed with flux more than not. L.A. changed complexion. The Office likewise. Seoul and Ciudad Whatever meet the Dark Continent and crash the White Spot.

L.A. changed. L.A. grew. The Office followed up. Representative justice—within meets without. Race. Gender. The Cold

Case Squad. Female victims probable. Three women to prosecute.

Cooley loved it. He was 54. He lived an L.A. lifetime. He
logged half-plus in the Life. He saw the big guns work and fade.
He met J. Miller "Gas Chamber" Leavy. Miller sent Stephen
Nash and Barbara Graham to the green room. Miller 86'd Donald Keith Bashor. Miller was a self-described gas.

Then was then. Now was now. Fuck nostalgia in the knee
cracks and neck. Now was better. Then had its place. The weave
warped inextricable. Then *and* now latched the L to the Life.

Public awareness was up *now*. Awareness meant accountabil-
ity. Reformer's zeal was in *now*. That zap of zeal elected him. He
grew up in the Life. It was BIG and circumscribed. He watched
the expansion. The dimensions dazzled him.

The Life. The Office. One force synonymous.

A thousand prosecutors. Nine hundred support staff. Two hundred and eighty cops. Thirty-nine regional offices. Thirty-nine
specialty divisions. The whole downtown octopus.

Expansion—concurrent with rising crime stats. The Life
meets the Life in proximity propitious.

You side with justice. You see the Other Life revealed. You
touch the dirt. You *feel* it. The slip into slime fuels you ambigu-
ously. It's delirious dispensation. It's the perverse perk of peeking
into purgatory. It reinstills resolve. It's a salutary salary de-
incentive. Defense lawyers outearn you. The Life lets you laugh
and not care.

You help victims. You punish wrongdoers. You poke through
their shit. The Life taxed you and tweaked you, vexed you and
vamped you, nudged you and nailed you nonplussed.

Cooley knew why.

It was the truth biz. You had to love it.

OLSON-SOLIAH PISSED BACKWARDS. He shitcanned Rampart.

Halloween day—she pleads guilty. She stays free on bail. The judge sets sentencing for 12/7. Possible term: 20 to life. Possible 5-year parole.

She pleads guilty. She splits the courtroom. She sees reporters outside. She says she's *not* guilty. She blames 9/11. I can't get a fair trial. Antiterrorist fervor, oh yuck!

Outrageous.

Unacceptable.

Cooley's DDAs responded. Michael Latin fumed. Eleanor Hunter said, "She's either lying in court or lying outside court to save face."

The judge called a hearing. It occurred 11/6. The judge lectured Olson-Soliah. "A guilty plea is not a waystation on the way to a press conference."

Olson-Soliah whined up 9/11. The judge asked her straight: "Do you wish your plea to stand?" Olson-Soliah paused. Olson-Soliah said, "Yes."

Cut to 11/15. Olson-Soliah proffers a sealed motion. It's unsealed and read. Olson-Soliah boomerangs. She wants to retract her plea.

"After deeper reflection, I realized I cannot plead guilty when I know I am not.

"Cowardice prevented me from doing what I should: throw caution aside and move to trial."

The judge set a hearing for 11/28. The judge postponed it to 12/3. The judge rejected the motion. His Honor Larry Paul Fidler, succinct: "She pled guilty because she is guilty."

Boom—sentencing on 1/18. DDA Latin, succinct: "It's time to face the music."

L.A. music. Johnny Justice and the Karma Kings—'70s rock. Potential upstate music—the Carmichael job.

Olson-Soliah dodged bullets. Cooley dodged some and caught some. Cooley shut off Rampart.

He held a press gig. Chief Parks and Sheriff Baca stood by. He announced his filing declinations. He'd signed 15. He might sign 30 more. He stressed Rampart's limits. Perez and his unit stood culpable. Trials and sentencing concluded/appeals in progress. Case closed beyond that.

There's no "endemic" LAPD corruption. Don't indulge witch hunts.

He stressed his Integrity Division. He detailed some new protocols. We roll out. We move on cop-misconduct charges. We probe. We prosecute valid beefs. Look for us—all officer-involved shootings/all custody deaths.

Fifty Rampart-related cases—dumped by New Year's. No new filings predicted. *It just wasn't there.*

Rampart—adios, motherfucker.

He got some praise. He took some hits. He tapped some long-term exhaustion. The conspiracy press fricasseed him.

Cooley the Cop Collusive. Colluder Cooley Culls Contacts. Cop Curtain Curtails Probe. Will Wicked Whitewash Wither Righteous Reformer's Prestige?

You can't control public perception. Shit—it just wasn't there.

Some defense lawyers responded. The corrosive chorus continued. It was "one huge look the other way."

No, we looked. We ran a Roto-Rooter ream stick through Rampart. It just wasn't—

Fuck it. It's fall in L.A.—some sunshine, some rain. Olson-Soliah dips to her destiny. The Cold Case Squad is setting up. Prospects prickle priapic. Ouch—prime those killers for some pain.

AUTHORITY MEETS JUSTICE. He grew up with the dream. Silver Lake—catch the view now to then.

The hills near downtown. Close to Chavez Ravine. Authority spawns injustice. Power dudes evict poor Chicanos. Power dudes build Dodger Stadium.

He grew up Catholic. Chief Parker went to his church. Parker was a reformer. Cooley knew it then. Parker kiboshed LAPD corruption. Parker was a lush. Wags called him "Whiskey Bill." Parker got drunk. Parker defamed Negroes. Parker pulled asshole stunts. Cooley did not know it then.

Cooley's dad was a Fed. Dad admired J. Edgar Hoover. Hoover collected pornography and dirty surveillance pix. Dad did not know it then. Likewise Cooley.

Silver Lake was half-ass diverse. White squares ruled. Homosexuals and Mexicans goosed the body count. Silver Lake was hilly. Wags called it the "Swish Alps." Nobody called J. Edgar "Gay" Edgar.

A good kids' place. Dig the hills and terrace views. Grow up illusioned. Disillusion right. Stretch out the process.

Cooley did it. He scored in school. He played kid sports. He sold the *L.A. Herald.* The *Herald* ran crime extras. Cooley hawked copies. Crime—the young lawyer's primer.

The Finch-Tregoff case. Caryl Chessman and the green room. The hot seat and J. Miller Leavy.

The *Herald* flogged the *Spade* Cooley snuff. Spade was a country fiddler. Spade and Steve were no kin. Spade was a hophead. Spade whacked his wife. She wanted to join a sex cult. Spade got mighty pissed.

Kids kidded Cooley. Spade had slit-eyes. Chinamen were Cooleys. Where's your rickshaw, Steve?

Crime scratched his skin. A prick—no big flesh wound. His life was full. School, four siblings, church. '60s tsuris bored him. *His* world was secure. The world at large *should* be. Dad was a Fed. There *was* a stable path. It brought joy and fulfillment.

He took it.

He graduated Loyola High. He entered Cal State L.A. Cal State ran no-frills. Cal State had a low rebellion quotient. He nursed a political urge. He ran for student body veep and got elected. The prexy got drafted. Cooley made prez.

He was the Man—some squaresville youth version. He was a

groovy youth figurehead. He confronted some radicals. He helped quash some half-baked revolt. The law scraped his skin. *This* flesh wound hurt. He applied to USC Law School. He got in. Let's train for the truth biz.

We'll learn theory and statutes. We'll learn to think legalistically. Let's learn to lasso the truth.

He studied. He gorged on test cases. He choked up minutiae. Law school—the Life writ small.

He honed his truth skills. It juked his appetite. He drooled for more adventure. It was '72. He doubled his workload. He joined the LAPD Reserves.

LAPD—the Life writ *bigggg*.

He took academy classes. He logged 264 hours. He augmented his law-school skills. He was young, dumb, and full of cum. Give me jeopardy and peril. Give me a black-and-white. Give me a badge and a gun.

They did. He got Newton Division—ruff, tuff, and non-Caucasian. He worked 3 to 6 shifts a month. He worked Saturday nites. He saw a gunshot victim bleed out on a pool table. The cat took one in the aorta. The cat's eyes pulsed and flatlined.

Newton kicked the youth out of him. He got in fights. He broke up fights. He rolled code 3. He read law texts. He popped his street cherry. He inhaled legal gobbledygook. He saw horror up close. He got used to it. The SLA pulled their shit. It was calamitous nonsense. He got no pinch-me portents of distant destiny.

He rigged a plan. He culled contingencies. Plan 1: Pass the bar. Plan 1-A: Become a Deputy D.A. Plan 2: Fail the bar. Join the Feds or go full-time LAPD.

Good plans. Lashed to his life sense and wrapped in his roots. He was 26. He was disillusioned. His ideals stood intact. He was book-schooled and street-smart and tricked out to try the truth biz.

He aced the bar exam. The D.A. needed prosecutors. Plans 1 and 1-A played out plenty good.

COOLEY WORKED. The '70s sizzled. The decade featured big hair and self-forfeit. Self-absorption reigned. L.A. was stoned. Criminals rapped sadness. Don't lock me up/help me adjust/I need rehabilitation.

It hindered truth detection. It made Cooley think. It made him weigh mitigation. It buttressed the truth as absolute standard. It undermined the truth as knowable up front.

It honed his shit sniffer. It taught him to gauge forfeit per person. It expanded his cop context. He moved past suspects and victims and fast patrol encounters. He whipped past his own white-ass world and Negrofied Newton. He read case law. He took specific fact patterns. He abstracted them. He revised them to fit breaking cases. He met diverse suspects and victims. He added witnesses and families in duress. He studied. He interviewed. He talked to cops cop-to-cop and cop-to-cop lawyer. He prepped for court. He plea-bargained. He litigated. He weighed his native rectitude against a growing compassion.

He learned. He lived the Life. He tried for the truth. The truth tricked him and trapped him. There's knowing the truth. There's proving the truth. There's the truth obscured by baffling fact patterns. There's forfeit fueled by traumatic circumstances. There's forfeit as furious fuck-up. The truth triumphs, the truth eludes, the truth preys on principles that protect the guilty. Every day/every case/every courtroom deal and judgment—simple truth, two-sided truth, truth misunderstood.

Misdemeanors, felonies, dope cases, assaults, burglary-robbery. Case law, plea deals, referrals, sentencing, justice. The Life socked it to him. Some trail of truth got him through.

He met a woman. They courted and married. Two kids followed. His career advanced. The Life and the Office—one force synonymous.

He toured the County. He wrote a dope-seizure text. He

Steve Cooley in his LAPD uniform in 1975. He served as a reserve officer for the Newton Street Division from 1972 to 1978. *(Photo courtesy of Steve Cooley)*

worked regional outposts. He ran Antelope Valley. He nailed a rape-o for a hundred years plus. Bam—the longest single-victim rape sentence ever. Truth-serving and well deserved.

Commendations accrued. Ding me with dinners and ply me with plaques. He litigated. He won in court. He forged friendships with fellow Lifers. D.A.s came and went. He studied Joe Busch, John Van de Kamp, Bob Philibosian, Ira Reiner, and Gil Garcetti. He ran San Fernando Valley. Said office was huge. Its size equivalence stunned. He tried special-circs murders. The Laurie Myles case went down. Cooley was on it.

It was a three-punk/four-month nightmare. It shocked the Valley. Two murders/three woundings/thirty robberies. They shot Laurie Myles in her car. Her young son watched. They parked outside a church. Her daughter was at Bible-study class.

LAPD got the punks. Cooley put them away. Two life-without-paroles. One 38-year jolt.

The truth—sometimes simple. Ask "Gas Chamber" Leavy.

The Simpson-Goldman snuffs occurred. Cooley watched the upscut. Gil Garcetti was D.A. Garcetti tried the case downtown. The jury pool favored O.J. O.J. walked. It was an outrage. Cooley caught the upshot.

The Office lost face. Public support dwindled. The office got shivved in the shorts. Garcetti got reelected. He won by a pubic-hair margin.

Cooley supported Garcetti's opponent. Cooley got punished and transferred downtown. He took over Welfare Fraud. It was a demotion and a shaft job.

He worked downtown. He saw Lifer discontent. He saw cop discontent. He saw public discontent *mucho* close.

He worked his shaft gig. He caught anti-Garcetti vibes. Rampart broke. Garcetti fumbled it. Gilded Gil glitched out. He had no system. He had no way to look/learn/listen/collate and cull.

The Belmont scandal broke. Let's rebuild Belmont Hi. Let's rename it a "Learning Center." Let's build on some choice downtown land.

But—

The land's faulty. It's fucking toxic. It's environmentally fucked. Taxpayer millions—gone already. It's a city contract. It reeks of collusion. It howls and stirs questions up.

Where's the truth? Where's Gil Garcetti?

Cooley extrapolated. Cooley ran fact patterns and flowcharts. Cooley countered current controversies in his head. Cooley got this idea. It was quixotic and Jimmy Carter-esque.

I'll run for D.A. I'll defeat the incumbent. I'll win.

■

He gauged the public mood. He sensed truth fiends out there. He sniffed shit in the *spiritus mundi*.

O.J. walks. Clinton walks. Rampart rages. Belmont Hi is Jack Webb's alma mater. Jack ran for class prez. Jack won insurgent.

Time trucks then to now. Circa '38 meets 2000. Insurgency runs in waves. It's yesterday once more.

He talked to his family. They said GO. He talked to aides and colleagues. They concurred.

He started early. He leaked word in spring '99. He put up a Web site. He hired a consultant. He beat potential candidates timewise. He glommed key-opponent status fast.

The media scoffed. Cooley hammered Gil Garcetti.

Garcetti sets up a Trademark Infringement Unit. Garcetti gets campaign cash from Guess? jeans first. A Garcetti backer's son hits the shitter. Garcetti reduces the beef.

The Life. Dig the traditions. Challenge your boss. Hold your job concurrent.

More challengers cliqued up. Cooley quashed their momentum. They came and went. Barry Groveman stayed. Formal announcements/fund-raisers/media brouhaha. '99 hits 2000.

March 7—the runoff election. A 50% plurality chills it. If Gil gets 50, Steve's fucked.

Cooley's a Republican. Garcetti's a Democrat. L.A. runs Democrat *biiiiig*. Garcetti paints Cooley as a manic malcontent. Garcetti infers right-wing nut and gun freak. Cooley brings up Lockheed.

Dig:

It's '96. Garcetti runs for reelection. The D.A.'s Office taps the County supervisors. Let's pay Lockheed 2.5 million. Let *them* run our child-support computer system.

Post hoc, ergo propter hoc:

Lockheed lobs Garcetti campaign cash. The envelope arrives a month on.

The clock clicked. Tick, tock to March 7. Cooley picked up endorsements. Garcetti and Cooley culled campaign cash. Garcetti looks like a Latin lover. Cooley's the "blue collar" call. It's disingenuously dunned—but it works.

Cooley hammered Gilded Gil.

Guess? jeans. Lockheed. The O.J. malaise as subversive subtext. Belmont. The Three Strikes Law—noxious nightmare.
Garcetti supports it. Garcetti hurls hypocrisy. Garcetti has a sup-
porter. His grandson stands on strike 3. Garcetti shoots him 16
months. That's inconsistent. It's *mandatory* life per strike 3.

Garcetti denied Lockheed. Garcetti tried to trim the timeline
in his favor. Garcetti spoke through a consultant. The consultant
called Cooley "a traditional disgruntled-employee candidate."
Such people "always make a mistake of thinking the public wants
to hear their laundry list of exaggerated attacks."

Laundry list, shit. No tickee, no washee. I'm no Chinaman,
but I'm a Cooley.

The list lurked and lingered. Cooley complemented it. He
sent off salvos of solutions. He launched them lawyerly. They
were complex *and* commonsensical. Mr. Blue Collar blurred
into Policy Pete.

It's March 7. L.A. County votes. Groveman: 330,429/25%.
Garcetti: 504,098/37%. Cooley: 509,750/38%.

No plurality. We fight to November.

They did. Cooley *had* the momentum. Cooley *built* more
momentum. Cooley *grew* from burly to stately.

Garcetti's attacks atrophied. Cooley opposes Three Strikes.
Bullshit—I want proportionality. I'm *not* passive on public scandals—Gil, don't shit me.

Cooley got the endorsements. The *L.A. Times*/the cop unions/
the *L.A. Weekly*. Ex-D.A.s stumped for Steve. The constituency
confounded. Cooley wrapped up the right and lured in the left.
Grassroots gravitas grabbed them. The man magnetized.

Garcetti got desperate. He did ethnic shtick. *Amigos y amigas,*
love me Latinate—my blood blends with you. He placed smear
ads. They kicked off with "Republican Steve Cooley." The
"Republican" rip rolled no ripples. Cooley rode a nonpartisan roll.

He debated Garcetti. They fought fifteen times. They jabbed.
They inveighed invective. Cooley's record—deconstructed/dis-

torted/revised. Gun control/Three Strikes/Guess? jeans/Lockheed.
Slick versus burly cum stately. You're soft on crime/no, *you* are—
middle-aged malice and a sandbox-shenanigan show.

It was overkill. It delayed and postponed. It fucked with the
foregone conclusion.

People loved Steve Cooley. It was genuflectingly genuine. He
hit the clear chord of *you and me.* He did it honestly and naturally
and effortlessly.

He won huge. Pinch me—you're the D.A.

THAT WAS NOVEMBER 2000. Cut to now—1/2002.

Cooley trekked floor 18. He touched wall cracks. He turf-
marked. He rehashed recent rebop.

The *Times* tainted him. Reformer's first year—few highs, few
lows. Joe Scott prestaged them. Joe released a memo. It ran 31
bullet points. It ran down Year One in detail.

Cold cases to hate crimes. Belmont to Rampart. Anticorrup-
tion to immigrant fraud.

The *Times* piece hit first. The memo stats ran piecemeal. The
Times got more cluck for the buck.

The truth was a *game.* Politics taught him. The truth was a
moral must and a shuck.

The Blake job—unresolved. The Cold Case Squad—looking
tuff. That Armenian hit job promised progress. Rick Jackson and
Tim Marcia rode it rough.

Rampart rang on rancorous. The conspiracy nuts won't give
up. The Public Integrity Division blew a case. Conflict of interest—you're out of the box.

The truth gets trashed sometimes. You're the Man now. You
take the shots.

The truth plays schizzy. Learn from it. Light some candles.
Light one for Gilded Gil Garcetti.

Cooley touched wall cracks. Subordinates said hi. They *all*
called him "Boss" and "Steve."

He crashed at his orgy desk. There's the view. Sip coffee and put your feet up.

The truth liberates. The truth vindicates. The truth kicks in late.

Sacramento moved on Carmichael. Then to now—26 years plus.

The Feds linked shotgun pellets to shells. The link led to an SLA hideout. Forensic confirmation—*waaaay* overdue.

The Sacramento cops moved. It's 1/16/02. It's synced to gnat's-dick-hair margin.

Emily Harris—popped at 8:02 a.m. Her ex Bill and Michael Bortin—popped at 8:18.

Tight spread—16 minutes/shotgun sharp.

Olson-Soliah slinked to her lawyer. She spent 1/18 in court.

She got sentenced. Bam—the car-bomb caper/20 to life. She got arraigned for Carmichael—211 and Murder One.

She pled not guilty. It didn't matter. She was karmically crucified, french-fried, and fucked.

There's the view. All crime all the time. Courtrooms and lock-ups.

Cooley gawked. Sometimes there's justice. Sometimes the plain truth works out.

Myrna Opsahl, God bless you—I'm glad I could help. We're all here on the Good Lord's dime. Someday we'll hook up.

Little Sleazer and the Mail-Sex Mama

The snuff vibed '70s. The slime factor, the cheap angst, the Valley mall bit. It should have been then. The Victim was young. The Suspect had a career.

The Herald flourished then. L.A.'s tattling tabloid as broadsheet. The Herald flew low. Crime reportage sans condescension. Bright flashbulb pix.

There's the Victim. She's ripe in acrylic tops and buckskin skirts. The Suspect's short. Short was in then. He's smug and cool. He's tall on TV. There's a bird perched on his cue-stick.

The tale demands a two-name title. The '70s ran rife with such. They lauded larcenous losers. They deified disaffection. They freeze-framed the freon cool as the System ate them up.

Rafferty and the Gold Dust Twins. Freebie and the Bean. The Duchess and the Dirtwater Fox.

Lascivious lovers. Furious fuzz. Hell-hurtling heroes and the fabulously fucked up.

Boffo box-office then. Mainstream moviemaking masquerading as maverick art. A prattling prophecy of "Nicole and O.J." and tabloid tell-all TV.

Then was then. Hindsight hinders and perverts perspec-

*tive. Deconstruction de-hinders. Nab some noxious nostalgia.
Move with the movie-biz metaphor.*

*It's a Hollywood story. The title crawls change. The same
shit applies then to now.*

They might indict the Suspect. They might discard assumption
of guilt. Leads might tweak them elsewhere. Clues could cull col-
lectively and radically ratify thinking. New suspects could slide in.

It's a mid-sized celebrity murder. It's the first L.A. job post-O.J.
Victim and Suspect lack Simpson-Goldman sizzle. They reign
rancorous and raggedy-ass. They won't mount a media Matterhorn. They define despair and ladle on lowlife ennui. Simpson-
Goldman bid you to vulture and voyeurize. It was filthy and

Actor Robert Blake, second from left, portrayed murderer Perry
Smith in the 1967 film *In Cold Blood*. *(Culver Pictures)*

fitness-crazed and fittingly fitted with money and sex. It set a pros-
ecutorial precedent that juliennes justice and trashes the truth to
this day.

Then to now. Seven years. Brentwood '94 to the Valley 2001.

Then:

The prosecutors' duty: Secure the truth and win or lose accord-
ingly. The defense attorneys' mandate: Win at all moral cost. The
O.J. prosecutors damned O.J. with circumstantial facts and DNA.
DNA is unassailably precise. DNA is boring science. The prosecutors overexposited it and put jurors to sleep. The O.J. defense
team caught their blows and punched counterclockwise. They
concocted conspiracy theories. They capitalized on a racist cop
nailed by the word "nigger" and craftily crucified him. They syn-
thesized a siren song of racial injustice and lashed logic with it.

The jurors dropped behind drama. The jurors reached out for
racial grievance and ignored the inviolate truth.

O.J. walked. Dig the dysfunctional dynamic. Then to now, dig
the dilemma.

Celebrity snuffs scare prosecutors shitless. The dramatic potential diminishes their shot to convict. Said potential is perennial.
The O.J. case redefined it. It was a shivering shock. It was hella-
ciously Hollywood. Reason versus drama in *this* town—no way,
Jose.

There's the truth. There's dramatic logic. There's age-old
movie themes. There's the victim as killer and the killer as victim
and the victimhood cult in L.A. The Victim's a sleazebag, the
Suspect's an *actor*—oh shit, we're fucked in L.A.

MAYBE. MAYBE NOT.

The L.A. D.A.'s a reformer. The post-O.J. malaise helped make
him. He'll follow the facts. He'll track the truth. He'll assess and
scrutinize. He'll indict or bop off indictmentless.

Said facts:

It's Friday, May 4, 2001. Victim and Suspect are newlyweds.

The marriage is six months in. She's 44. He's 67. They lack that newlywed glow.

She got pregnant. He got pissed. They considered a scrape. She slept around. A DNA test nailed his daddyhood. They got hitched and had a baby girl.

They shacked apart. They had two pads on his property. He made her sign a prenup. She swore off bunco schemes. She vowed to drop her known-felon buddies.

Said Friday:

8:30 p.m. Victim and Suspect nosh at Vitello's restaurant. It's a mid-range dago joint on Tujunga. The Suspect's a regular. There's a pasta dish named after him.

They live nearby. They drive up in his Stealth. They park a block away. Why dat???—there's spaces much closer in.

They eat. They split to the car. The Victim gets in. The Suspect unkinks a brain cramp. Fuck—I left my gun in the booth!

He packs a roscoe routinely. He's got a carry permit. The Victim is a larcenist. The Victim has enemies. You gots to protect yo bitch!!!

He hotfoots it back to Vitello's. He retrieves his rod. *He* recalls it vividly. No eyeball wits confirm it.

He bops back to the car. He sees the Victim. She's got a gunshot head wound. She's slumped in the seat.

Panic now—

The Suspect runs. The Suspect crosses the street. The Suspect bangs on Sean Stanek's door. Stanek knows the Suspect by sight and reputation. The cat's a local habitué.

The Suspect begs help. Stanek calls 911. They run to the car. The Victim gasps. Her eyes roll back. Her window is down. There's no shattered glass.

Panic City—

The Suspect runs to Vitello's. Eyewits recall *this* trip. The Suspect is frantic. He begs water and gulps it. His wife "got hurt or mugged or something."

The restaurant boss wants to call 911 quicksville. The Suspect says it's redundant. He walks to the car. The victim is insensate. He starts vomiting in the street.

Paramedics arrive. The LAPD shows. Code 3 service—seven minutes to the scene.

The Victim expired. Cops braced the Suspect streetside. Cops braced him at his crib. Cops braced him for five hours straight.

He declined a polygraph. He took a gunshot residue test. Results: inconclusive. He'd handled his carry piece.

He denied all guilt. He detailed the Victim's bunco scams. He flung the fuzz a nebulous knot of her nameless enemies. His blood pressure pressed up *prestissimo*. He hospital-hid overnight. He hired a crack criminal lawyer. Said shyster shivved and sheared the Victim postmortem. The Suspect sulked submissive. The Suspect submitted to search warrants and gave up his guns. They passed ballistics tests *bellissimo*. Cops carted off cartons of the Victim's belongings. They cried out her criminality and signed in as sick souvenirs.

Days dipped by. A dumped Dumpster delivered the murder piece. The bin stood near the crime scene. The bin was deep with debris from May 4th and 5th. The roscoe reeked of gun oil. The roscoe was fingerprint-free. The roscoe's registration remained anonymous. No way to sully the Suspect. No way to hitch him to some hired hit man.

The Suspect was subsumed by sadness and wracked with regret. He doted on his daughter. His mouthpiece maligned her mother. The Victim's family shagged a shyster. A PR war waged. Cop PR dithered disingenuously. There's the Suspect suspended as a *non*-suspect—just like O.J. was at first.

The snuff vibed '80s. The heedlessness, the self-absorption, the glut. Time-trip then to now and dig the disjuncture.

Little Sleazer at fifty. Pint-sized and pumped with allure. The Mail-Sex Mama looking gooooood.

Robert Blake, left, covers his face as he arrives back at his Studio City home with his attorney, Harland W. Braun. *(Luis Sinco/L.A. Times)*

Ron Reagan's in the White House. El Jefe hails from Hollywood. Cocaine comes to conquer. L.A. blurs in the blowout and pounds with postnasal drip.

The era etched early earmarks. Plea bargains began mounting up. I'm a victim/I'm an addict/don't judge me cruel. All this excess engulfed me.

Dope delivered the deus ex machina. Dope molded mitigation pleas. The boom era boomeranged with furious forfeit. There's Little Sleazer and the Mail-Sex Mama trapped back in time. They're coked up. They writhe in relinquishment. They're pouring out postnasal drip.

It's a Hollywood story. The title crawls change. The same shit applies then to now.

Little Sleazer is an actor. All actors are fucked up. They *are* their art. Their gift is impersonation. It's nonmeditative art. The goal is to become something you're not. The goal entices narcissists. The cessation of self bodes warm. It's a riff on Woody Allen's line: "My one regret is that I'm not someone else."

Good actors impersonate across a wide character plane. Their mental gifts and neuroses mesh. *Bad* actors run with their egos unchecked. They rage effusive and grotesque. *Successful* bad actors tailor their personas to the media marketplace. They possess physical grace and/or outsized presence. Their need to impress manifests as dynamism. Their effusiveness stops short of desperation. Their grotesquerie seduces more than repels. They become themselves hyperbolized and repackaged for large and small screens. Successful bad actors push *one* creative envelope. Their drive is conscious and unconscious and ruled by casting-call nods. Successful bad actors find roles that allow them to *be* themselves and explicate their offscreen potential.

Little Sleazer plays killers. He plays them with hambone humanity and the requisite reptile rage. He chewed scenery as Perry Smith in *In Cold Blood*. Sawed-off serpent Smith had an abusive father. Little Sleazer copped to the same. His performance was silly symbiosis. It's all tics and mugs and squints and goofball grins. It recalls real-life rodent Charles Schmid, "the Pied Piper of Tucson." Schmid killed teenage girls in the '60s. He was short, dark, and narcissistic. He wanted to be an actor. He wore eye shadow. He jammed tin cans in his boots and boosted his height.

Little Sleazer as Smith via Schmid. The four *In Cold Blood* victims plus the Pied Piper's three. Little Sleazer as current murder suspect. Little Sleazer's rap on murder in *People* magazine:

"A murderer only becomes a murderer after he or she kills somebody. But what are they before they're on death row? They're you or me."

Jive wisdom. The universal-guilt chestnut. Nonjudgmentalism as actor's creed.

Little Sleazer on murder redux:

"I have played a lot of people who killed. I have been on death row. You know, I have never met a murderer in my life. That's because there ain't any. There are people who crossed the line. Some of us don't cross the line."

Wooooo! Heavy shit. Sinatra might make it work. A shrug, a Pall Mall, a martini. A sharkskin suit from Sy Devore. The frail frame that boffed Ava G. The Chairman, maybe. He granted grace and gravity to the sheerest of shit and stung you with style. Little Sleazer—no, *nein*, and *nyet*.

He's lachrymose killer Perry Smith—that crap-your-pants cry-baby. He's funky führer Jimmy Hoffa toned down for TV. He's family slayer John List—he didn't kill no one, there ain't no killers, there's just you and me.

Little Sleazer played Baretta. He frappéed us frigid and fried us with that bird on his cue. He was fortyish. He was *cooool*.

Cooool is childish. *Cooool* is nonsense. *Cooool* is the pinnacle of male-gender jive. If you don't know it at forty plus, you never will.

Combine coolness and rage. Merge them maladroit. You get the psycho default mode of bad actors.

Who tend to indulge bad habits. Who tend to disdain inhibition. Who tend to confuse their lives with their roles.

The Mail-Sex Mama's mama on her brief son-in-law:

"He would be real nasty and sometimes he would be sweet. She liked him when he was sweet. I told her that he's an actor, and how is she going to know when he's acting?"

SHE DIDN'T. *She* was acting. Her wife-coquette performance blunted her to cues. *She* was a narrow-range actor. She deployed her fading assets. Her default mode was sex.

She was a con. She ran her short con from mail drops. She

read lonely hearts and singles mags and made her marks from plaintive pleas for poon. She placed classified ads. She sent out skin pix and dunned dolts for money. Her long con was celebrity marriage and judiciously unplanned pregnancy.

She was a hell-bent harlot. She hailed from New Jersey. She died a month shy of forty-five. She wanted to be an actress. She wanted to marry a movie star.

She married a Jersey guy. They had two kids. She boogied. He watched the kids. She pursued "careers."

The law nailed her. Bad checks/Jersey/'86. Dope busts in '88 and '89. A widower answered her ads. She married him in Nevada. He gave her a roll of quarters. She split. He never saw her again.

Check beef #2 — 1994. Jail time and a move on. Arkansas beckons. Ditto the fuzz. Stolen credit cards/'96/a fine and probation. California beckons. She stalks Jerry Lee Lewis. She has a daughter. She claims that Lewis fathered it. Lewis denies it. She declines a blood test.

She has a thing with Marlon Brando's son, Christian. Christian is a killer. He capped a cat named Dag Drollet and did joint time. Jerry Lee Lewis is nicknamed "the Killer." Little Sleazer plays killers and denies that killers exist.

Thrill to the theme. Preview the prickles of prick-teaser destiny.

The Mail-Sex Mama moved on. She placed classifieds. She kept a journal. She made notes to stalk Sugar Ray Leonard and Gary Busey. She stalked retreads within the realm of reason. She dug the dynamic of diminishing returns.

She looped Little Sleazer. She sent out "Hi, single guy" letters and pix of her twenty years back. Her meshuga marriage moldered as misalliances do. Little Sleazer righteously resented her. She fitfully feared him. She kept an address book. There's sweaty Jimmy Swaggart and paralyzed pussy poo-bah Larry Flynt. There's freewheeling Frankie Valli and some doofus from *The Dukes of Hazzard*. It's a dizzying D-list descent. It's a hopped-up heap of hopeless hope.

Hope springs infernal.
Right up to May 4, 2001.

■

The snuff vibed '90s. *The Clinton climate, O.J.'s ogrehood, victimhood visions reprised. It should have been then. The Victim was younger. She's white trash worthy of Bill C.*

Little Sleazer played John List then. List lived in New Jersey. The Mail-Sex Mama was born there. Likewise Little Sleazer. It's sinister symmetry.

John List killed his family. He wanted to move on. There ain't no killers. There's just you and me.

Blow jobs ain't sex, but I came on her dress. There ain't no perjurors or obstructors. There's just you and me.

Dig the decade. Tally the tabloid toll. Pry the precedents free. O.J. walks. Michael Jackson slimes loose. Little Sleazer could wiggle. Celebrity deaths and good things both come in threes.

It's 2002 now. May 4th is ten months gone. Some cases build slow or evaporate. That means there's more or less than you see.

They might indict. They might not. New suspects might bode and retreat.

He's got the kid. He's a single dad. O.J. got the kids. It's a single-dad symphony.

Murder is always wrong. Fuck mitigation madness. Fuck the vicissitudes of victimology. Killers exist. There are too many and precious few. They ain't you or me.

Little Sleazer and O.J. should talk. They could meet at Vitello's or Mezzaluna. O.J. knows the drill. They could share spit. O.J. could cuddle and counsel and instill inspirationally.

Hang in. Act your way out. Pose with your daughter. Lies and circumstance might click your way. You might get lucky.

I've Got the Goods

We want the goods.

Who knows who. Who *blows* who. Who's got the pull and the gelt.

Who's got the size.

Who's got the habit.

Who's got the appetite.

Family dirt doesn't count. Shared blood means shared secrets and reciprocal pacts not to tell. Friendship entails codes of silence and threat. Don't dish my dirt or I'll dish yours and I'll dip deeper yet.

We're the vigorous vultures of verisimilitude. We feed off the luridly authentic. It makes us feel alive.

We require a dish-dipping disjuncture. Distance on our disillusionment. We can't carve carrion too close to ourselves. It subtracts the Allure from Alive.

Dystopian dish demands a dynamic. Demigods to devirginize. Star-stamped stand-ins for you and me.

The dynamic digs deep. We want our demigods divinely deigned and delivered defiled. We want them to soar above us and *be* us under the skin.

Godlike. Attainable. A confounding contradiction.

Only fools want to fuck movie stars and models. That anoints us a fool nation. We want Rita Hayworth in *Gilda* and Rita with the DTs. We want Rock Hudson in *Giant* and Rock at the Lavender Lounge.

Some savvy publications have exploited this need. They debuted in the early '50s.

The scandal rags.

Confidential/Rave/Whisper/Lowdown/Top Secret/On the Q.T./ Hush-Hush.

Cheezy covers. Tall print. Clashing color schemes. Jarring shades that agitated the eye.

Cheap paper. Typos and misspellings. Back-page ads.

X-ray glasses. Sex guides. Home law school.

The rags raged. The rags ran concurrent with the Red Scare. The rags subverted thought in a subversion-minded era. The rags hit right on cue.

The movie biz was 40 years old. Toga epics and musicals reigned. Film noir redistributed paranoia.

Nightclubs held sway. TV was new. It fed us jingoism and pap. Joe and Jane America lived through the Big War and got sucker punched by Korea. They dug the boom economy and bought the party line. They suffered night sweats. They built bomb shelters. They sniffed the cultural air. They developed an Us-versus-Them thing.

It encompassed the Reds and the Negroes. It indicted the Mob and the foreign unwashed. It bowed to the Glamour World and ceded their right of access.

The Glamour World was a confluence. It publicly cohered in the '50s. The scandal rags linked the divergent strands and mythologized the players. The rags built the world from photo files and innuendo.

Socialites. Film stars. Politicians. Jazz horns and playboys. Mobsters with crossover appeal.

The celebrity matrix. Revised and deconstructed for rube readers of a distinct demographic.

The estranged. The horny. The bereft and aggrieved. The worshipful stargazer ablaze with self-hatred. The chronically optimistic.

The rags were cynically optimistic. The rags were prophetic. The rags presaged the media age and the age of tabloid TV. The rags told us that the Glamour World was Our World hyperbolized and restricted for those with coin and good looks. The rags ran rancorous and riffed off their readers' resentment. The rags ran riot with one rich subtext.

THEY are YOU. YOU could get lucky.

Joe and Jane Reader, rejoice.

The rags ratted out Johnnie Ray's men's-room misadventures. They were sneeringly snide and priapically pro-gay in the pre-pride era. The rags ran Ava Gardner's murky memoirs of miscegenation. It reviled racists and revitalized race-mixer rectitude. The rags roasted rabid Sonny Tufts. Sonny bit showgirls on the thighs. The rags routed showgirls out of harm's way. The rags put Sonny on a choke chain.

Disillusionment is enlightenment. Some pundit popped that platitude and clipped a clear chord in our souls.

The rags boomed for six years. They explicated the Glamour World. They enlightened. They emboldened. They obfuscated. They told trenchant truths and launched and licked libel litigations. They raised rubber and scored skidmarks on square America.

They gave us an alternative American family. They rebutted Ozzie and Harriet. They reinforced rapacious buffoons like Sergeant Bilko. They stamped stereotypes in stereophonic sound. They violated their own validity with loopy lyrics like the ones on this page. Scandal-rag language distanced and seduced. It read as contemporaneous satire. Rag writers moralized. Rag writers attacked Reds. Rag writers rallied behind the restrictions of their

The rags loved to go after marginal Hollywood characters, like Johnnie Ray, a crooner who, the mags would allege, was involved in homosexual high jinks. *(Culver Pictures)*

time. Rag writers wistfully winked and inferred a more insidious intent.

Scandalanguage. Scopophiliac. Scarifyingly complex and multi-faceted in motive.

The scandal-rag family of the '50s is the dysfunctional family of today. Their voyeuristically viewed behavior is the hyper-analyzed behavior of today. The sedate backdrop of the '50s gave it a compensating panache. The hopped-up pace of the '90s depletes its power and underscores the behavior as prosaic.

Dipsomaniacs, hopheads, nymphos, fruits, dykes. Satyrs, Commies, miscegenators, hoods, provocateurs. Car wrecks, bar brawls, paternity suits.

Gang bangs. Three-ways. Toilet-stall assignations. Euphemized for the censors. Scandalanguaged to tell you *exactly* what it meant.

With appropriate pix.

Mug shots. Nightclub snaps. Outtakes from low-rent paparazzi.

Booze bloat. Stretch marks revealed. Loose shirttails and gaping flies outside whorehouses.

THEY are YOU. YOU could get lucky.

The scandal rags gave us the epic of hijinks gone wrong. They titillated. They linked US to THEM. They proudly promulgated the egalitarian spirit. They mocked celebrity culture. They put the "id" in "idiot." They underscored the "I" in "Idolatry." They mainlined a message in ellipsis.

Only character counts.

I dug the rags. It started about '56. I was eight years old.

I lived in L.A. I was a fucked-up child of divorce. My dad was a Hollywood bottom-feeder. He used to work for Rita Hayworth. He told me he porked her.

I allegedly met Rita at a hot-dog stand. I was three years old. I allegedly spilled a grape drink in her lap. My dad said there was a dyke bounty out on Rita. He did not explain what that meant.

My dad worked for a schlock producer named Sam Stiefel. My dad told me Hollywood tales. My mom disapproved.

She was a drunk. Her boyfriends looked like film noir psychopaths. She sent me to the Lutheran church.

Martin Luther would have been a scandal-rag fave. He talked to himself and talked to God on the john. He kicked papal ass and renounced his celibate vow. He had beady brown eyes like my own.

I dug Luther's story more than the Bible. The prose style was flat. I preferred *Whisper* and *Confidential. That* was literature.

My dad left his copies out. I got the goods. It corrupted my imagination.

My Sunday-school class went to see *The Ten Commandments.* I fidgeted and dozed. Yul Brynner played the Pharaoh. My dad said Yul was a poonhound. He had the goods.

I read a rag piece on Porfirio Rubirosa. "Rubi" was a shitbird. He hailed from the Dominican Republic. His dad was a wheel. Rubi ran guns. Rubi ran a white-slave racket. Rubi wrecked cars and married heiresses.

Rubi lived in the rags. He rarely made the mainstream press. I asked my dad about him. My dad had the goods.

Rubi had a monster shvantz. It caused internal damage. A Rubi conquest called it "Yul Brynner in a turtleneck."

I put it together. Yul Brynner was bald. I now had the goods.

The rags worked their voodoo on me. They showed me the adult world unvarnished.

Money was everything. Sex was everyone's secret. Sex was taboo. Fucking precipitated childbirth. This implied a wholesome endeavor. I didn't believe it. The rags said otherwise. I caught my mom in bed with a man. It looked like a scandal-rag pic.

The pictures scared me. High-contrast black-and-white on pulp paper. Flashbulb glare as truth.

Every photo reduced beauty. Every photo tagged the price of fame.

THEY are US and THEY will die young.

The rags died slow.

They beat back lawsuits. They pissed off people with pull. They pissed off movie magnates and publicity flacks. The rags outed homosexual actors. Flacks traded dope on minor stars to protect their high-end homos. Rock Hudson remained sacrosanct and un-outed. Some Rock lovers took the Rock's fall.

My dad had the goods on Rock. I had a crush on a 4th grade girl. She slathered the Rock all over her notebook. I told her Rock was queer. She said, "You're just jealous of him."

Outing minor actors was the rags' bread and butter. Stars rarely got nailed. Rock Hudson remained untouched. *(Universal/The Kobal Collection)*

The studios built up a slush fund. They targeted *Confidential*. They tied it up in litiginous tape. Maureen O'Hara sued *Confidential*. They said she groped a guy at Grauman's Chinese.

She won her suit. *Confidential* doused the heat on its sinuendo. The other rags followed. Their collective circulation fizzled. They flatlined into the '60s.

The decade was not kind.

Rubi kicked in a car crash. The new Prez had sex shit in his closet. The new Prez was too powerful to fuck over.

'50s sex was a leer and a gulp. The rags capitalized. '60s sex was a wink.

The rags flourished under suppression. Bad juju spawns subversive literature. American culture was reconfiguring. The rags couldn't keep up.

Hootenannies. Folk music. Deep roots on the left. A globalistic message.

Foreign films. Wild stuff that glorified adultery and ennui. Moral turpitude imported from Catholic countries.

JFK in the White House. His implied message: Be cool like me.

Sex spoofs on screen. Beehives and bikinis. The American male as a pussy-whipped shlub. The implied message: Don't sweat it—it's the human condition.

The Twist. Negro music for white stiffs. Interracial dancing on TV.

The rags couldn't compete.

They latched their lenses on foreign film stars. They spilled their sordid stories.

Snore.

They lobbed softballs at JFK and the Rat Pack.

Yawn.

They exposed Dr. Feelgoods and their loose prescription plans.

Snoresville, U.S.A. Joe and Jane America *had* their pills. They didn't want to know from the dangers.

JFK bought it. America bought that jive "Loss of Innocence" line. The Vietnam War raged. The civil-rights struggle mulched the "m" off "miscegenation." Joe and Jane's kids became freaks. Some geek coined a term: "the Sexual Revolution."

The rags were passé. Everybody was stoned and fucking. They got their titillation firsthand.

They didn't want the goods. Gossip was uncool.

The rags died.

■

I survived without them. I had the goods. I was one unhip cognoscente.

I had the dirt, the dish, the scopophile skank. No one cared. They had their own sex lives and dope habits. The rags were prophetic. THEY were US. The Glamour World had merged with the Real World—at least in L.A.

Dubious mortar. Sex and dope. Promiscuous egalitarianism.

The whole city was bombed. It was fried, fragged, zorched, zonked, blitzed, and blotto. It stayed stoned to the late '70s. I stayed stoned and stupefyingly chaste. I had the goods. It was innocuous information.

I utilized it twice.

I spotted an actress on Wilton and Melrose. She had a flat tire. She looked helpless. I knew she was a nympho. The rags said so.

I was bombed. She was bombed. I changed her tire. I suggested a drink at her place.

She said no. She gave me a dollar and a pat on the head.

The goods did me no good.

I was hitchhiking. I was bombed. A car pulled up. I recognized the driver.

He was a name actor. The rags ratted him out. A buddy confirmed it. He had firsthand knowledge.

The actor craved young males. He was indiscriminate. He picked up hitchhikers. He offered them cocaine and head.

I declined his ride. The goods did me *some* good.

■

I cleaned up my life. L.A. stabilized and de-stoned. The rags resurrected in partial spirit. They metastasized into supermarket tabloids.

I noticed them in the early '80s. I'd quit shoplifting. I was walking through check-stand lines.

I watched housewives shag the tabs. I watched hipsters goof on them. I read over their shoulders. I glommed the gestalt.

The tabs pushed minor gossip. They dick-teased their readers. The headlines promised spice. The text was coitus denied.

Bait-and-switch. Buy the tab off the headline. Jump from implied incest to kids rescued by movie stars.

The tabs pushed the lives of monarchs and TV actors. The tabs reported cancer cures and mystical amulets. The tabs reported double-digit births. The tabs tattled tales of thousand-pound women confined to their beds. The tabs detailed abductions to Mars.

The tab readership was the rag readership expanded and lobotomized. Tab readers craved reassurance and surrogate lives more than they craved the goods. They did not want their idols de-idolized and rendered attainable by chance. They wanted their fear of death assuaged. They wanted their disbelief smothered. They wanted to blunt their boredom with yarns of the gilded and blessed. They wanted to extend their realm of possibility past *all* sane boundaries.

The tabs delivered.

Amazing rescues. Chocolate diets. January-December romance.

Miraculous healings and saves at death's door. Firsthand sightings of God.

Full circle.

The rags disillusioned. The tabs reillusioned. The rags proferred sex in a sexless time and succumbed to sex abundance. The tabs metamorphosed from profligacy. They offered a fulsomely lunatic love.

Outsiders crave the goods to grease their way in. The rags said you might not want to go there. The tabs showed the insider's world as one of your limitless options.

The rags and the tabs showed their venal colors. The rags and the tabs showed some balls and some heart. The tabs pandered lower and kinder. They warmed more souls and showed more legs in the end.

AMERICANS ARE SUCKERS for dish and redemption. The tabs and the Bible notch big numbers still. The goods remain the goods. Hard data to hoard in yearning—or judgment.

Tabloid TV slimed out of the rags and the tabs. Large-scale entertainment reporting hatched concurrent. TV shows and magazines devoted to gossip and scandal. Chroniclers of the NEW Glamour World.

Puerile actors and rock stars. Fashion moguls with anorexic models in tow. Doomed and fatuous royals. Homicidal halfbacks. Sex-harassing politicians.

Entertainment reporting arrived at a wild-ass juncture. Movies were bad. Mindless blockbusters ruled. Stupes reveled in their brainlessness. They wanted to know all about them.

It was voyeurism sans sex or soul. The goods as box-office numbers and deal memos revealed. The deal as the foreplay. The boffo opening weekend as the climax.

Glamour World arrivistes: feral film execs and agents. Officious and prim. Seductive because they choose what movies get made. Sexy names in a prostitute's trick book.

Entertainment reporting merged with tabloid TV. Film criticism was subsumed by back-page plot summations and televised yeas or nays. Hard news got mauled in the flow. O.J. updates ran between premieres and bikini-waxed starlets.

Narrative lines blurred. The late-breaking goods:

The Glamour World *is* the Real World for stupes. Conglomerates dictate the aesthetic. They own the TV stations. They own the film studios. They run the entertainment mags. They collude in their shared interest.

The dish is an advertisement.

Let's huckster the new epic of hijinks gone wrong. Let's pull for the kids in our dysfunctional brood. Let's juke our ratings and bait the stupes out to the multiplex.

Robert Downey's in the slam. His new flick debuts next week. O.J.'s got a new babe. Will he off *that* one? Buy his doofus comedies on DVD.

Our kids are unruly and beautiful. They eat the poisoned fruit that we're afraid to touch. We're their flunkies and their enablers. We cosign their shit. We buy them their dope and urge them to drive drunk.

We've got the goods. It allows us to live vicarious and judge harshly at whim. It makes us feel alive.

Our new brood is soporific. Everyone's got their goods. That tops the "t" off "titillation" and vaps the "v" off of "voyeur."

I don't want the new goods. I live in Kansas. I don't want to exploit movie stars with flat tires. I'm a Lutheran. I live by the scandal-rag message in ellipsis.

Only character counts.

I'm full of Midwestern fervor. I judge sternly. I hate Bill Clinton. I love Bill Bennett and Bill O'Reilly. I mess with notions of the Lutheran ministry. I know a pastor of some renown. He said he could get me into divinity school. They'll waive the high-school-diploma requirement in my case.

My wife finds this calling dubious. She sees me as a man of soiled cloth. I wouldn't hack divinity school. I'm too joyous and profane. I see God in foul language and sex. I'm more L.A. than Kansas City. The Lutheran Church would disdain me. They'd quash the dirty tales I write for GQ.

The notion persists. The calling calls. My wife has successfully countermanded it.

She's got the goods on me. She'll go to the tabs in a hot fucking flash.

The Trouble I Cause

Blind Item. *Hush-Hush* Magazine,
March 1957 issue.
COP CONTRETEMPS —
CALL IT COERCION OR ????

We won't waste words. What paparazzi-plagued
police department deploys proactive propaganda via a vivid
TV show? Said show: sadly sagging into retrograde ratings. A
ripe rumor: The star of the stale show shivers in the shadow of
a politically potent police chief.

The chief chirps. The star stutters and stammers. That's the
standard stamp of their relationship. Hot news: Has the hell-
bent El Jefe handed the star a startlingly malevolent mandate?

Item: A certain PD circumvents civil rights routinely.
During the Depression they deep-sixed the dispossessed and
deported them to distant states or whipped them into work
camps. The cops called it the "Bum Blockade." It kept hungry
hordes out of Hollywood. It hustled homeless herds out of

Hermosa. Hell—it kept a scintillatingly sinful city cosmetically clean.

Item: Has the pissed-off police chief told the stuttering star to scrawl a scurrilous script? Will said script scrutinize the Bum Blockade and blasphemously blast the need for its reinstatement? Do you smell a smoke screen to finagle a Fascist agenda? Will the servile serfs of a certain PD implement it?

Remember, dear reader, you heard it first here: off the record, on the Q.T. and *very* Hush-Hush. . . .

1.

Jack Webb: a jejune jerkoff jacked around by the LAPD. A punk pawn in the paws of Chief William H. Parker.

A script reader skimmed me the skank. She perused paper at Paramount and perched in my pocket. I owned her. She dove dusky girls at a dyke den in Duarte. I had snappy snapshots.

The script was surreptitiously submitted. Jackoff Jack wrote it. Sapphic Sally noted notes in the margins. She pounced on the PARKER penmanship.

She recognized the round R's and tall T's. She'd dragged herself through three years on *Dragnet*. Parker penned moronic margin notes on all the scripts she screened. She hated Jumpy Jack. Jack tried to juke her into bed with a muff-munching mulatta. Jack loooved to watch.

I paced around my pad. I mixed a morning martini. It mingled through my membranes and mesmerized me. The March issue was a motherfucker. I rained rancor on a randy boy who rammed Rock Hudson. I blasted that blind item.

Dick Contino called me. He dished more dirt. Baaaad blood bopped between Bill Parker and Juvenile Jack. It bipped back to '54. Parker partisaned Bum Blockades then. Parker the facile fascist with fangs. Jive Jack the unctuous *Untermensch* under his thumb. Dick demurred on more details. Impetuously implied:

Jack Webb was so convincing in his role on
Dragnet that the LAPD would receive
constant calls asking for Sergeant Joe
Friday's help. *(Los Angeles Times Collection,
Department of Special Collections, Charles E. Young
Research Library, UCLA)*

Parker pulled the puppet strings and pitted his will against
Webb's. Webb wiggled, withered, and wailed, "What do you
want?"

I mainlined my martini. It seared my cerebellum and pinged
my pineal gland. It was godlike good to be Danny Getchell—the
scandal-scamming Scopophile King!

My living-room door lurched loose. It levitated. It lolled off its
latches. It creaked, crashed, and flew to the floor.

Look: LAPD Sergeant John O'Grady.

He bristled. He brandished a Browning pump. He brought the butt end down and bumped the bulge in my BVDs.

I retched and ran out of breath. I belched up bile and Beefeater's. My shag rug shot up and hauled me down in a heap.

THE LINCOLN HEIGHTS drunk tank:

An inferno. Incontinent inebriates installed within. Howling hopheads. Wetbacks and wienie waggers. Misanthropic misdemeanants crammed in a crap-crusted crawl space. Sixty sunkenfaced sub-felons sunk in a subterranean shit chute.

Bars. Stainless-steel staves. Sticky stained and sealed with semen. Cement walls. A flat floor flecked with floating phlegm flakes. Catty-corner off a catwalk: the INS tank. *Mucho* Mexicanos mopped up by the *migra*.

My head hurt. My balls boinged. O'Grady ossified me. He planted righteous reefers on my ass and popped me for Possession. He blitzed me for that blind item.

I stood by the stainless-steel staves. I fretted. I froze in a fresco of frustration. I was fundamentally fucked. I'd landed in the lurid lurch of LAPD limbo.

Winos wailed. Hopheads howled. Homos humped in a hot heap. Sheriff's shits moved Mexes out of the *migra* tank. Jungle John O'Grady assisted.

The shits chatted up the cholos. "You want *trabajo*? You want to be in a movie?" The cholos chained cigarettes. They chomped their chancre sores and chewed on the offer.

The shits shot back to the drunk tank. They walked up to wickedly wasted winos and whispered. The winos wiggled and went wow! The shits ripped off their wristbands. They scooted a scurvy line out to the catwalk.

O'Grady observed. I orbed in on him. O'Grady ordered the Sheriff's shits about. They moved the Mexicans. They led them to a loading dock. The winos wiggle-walked their way.

I felt squirrelly. I squinted square at the dock. O'Grady squawked at the Sheriff's shits and shoved his weight around. The shits whipped on the winos. They manhandled the Mexes. They ripped wristbands off four choice cholos. They chewed out four chumps and sidled them in a side door.

I got the gestalt. Troublesome *trabajo*. A movie or the *migra* and a march to Mexico. A chilling choice for Charlie Chorizo.

A truck trundled up. The back bed dipped down to the dock. O'Grady growled gruff. He grabbed wetbacks and winos and herded them wholesale.

Movie meshugas. *Bum Blockade*—a blighted blockbuster for LAPD? Threatening threads thrown down at ME.

I paced. I skirted scurfy scamsters and chirpy child molesters. I was framed. I was french-fried and frappéed. I was fright-fraught and frazzled.

I heard hard voices wafting out a wall vent. I crawled over two crybaby creeps crapped out by the john. I jumped on a jigaboo's head and vaulted up to the vent. I heard John O'Grady grandstand gratuitously.

"We'll take two birds out with one stone. The pretty boy and Getchell."

The jigaboo jiggled. I jerked into jitters and jumped off his head. I jostled a junkie draped on a drag queen.

I paced. I plodded and plotzed. Deputies dipped through the tank. They read wristbands and ran inmates into court. Sixty sullen sub-felons sank down submissive and slinked toward a nudge from the judge.

I was alertly and alarmingly alone. I was the Stranger—stranded and stripped bare. It was existential exile. I was freaked out like that frigid frog Camus.

The bars banged and boomed. They sluiced and slid. A pouty punk with a pompadour popped in. The bars bashed shut behind him.

I moseyed up. I moved in and made him.

Harry Hungwell. A hunky homo. A hophead. The studly star of Stan Stevens's flick *The Greek Way*.

Harry hated me. I hung his handsome hide in *Hush-Hush*. I hipped Hollywood to his homophile habits. PRIAPIC PROSTY PRIED OFF PRINCE SAHEED AT ALL-BOY BORDELLO.

I said, "Hi, Harry. What's shakin', Daddy-o?"

Harry hiccuped. Harry heaved. Harry twitched and twanged and ran red in rage.

I read his wristband. Fuck—555 PC.

The code numbers numbed me. Possession. Paraphernalia. The narcs nabbed Harry with heroin and nailed him with needles.

Harry said, "You framed me. O'Grady said so."

I laughed loud. "Back off, bun boy. O'Grady framed *me*."

Harry hurled my way. He lurched and lunged and shagged a shiv from his pants. A black book blipped out and flew to the floor.

I jumped back. I judo-chopped. I jabbed and jammed and julienned Harry. I humped heavy hurt. I ripped and raked and raised welts. I hammered Harry with hapkido and japped him with jujitsu and tore him up with tae kwon do. I sheared the shiv from his hand and socked an eyeball out of the socket.

Harry screeched and screamed. He spun and spasmed like Sputnik on speed. He listed and lolled and launched into one-eyed orbit.

Fuck—fuzz at five o'clock. Big bulls barging down on the bars. Setup—the Sheriff's shits shot Harry in to shank me. O'Grady ordered it.

I hunkered down. I hid behind hysterical Harry. I bagged his black book. I throttled his throat and shoved him up to shield me.

I ran. I held Harry. The Sheriff's shits shot through the bars. Harry hemorrhaged and absorbed ammo. He buckled behind buckshot and slumped slow with slugs.

I jumped on the john. I hurled Harry down. Bullets bit his balls and popped off his patellas. I shook and shimmied up the wall and vipped into the vent. I blasted my way into black.

2.

Vibrating vents to silt-sifting sewers. A manhole maze under L.A.

I slogged slow. I swam swift. Currents curtailed and carried me. I flew through flipped-out flotillas.

Fetid fetuses and hamburger husks. Rats like Rin Tin Tin. Squishy squids and squashed beer cans.

I paddled with a propeller piece and steered with a stick. I soaked my way soddenly south. I was aqueduct-adequate and sewer-certified. I played a plump pimp in *He Walked by Night*. Bad guy Basehart buys it by Ben Hong's herb hut in Chinatown. He's the undulating überfiend under the Broadway Bridge.

I looped through Lincoln Heights. I churned through Chinktown. I crested on a crosscurrent and crashed at Chavez Ravine.

I meandered out a manhole. I bopped to Ben Hong's. Chinks checked me out. Slanty-eyed slicksters with pierced pigtails and pointy-toe shoes. I shivered. I shook. Shitballs shot off my shirt.

Ben Hong handed me a hophead highball. Boss belladonna buttons and monster ma huang. I chugged it. It churned through me. I charted my chance to chisel and cheat my way free.

I owned Bad Ben. I quashed a quixotic *Hush-Hush* piece on his perverse peccadillos. Ben poked Peking ducks with his peewee pecker. Ben dicked ducks from Shanghai to Sheboygan.

Ben hid my *Hush-Hush* bug gear. Ben bowed and beamed and bent to my bidding. He brought me a big bowl of Hochohan soup—hard on the hoisin. I hauled out Harry Hungwell's black book.

I tripped through his tricks. Harry was heavy hung and cooly connected. He trick-trucked with all the hot homos.

Rapacious Raymond Burr. Robert Taylor—ribald and right-wing. Dirty Dave Garroway. Adlai Stevenson—standard stands at the Statler. Randy Randolph Scott—rump wrangles at his ranch in Rio Ricondo.

I tracked tricks. I nabbed names. Harry played hide-the-hose with half of hip Hollywood. He mowed his meat on Monty Cliff. He laid the linguine on Leonard Bernstein. He boffed butch Burt Lancaster at Leo's Lavender Lounge.

Two no-name names and numbers nudged me. "Jack" and "Bill."

I called Carla Cardiff—my cop communications contact. She noodled the names and numbers. She ran them through her reverse book.

Holy *Hush-Hush* Hannah—

Jolting Jack Webb. Wicked William H. Parker.

I BORROWED Ben Hong's Hudson Hornet. I parked by Parker's pad on Parkman.

Dusk dimmed down. Twilight twirled and slid through slits in the smog. I bopped behind belladonna and metastasized with ma huang. I was hopped up and homicidal.

Parker popped out of his pad. He poured himself into a Pontiac and punched it. He was bleary-eyed and blotto. He blew a red light and raised rubber.

I sidled up to a side window. I screwed off the screen and scrunched my way in. I listed and landed on the living-room rug.

I heard gravel growls. I flipped on my flashlight. My beam beat down on a beady-eyed bull terrier.

I tossed him a taste treat. Ben Hong's lichee-nut lollipop laced with LSD. The hound hooked it down and humped a hand-sewn hassock.

I peered around the pad. I slinked and slunk and surveilled surreptitious. I pored through piles of Parker's papers. I caught his coruscating correspondence.

Parker pen-palled with punk patriarchs in Paraguay. He kept carbon copies of his own nasty notes. He fulminated to Fulgencio

William H. Parker, appointed chief of police in 1950 and serving until his death in 1966, molded the LAPD's paramilitary image that would earn the force both fame and infamy. *(Los Angeles Times Collection, Department of Special Collections, Charles E. Young Research Library, UCLA)*

Batista. He waxed weepy to Juan Perón. He ballyhooed Bum Blockade to rasty Rafael Trujillo. He lavishly lauded the "LAPD Reich" and lachrymosely lamented likely losses in the '58 elections.

?????

I pawed more papers. I shot through shelves and drove through dressers and drawers. I found a fat file: "'58—Senate/Governor's Race."

I read it—red-eyed and *rapidamente*.

Facts. Fatuous fancies. Prissy prognostications. Doleful dope on the cancerous candidates.

Idiot incumbents: Governor Goodwin J. Knight and senescent Senator William F. Knowland. Retards. Retread Republicans. Late-breaking lowdown: Both boobs plotted a ploy to ply themselves with more power. Noxious Knowland would seek the governor's seat. Goody Knight would swing a sweet switcheroo and sententiously seek the Senate.

Bodes big, but:

Goody and Boiled Bill boasted paltry poll numbers. The numbers negated them and nodded to their obvious opponents:

Senator Clair Engle—a Democratic demagogue. Attorney General Edmund G. "Pat" Brown—a dipsomaniacal Democrat diva.

The file fulminated:

Pat Brown bristled and broiled with hate for Bill Parker. Brown brewed a brilliant plan to broast him—if he got his gloves on Goody Knight's governorship.

Pat patterned a plenary plan to plow the LAPD. Fuck—full-scale floodlights on their fascist agenda!

The file text turned torrid.

Parker paid heavy headshrinkers to hatch populist polls. Their freakily Freudian findings:

Cal Californian calls it this way. Carla Californian concurs. We want Homeric heroes to love and lead us. Menschy men with magnetic machismo. We want magnanimously male MOVIE STARS.

Ooo-hooh, Daddy-o! I was digging it all, Democratic!

Torrid text. Followed by: filched tax returns.

Menschy men:

Doofus Duke Wayne. Holy Hank Fonda. Randolph Scott and Robert Taylor—turgid turd burglars tracked from a trick book.

I read the returns. Doofus Duke—solidly solvent. Holy Hank—

in hock on stiffed stocks and half-breed haoles hatched in Hawaii. Robert and Randy—rolling in rice.

Oooooh, papa-san! I was paring it down, paranoiac!

JACK WEBB LIVED in a lurid lanai in Laurel Canyon. A lavish lean-to off Leawood and Lotus Lane.

I slid my sled slow to the curb. I bipped the back bumper of a big Bonneville. Fuck—a furtive fuzzmobile with fish fins and a wiggly whip antenna.

I loped around the lanai. I leaned low and lurked under wide windowsills. I popped up and peeked the pad. I spotted Jive Jack and John O'Grady.

Simmering silhouettes. Bad boys backlit by lava lamps and low shadows. A TV cop caught in a conundrum. A goon who got Getchellized.

Webb waved a scrawled-up script. O'Grady groused and grew grave. I loitered and listened.

Webb said, "I want Ronald Reagan. Randy Scott's too swishy to play a cop."

O'Grady sneered snide. "We've got no wedge on Reagan—and he won't work for the low coin the Chief's paying."

A ripe revelation ripped me:

Harry Hungwell's whore book. One wild wedge on Raw Randy Scott.

Webb whined and whinnied. "Johnny, have a heart. I don't want to direct this fucking lox."

O'Grady said, "Shitfire, Jack, you have to. You direct *Bum Blockade* or Parker pulls the LAPD's sanction on *Dragnet*."

Webb withered. "Okay, I'll do it. Jesus fucking Christ."

O'Grady groaned. "No, Danny Getchell."

Webb said, "What's that cocksucker got to do—"

"He killed a fruit hustler at the Lincoln Heights tank. The D.A. just issued a warrant. The first cop who spots him will waste his alliterative ass."

Cowabunga! Call it cold—cop conspiracies colliding—

Webb whistled. "That fuck will rue the day he wrote that blind item."

O'Grady said, "Rue, shit. You just be at the set at midnight. We're hijacking a load of wetbacks and bringing them in to play bums. Between them and those humps we got from the tank, we'll have enough extras."

A telephone trilled. O'Grady grabbed it.

"Yeah?"

Scintillating silence. O'Grady—grossly gruff.

"Listen, Pancho, you'll do as you're told. The truck's crossing the border at eleven. We'll take it down in Chula Vista."

Simmering silence. O'Grady: "Yeah, what's the plate number? . . . DDX089. . . . Yeah, right."

I went slit-eyed. I sluiced back to my sled and slid in. I sliced south—silent and psychopathic.

3.

I tripped into the truck near Trejo and Tregundez Streets. I tipped in tanked on tequila.

The truck trundled and shook on shot shocks. It shimmied by sharecropper shanty shacks and rocked through ruts in the road. I popped in off a pogo stick. Dig my distinct disguise:

A somber sombrero. A sexy serape. Sandblasted sandals and a zany Zapata 'stache.

The wetbacks welcomed me. We quaffed Cuervo and chewed cheese chimichangas. I said "*Sí, sí*" every six seconds. The beaners bought me as one bad *bandido*.

We bopped over the border. We chugged into Chula Vista. We violated vital immigration laws. We hid under heaps of hashish hunks and chests of child smut. We bit through burlap bags and hooked into the hash. We vizzed through vivid visions. Visitations with the Venal Virgin of Vera Cruz and other vapid shit. We hash-howled through one hot hijack.

Some fucked-up fuzz futzed with the truck. They cadged into the cab. They badged the burrito boy behind the wheel. They pistol-whipped the *puto* and poured him out on the pavement. I heard it through holes in the hash heaps.

The hijackers hauled ass. One rascal said, "Rio Ricondo—*rapido*." One jackal said, "Jack's shooting night for day."

Rio Ricondo. Risqué Randy Scott's rancho—

The truck trudged tranquil trails and cut through coastal canyons. It hung hairpin turns and hit high heights. I tore the tarp by the tailpipes and took in the view.

Rich ranch land. Ridges rippled with rivers and roaming roans. A red-rocked ranch right up the road. Arc-light glow glaring.

Nail it now—night for day.

The truck stalled and stopped. The wetbacks snoozed and snored. They were hovering high in Hash Heaven.

I tapped my eye to the tarp hole. I saw a skimpy crew. Skeletal and skanky. Scabs hired cheap. Scads of scabby winos. Mexicans moved out by the *migra*. The recidivists recruited and run in from Lincoln Heights.

Jack Webb in jodhpurs and a jersey. Shitty Sheriff's shills with shouldered shotguns. Two rangy rump rustlers resplendent in LAPD blues.

Rough Randy Scott. Rabelaisian Rob Taylor.

Webb warbled, "Action!" A Panaflex panned. It whirled wide and dipped to the door of the ranch house. Rangy Rob ran up. He rang the bell. Raw Randy rolled up rasping. The blue boys booted the door down. Dig the cell block set sunk within.

Bare bars stuck to steel stanchions. Seedy cement. Cruddy creeps passed out on pallets. Lovely Lincoln Heights—revisited and revised.

Rob said, "We've got to get these panhandlers and welfare jerks off the street."

Randy said, "The Communists use them to undermine our way of life."

Rob said, "We've got to reestablish the Bum Blockade. It's the first line of defense between us and the Fifth Column."

Jodhpur Jack yelled, "Cut! Print it!"

A greasy grip hauled a hose up to the truck. Jingo Jack yelled, "Wake up, you illegals! It's movie work or a trip back to T.J.!"

The hose heaved. Water whacked the truck. It doused the dozing Diegos and hauled them out of Hash Heaven. We got sprayed, spritzed, and sprinkled. We got swizzled and swacked. We hit the ground on our huaraches and hurtled.

I hunkered by a hibiscus hedge and hid from the heaving hose. Sheriff's shills hemmed in the *hermanos*. Hardheaded harness bulls with Remington riot pumps.

The spics spotted the cell block set. Their hackles hopped. Their lazy lids levitated and hitched up to their hairlines. Their hashish-hallowed hearts hardened in rigorous rage.

Joo don' juke Juan Wetback into no jail.

They pulled stabbing stilettos and mini-machetes. They shook out shanks and shears. They flew at the flank of Sheriff's shills with shotguns.

A shuddering shitstorm shook Rio Ricondo. Double-aught deershot disinterred. It decimated and disemboweled and detached dicks as it dispersed. It mowed down the Mexicans and mulched them into movie-set menudo.

Panic. Pantheonic pandemonium.

I ran toward Randy's ranch. I crashed through the crew. I capsized cameras and lunged into lights. I jostled Jack Webb. I rammed Randy and Rob. I grazed grips and ground them into the grass.

I saw a paved parking patch. I popped by Packards and Pontiacs. I detoured by Daimlers and Dodge coupes. I jumped in the back of Jingo Jack's Jag.

I nuzzled under some newspapers. I cringed craven and cried out to Christ. The ignition ignited. The Jag jumped. Jerky Jack ratched rubber and ran a rabid rosary.

The Trouble I Cause

The Jag jammed. Jack razzed us out of Rio Ricondo. I latched onto a lug wrench. I creased Jack's crewcut crisp. His cranium cracked. I crawled into the front seat. I whipped the wheel and braced the brake and clawed at the clutch. I jerked the Jag into a ditch.

Jack was wedged into a wind wing. He sniveled. Snot snuck out of his nose. Blood blended in. His scalp was scoured down to his skull.

I said, "Tell me, Daddy-o. All of it."

Jack jabbered. "It's fucking Parker. He's had these fucked-up plans since '54. He thinks this *Bum Blockade* lox is a winner. It's his power play. He's got dirt on Taylor and Scott. They were boning that queer you killed. Parker coerced them into the flick. He wants to shove Bill Knowland and Goody Knight out and run Taylor and Scott for governor and the Senate. He thinks the voters want heroes. He wanted to get Ronnie Reagan, but that geek's too fucking boring and clean to extort."

I jabbed Jack in the genitals. "What's Parker's pet vice? That sick hump's got to have one."

Jack laughed licentious. "He doesn't have one, you fucking parasite, so you've got no way to hurt him."

4.

The metaphysic mauled me. No vulgar and vacuous vices.

The notion noodled my noggin. It nattered and negated and hatched holes in the *Hush-Hush* aesthetic. Humans humped and howled and hid their most hideous secrets. Men made mincemeat out of moral vows and pronged their pricks primeval. I stood steadfastly strong in my rector's rectitude. I delivered disillusionment as dystopian dish. I crucified crafty creeps and crowned myself Christlike. My magazine mandate: Track and trumpet the truth triumphant.

I holed up in the Hawkshaw Hotel in Hawthorne. I hooked down hair tonic and buzzed behind Benzedrine. Jack Webb was chained to a chair. I doped him down and delivered him docile. I hooked him on heroin and closed him up in a closet.

I was full-sized fucked. I had to frag myself free of the fruit-hustler frame and lunge from the lurch. I had to whip a wedge on William H. Parker.

My brain broiled down to my brows. My synapses simmered. The voices of various vices violated me.

Vile vocations. Vigorously venal—

It *Hush-Hush* hit me.

Call Cal Conners—that putzy pedophile at Pacific Bell. Pull Parker's phone-call file.

I called Cal. I owned him. I snared him out of a snuff-flick snafu. Cal collared the call sheets and called me back collect.

He ran down a numbing nab of names and numbers. Cops and coroners. Contractors and congressmen. Conservative columnists and dithering dictators in the D.R. I daydreamed. I dozed. I licked my lips and lopped lice off my balls.

Cal said, "I saved the best for last. Parker called Minnie Roberts's Casbah thirty-four times in the past two years."

The Casbah—a cool coon cathouse in Compton. A sepia sin spot. Jungle jazz and jive. A race mixer's rendezvous. Man-o-Manischewitz—a mecca for miscegenation!

Bim, bam, bingo—it ALL cohered copacetic.

Pat Brown capered at the Casbah. Call it calm—*Confidential* caught Pat with two Congo cuties. June '55—DEMOCRAT DALLIES WITH DUSKY DELIGHTS.

Oooooooh, Daddy-o! I was reining it in, repugnant!

THE CASBAH CAROUSED by night. Ten hot-sheet holes above a sweltering sweatshop.

I breezed through in broad daylight. Luscious Latinas cut condoms on long latex looms. I undulated upstairs. I moseyed by Minnie's office. I jacked the janitor up and bought him off with a big bag of boo. He opened the office and bid me bye-bye.

I dissected the desk. I dragged out the drawers and culled the cubbyholes. No ripe rosters or ledgers and lists.

I flung up the floor rug. Flies flicked on a flat safe. I ditzed the dial and notched numbers. I caught the combination.

I hooked up the handle. I dug deep and latched on a ledger. I pawed pages and pounced on Pat B. and Bill Parker.

Minnie Roberts wrote rancorous notes. She patronized Pat Brown. She parodied Parker.

Pat poked haughty high yellows. Pat politicized as he poked. Pat put out his policies to Polly and Pauline—two quixotic quadroons. Pat talked too much. Parker picked up on his penchant. Parker's pet pit dogs manhandled Minnie. They enterprisingly entrapped her. Minnie was mush. Parker's pits bugged Pat's regular room. Parker policed Pat's passion and heard him address his agenda. A wicked woman stenographer stood by and notched notes. Name it now—Pat popped off about his private probe of the LAPD. Parker puckered and pocketed the data. He hatched his hokey hero plan. He pollinated politicians. He seeded seedy movie stars and blackmailed them blasphemously. *Bum Blockade*—priceless propaganda. Starring roles for two steamy stallions stamped for the statehouse and Senate.

I chewed on a checked entry. Ping—Pat was poking Polly at 8:00 tonight.

I went to work. I toked some tea with the janitor and assured his assistance. We coursed through the Casbah.

I tossed tools and tore through termites and whipped wires through walls. I rewired Pat's room and rigged a reverb route right back to Parker's. I wire-wiggled whipcords into a messy maintenance room. I hooked up a hi-fi hitch and spindled up my own speakers. I could hear ecstatic exclamations and send sound every which way. I could broadcast with bristling bravado.

Danny Getchell. The Demon DJ on Radio K-FUCK—about to abort history.

———

I HUDDLED BY my hitch. I hid behind hot headphones. I massacred myself with mary jane and perched with my Polaroid.

7:10, 20, 30, 40—7:59.

Speaker 2 sputtered. Pat Brown panted: "I hate those goddamn stairs."

Polly pooh-poohed Pat: "Don't complain, baby. Give me a dose of that Democratic love."

Pat popped a gut. Whore humor—ha! ha! Speaker 1 spritzed. Boss Bill Parker said, "Unzip me—the son of a bitch is talking already."

Holy hard-on! Hear that hate—heavy on the homoerotic!

Speaker 2 spunked. The stenographer stammered. "You're all bunched up in your shorts. You should wear boxers. Jockeys are strictly for kids."

Speaker 2 sparked. Polly pouted: "Come on, Pat. Pour me the pork."

Speaker 1—sticky with static. Pixilated Parker: "Get a grip on that thing and tell me it's big, or you'll never make sergeant."

The steno stuttered. "It's soooooo big. It's got a head like a Nazi helmet."

Speaker 2—crackle crisp. Passionate Pat: "Let's take off our clothes. I want to talk politics." Poli-sci Polly: "Tell me bad things about Parker. You know, all the colored folk hate him."

Speaker 1 spurted. Parker—palpitating with paws on his pud: "Faster, he's getting to the good part."

The steno—starting to steam up *my* stones: "You're bigger than Jack Webb. You're bigger than my husband and all Negro men. Shit, it's flopping out of my hand."

Pat Brown—prophetically precise: "Parker can't get it up for man, woman, or beast. I heard he's hung like Napoleon. They won't be able to find it when they autopsy him."

Bill Parker—surfing the semen sea of self-loathing: "Jesus, I'm almost there!"

I wiggled wires. I circumscribed circuits. I rigged reciprocal reverb and sent sound to both rooms. I picked up my Polaroid and flew off the floor.

I hammered down the hallway. I banged both doors off their bolts. I found the fetching foursome perched in Pat's parlor.

Pat was knock-kneed nude. Parker's pants pooled at his patellas. Polly was baby-buff and tantalizingly tan. The stacked steno stared at her — savagely sapphic.

I popped one perfect Polaroid. Insurance for loss of life or limb. I buried it by a burger stand at Beverly and Berendo.

Parker and Pat patterned a pact and pulled back from their sinful symbiosis. The Republicans ran Knowland and Knight. They lost in landslides. Pat Brown gnashed Knowland and got the governor's gig. Parker bumped Bum Blockade off his demonic dance card. Ribald Randy and Rob rustled rumps and refrained from politics. They weren't Homeric heroes here at Hush-Hush.

Ronald Reagan ran for governor. He incinerated incumbent Pat Brown. Reagan reigned as our 40th President and retired to a ranch like Rio Ricondo.

Draw your own corrosive conclusions.

Part II

RICK LOVES DONNA

Hollywood Fuck Pad

1.

I died in a futile gunfight. Others fell before me. This is for them.

My promotion/transfer slip arrived—Hollywood Patrol to Hollywood Homicide. Holly*weird*—rectal-raped runaways, cocaine killeristas, fag-in-the-bag body dumps. I was 31. I had four years in patrol. I was testosterone-torqued and pumped. It was fall '83. Ray-Gun was Prez. Gates was Chief. *Dragnet still* reran. O.J. was a Westside splib. Rodney King was a cannibal couched in the Congo. LAPD was King!!!!!

Russ Kuster ran Hollywood Homicide. He took no shit, he brooked no shit, he brooded over bonded bourbon nitely. He favored Reuben's, the Firefly, and the Hilltop Hungarian. Holly-wood hemmed him in. He shit where he ate. He kept a condo on Cahuenga. He warred with his wife there. They battled over his bitches and his Walpurgisnachtian workload.

I grabbed Russ in the squadroom. He checked out my rhino

Russ Kuster ran Hollywood Homicide until he was killed in the line of duty on October 9, 1990. *(Photo courtesy of the LAPD)*

regalia. I love rhinos. I've got a faux-rhino gunbelt and faux-rhino boots. My faux-rhino bedspread captivates cooze. I fucked a rhino once. A street creep slipped me a hash brownie. I flew Trans-Zulu Airways to Zimbabwe. It was so *goooood*.

Russ said, "You look like a fucking pimp. You may be useful here."

"I welcome the opportunity, boss. And I figure a flamboyant appearance will help me on the bricks."

Russ nodded. His teeth were nicotine-napalmed and notched down to nubs. He was stripped and striated by stress.

He lit a cigarette. "Your partner's Tom Ludlow. You know, 'Phone Book' Tom. He's got 22 notches on an old Yellow Pages. It's against the regs, but it gets confessions. I'm not saying do it or don't do it. I'm just saying it works, and I demand results, and if you don't produce, you'll be working the AIDS car and wearing triple-strength rubber gloves like a fucking proctologist. You ever pick up an AIDS vic?"

"No, boss."

"Their limbs tend to drop off. Do a good job here and don't subject yourself to the experience."

I clicked my heels. Russ loved Wehrmacht protocol. My faux-rhino gun buckle rattled.

Russ said, "We need a fuck pad. We've got 14 married cops who need a crib for parties and nooners. We need five bedrooms for a hundred a month tops."

I laffed. "Slum pads go for twice that."

Russ smiled. "Imagination or coercion always works for me. No killing, though. We're still taking heat for that old granny those guys waxed in Newton."

HOLLYWOOD. Home of hipsters, hugger-muggers, and hermaphrodites. My hutch since '78. I knew every crack-pipe crevice. I worked Harbor for a year and humped home. I knew the hookers, the homos, the heist men. Methheads met my eyes and meandered. K-Y kowboys kringed. My F-car featured a faux-rhino horn. Illegal, but effective. It glowed like a priapic prism.

I cruised the hot-sheet huts on Sunset. No five-bedroom pads, rats like Rodan, staphylococci-stiff sheets. I cut south on Highland. Dave Slatkin ran the LAPD Animal Shelter. It was an ex–head shop. Some diesel dykes ran it. We popped them for paraphernalia and pried up the property.

I pulled up and walked in. Dogs drooped on confiscated couches. A malcontent mastiff growled. A baleful bull terrier snarled. The shelter was Dave's passion and an LAPD ploy. We raid meth labs and rescue guard dogs. Dave goo-goo-talks them and ladles on the love. We train them to kill burglars and find them good homes. They wear breastplates with "Trained to Kill" logos.

Dave smooched a brindle pit. I said, "Jane mind you bringing fleas home?"

"She wears a black-studded flea collar. It's kinky shit."

I yawned. A Dogo Argentino pissed on my shoes.

"Russ Kuster's got a job for you. He's got me searching for a fuck pad. He wants you to bring some station trusties in and GI the place."

Dave yukked. "Don't tell me. Five bedrooms for a C-note a month."

"That covers it. Any—"

"There's some SRO cribs on Tamarind north of Franklin. Junkie squatters, the shits. You know Harry Pennell?"

"No."

"He works Wilshire Patrol. He's black, and he's got a scam going. He tries to rent pads in Brentwood. They say there's no vacancy, and he sends a clean-cut white cop in two hours later. It's a moneymaker. They rent to the white cop, and Harry pops up with his hands out."

"Can he meet me—"

"I'll tell him Tamarind and Franklin in an hour."

The Dogo sniffed my crotch. He grew a wicked woody. I shooed him off.

"Russ said you can forensic the place. He thinks it's useless, but he's willing to indulge you."

Dave sighed. "I know Hollywood history. Russ doesn't. Those places were abortion mills back in the '50s. I'll bring in some luminol and turn up some blood."

"Have fun. I'm working a movie gig at the Academy tonite."

"Feature?"

"TV job. Rookie partners develop a jones for each other.

They're both married to ranking brass. The male's CO tries to rape the female. She wastes his horny old ass."

Dave picked his nose. The Dogo snagged the nugget. I said, "What do you feed these fuckers?"

Dave said, "Trusty chow. We've got stuffed bell peppers and kielbasa today."

The bull terrier laid a fart. I splitsvilled quick.

HARRY PENNELL WAS fat. He wore a green leisure suit and a purple newsboy cap pinned to a wide-wing Afro. He wore a "Kill the Pigs" button. He tucked his piece and badge in his pimp boots.

Harry bragged *bravissimo*. He owned a car wash, an AIDS test clinic, and a dyke bar called the Munch Box. He owned two wetback garment mills, three roach coaches, and six he-she outcall whores. He got away with "boocoo shit." He possessed a "notable" fuck flick. Dig: a deputy chief's wife's going down on a meter maid at Claire's Clam Club.

Harry laid the scam out: 1. He hits the pad. 2. He flashes a roll. 3. He lays out his "bitches" and his late-nite parties. 4. The Vacancy sign disappears.

I walk up. I rap my Klan konnections and ties to the fuzz. I stress black rape-os, black slashers, black hot-prowl artistes. I stress the *good* news: cops around the clock. I stress the *bad*: five bedrooms/a yard per month tops.

It took eight hits. Eight peepholes slid back. Harry smiled. Eight peepholes shut. Peephole 8 paused. A brazen biddy wedged the door. Harry got "stable" and "fine hos" out. The door slammed. I rhino-rocked up. I badged the biddy. I riffed on the "Negro crime wave." She said, "Prove yourself. I've got four lowlifes behind in their rent. If you evict them without all that paperwork, I'd be obliged to say yes."

I followed the smell. Burnt matches/crack-pipe ether/unwashed flesh. I tracked two hallways upstairs. A pit bull lounged on a landing. He growled gravel-gruff. I chucked him my lunch: Fritos and two candy bars. He snarfed down. I hurdled him and followed the stink.

There's a door. Let's kick it in.

I did it. Dig the three spiked-hair neo-Nazis. Net weight: 160. Gender: a tough call. Dig the crack pipes. Dig the crackheads entrenched on Cloud 9.

Dig the open window. Dig the rosebushes below.

I chucked them out. They weighed bupkes. They hit the bushes soft. Bush thorns slashed them new tattoos. Bush billows muffled their falls.

WE GOT THE PAD. My race jive helped. I concocted "the Negro Nabob," "the Negro Nookie Nabber," "the Black Blasphemer," and "the Sepia Succubus." Granny agreed: five bedrooms/one C per month. Numerous cops/round-the-clock access/ raucous behavior—boys will be boys.

Granny showed me the crib. 3-story, warped wood and beamed ceilings, bedrooms off central hallways. A downstairs hi-fi rigged with Lawrence Welk and Mantovani.

It *all* worked. Thick walls, privacy between rooms. Dave warned me: Harry installed wall peeks and shot infrared footage for *Bushman* magazine. I told Dave I'd mock-bust him as "the Negro Nookie Nabber."

I checked the walls and wainscoting. Dave might be right—the dark flecks might be old blood. Dave *knew* Hollywood crime. Dave insisted: mayhem metastasized south of Sunset and nudged its way north of Franklin. He loved to test old houses. He got visions sometimes. Not psychedelic shit. More like wisps, whines, whispers, and whimpers. I'll say it, rhino-reluctant: Dave's a hopped-up hip hybrid. He's a demon dog worshiper. He's a vibrant visionary. He cleans pads for Russ Kuster. It's a ploy. He's got five years on. He wants Hollywood Homicide. Two master's degrees, visions, a psychosexual seismographic history of L.A.— he might make it *faaaaast*.

I grabbed the pit bull and took him to lunch. We shared three oki pastrami burritos. I dropped him off with Dave. It was love at first bite. He chomped Dave's billy club. Dave let him have it as a chew toy. He put him on an IV drip. The tube fed him beef broth and K-9 meds. I mentioned the blood flecks. Dave said he'd glom some trusties and forensic the pad.

"I'm having visions, Rick. I'm seeing a tall, gap-toothed guy from the '50s. I get the feeling he's pretty obscure. He won't be on computer programs. I might have to go to the *Times* morgue."

I yawned. "I've got that gig tonight?"

"I heard the female lead's a fox."

"You got visions I'm about to get lucky?"

Dave said, "Frankly, no."

HOLLYWOOD HEMMED *ME* IN. *I* shit where I eat. I eschewed Simi Valley. Orange County de-orbited me. The kool Kuster kustom: Bop your beat, know your neighbors, interdict them instinctively.

I lived in a mock-Egyptian courtyard. I prized its proximity. I read in the John C. Fremont Branch Library. I lived near Harvey Glatman's photo-death den. Dave Slatkin had Glatman visions. They astounded early psychic researchers. He lived in Whipdick, Wisconsin. He was 4 years old then. L.A. visions whipped him west and formed his cop calling. He linked old evil to still-standing structures. Cops are skeptics. Dave skewered their skepticism. Dave found Barbara Graham's hypo kit behind the Hollywood Ranch Market. Dave found Black Dahlia rubber receipts in a vent at Owl Drugs. Hollywood—insidious instigator of morbid myth. Why work anywhere else?

And dig this:

I'm laying out love vibes for THE WOMAN. I know this much. She won't be a Hollywood habitué. She'll get the gestalt going through.

■

Arc lights popped at dusk. Day-for-night delivered. The Academy lit up.

The main building/parking lot/gym. The Elysian Park Hills. Ravines, gulleys, and snaky pathways uphill. The hills magnetized fruits. They got micro-close to malignant male authority. It was self-serve self-loathing. Rump rangers rutted in parked cars close to the cloister of cop academe.

We were fruit-free tonite. The lights looped east to Chinatown and Sunset Boulevard.

I wore my uniform. I carried a walkie-talkie. The gig prohibited rhino regalia. I humped the homo hunting ground. I dragged a litter bag. I snagged French ticklers, discard dildos, amyl nitrate poppers, S&M bar matchbooks.

The arc lights popped off. The hillside shot to sharp shadows. My walkie-talkie bipped.

I picked up. "Jenson."

"It's Bobby Keck. They're dousing the hills and lighting up the bar. Come on up and meet the cast."

I rogered and hitched up my gunbelt. My mini-gut flared and flattened. LAPD likes lean lines and cut contours. I find it homophiliac. It deters ham-hock dinners and donut desserts.

I walked up to the bar. Grips hauled boxes. Lighting louts lit lamps. I saw two civilians in cop blue. I recognized the man.

His lineage loomed large. The baldness, the big beak, the Latinate looks. He was the seething seed of Luis Figueroa and Rosemary Collins.

I recalled my casting sheet. "Figueroa, Miguel D." The woman pirouetted and provided a profile. That's her: "Donahue, Donna W."

Call it cold: D for Man Destroyer. D for Detour to Heaven. W for Wickedness and Winsomeness as one.

She was svelte. She had dark hair and hurricane-hurled hazel eyes. Her gunbelt hung low and hugged her hips hard. Her badge hid her left breast and hinted at hammering heartbeats.

I walked over. I reinvented myself as rhino raconteur. I rehearsed gunfights and righteous 211s. I killed a hot-prowl rape-o last year. My faux feminism might impress her.

I opened my mouth. Donna Donahue detoured me.

"Are you a real cop or an extra?"

I said, "I shot Huey Muhammad 6X, the infamous hot-prowl rapist. I wasted two wetbacks — I mean 'illegal-emigrated Mexican-Americans' — during a daring, short-range shootout at Taco Tom's on Hollywood and Western."

Miguel Figueroa said, "Wow." He checked out Donna Donahue snakelike.

Her heartbeat hammered. Her left breast lurched. Her badge bumped and boinged.

My rhino horn hardened. Figueroa stared at me. I said, "I had a big thing for your mother. I used to dig on her in the '60s."

Figueroa laughed. "Maybe you're my daddy."

Donna said, "What did the thieves at Taco Tom's get?"

I squared my shoulders and sucked in my gut. My belt slackened and flattened my fly. It undulated and unfurled. My Jockey shorts showed. They bore the Burger King logo: "Home of the Whopper."

Figueroa yukked. Donna demurred. Her hazel eyes hooked up to my blues.

"What did the robbers at Taco Tom's get?"

I smiled. "Nine dollars and a burrito tray. They burned their hands on the tray and dropped it."

Donna's jaw jumped. "And you *shot* them for *that?*"

I winked. "They were after the chimichangas and quesadillas. I had to nip that in the bud."

Donna howled. Figueroa yukked. I ran my zipper up *rapida-mente*. A megaphone geek walked up. He vibed director.

Figueroa said, "Officer Jenson iced two cholos during the famous Taco Tom's heist."

The director sneered. "Amnesty International condemned that shooting. Those robber guys had twelve kids between them."

I sneered. "Planned Parenthood commended me. I shot them in the back, by the way."

Donna smiled. Her every glimpse hurled me to heaven.

The director said, "You think you're a tough guy, don't you?"

I winked at him. "I'm your daddy."

Figueroa winked at me. "Don't be embarrassed. He's my daddy, too."

The director *seeeeethed*. "Let's go. We're doing the patrol car scene next." Donna and Figueroa walked. Donna wiggled her fingers over her shoulder. I blew a kiss at her back.

A PRODUCTION SLAVE gave me a headset. It provided cop-car access. Donna and Figueroa play patrol-partner lovers. They cuddle in their cop car. They're married to deputy chiefs. It's gotta go bad.

I hooked on my headset and laid around the lounge. There it goes: snap, crackle, radio pop. The director: "Let's rehearse, kids."

One arc light popped on. The luminous vapors crossed the hillside. Fruit Alert: butt bangers in backseat bliss. They're bouncing cars. They're tearing tailpipes. They're shearing shock absorbers.

My headset stammered static and cleared clean. Donna said, "Get your tongue out of my mouth, you cocksucker."

Figueroa said, "Come on, baby. This is the Stanislavsky method. This is shit I learned at the Actors Studio."

Donna said, "Like father, like son. Your old man hit on me on *Hawaii Five-O*."

Figueroa waxed winsome. "He taught me everything I know.

He taught me acting, culture, music. Then he hit on my girl-friends and took them away from me."

Self-pity and woe—standard Stanislavsky.

Donna said, "I heard he's hung like a mule."

Figueroa yukked. "Like the Big Burrito at Taco Tom's, baby. 'Accept no substitutes.' "

Donna: "I'll call him. Hey, Luis, tell me how you did the wild thing with Rosemary Collins before I was born and confirm my theory that size skips the next generation."

Miguel: "No, baby. It grows. *El chorizo mucho grande por amor.*"

I heard rustling sounds. I heard a gunbelt snap. I heard a zip-per unzip. I heard Donna dead cold. "Chorizo to cocktail frank in two seconds. My dad said, 'You're going to Hollywood, so you might need this.' "

I pictured it—a Swiss Army knife—prongs, probes, and prick reducers. Figueroa said, "Don't cut me, baby. I need what I've got. Shit, I've got a migraine. I get real motherfuckers."

Donna said, "Check these cars out. It's like a drive-in movie with no screen."

Figueroa groaned—oooh, my fucking head. Donna said, "It's gay caballeros getting their jollies. How do you shoot around something like that?"

I knew.

The hillside sloped down to a reinforced ravine. Cars drove up easy. They wiggled up winding driveways and dirt. Cars went down hard. They grabbed grass. They tore tree trunks and bumper-carred and banged the ravine. Quantum queer evictions ratcheted cars *into* the ravine. Garlands of garbage goosed them to the L.A. riverbed.

I ran outside. I yelled, "Lights." Two dozen arc lights glare-glazed the hillside. I rhino-rampaged and hit cars.

I baton-bashed windows. I yanked emergency brakes. I glimpsed *fruitus interruptus*. I heard yelps, yowls, yodels, yammers, and yells for help. Cars skidded and skittered downhill. Cars blew by the narc arc with Divine Donna and Masher Miguel.

Donna got out. Donna jumped on the roof of her car. She saw Ramblers roll and rip the ravine. She saw Dodge Darts ding trees and die dead. I watched her. She watched the ravine collect cars. She's got hurricane-hazel eyes. She's got dark hair pageboy-styled. She's got her legs dug in. She's all LAPD wool stretched tigress-tight.

Miguel got out. He stood and watched the homos hurtle hell-bound. He watched the ravine. A T-Bird toppled in. Transaxles dropped off driveshafts, drifted, and dragged rubber wrappers.

Miguel said, "I'm getting off on this. You know what Luis always says, 'Homos expand the pool of fuckable women.' "

I looked at Donna. How fittingly Freudian-frazzled: *the* erotic image of my life as a COP.

A Bonneville banged the ravine. I heard three gunshots. I saw a man run.

Donna jumped off her car. She said, "The arc light was on him. I got a good look."

FRUIT SNUFF: A species of HOMOcides vulgaris, inimical to Shine Killing. Fruit Snuff vs. Shine Killing—a primer.

Fruits killed in Hollyweird and Rampart. *This* murder vibed panic and self-loathing. The killer's id went "Ick." His superego sermonized: Don't fuck men in purple Pontiacs/don't fuck men at all.

Fruits killed like prima divas pacing. They paced. They smoked. Joan Crawford crawls to the edge. She grabs a knife. She stabs her lover 91 times. Fruits *over*killed. Fruits dug the term "multiple stab wounds." The faithless faigelah is dead. Feel better now?

Shine Killings went down in '77 and Newton. Shine Killings went down *fast*. Willie owes Shondell 10 scoots. It's a crap-game debt. Remember—we rolled behind Muhammad's Mosque #6.

The men mouth multitudinous "motherfuckers." Willie gets bored and shoots first. Pow! Shondell be walking that deep River Styx. He's close to Mecca or Mama or the Big Liquor Store. We follow his blood drops. He's almost dead. He sees Saint Peter. Saint Peter's guzzling Schlitz malt liquor and wearing a porkpie hat. We get there. We say, "Who killed you, homeboy? Tell us fast." Shondell says, "Willie X." That's how we grab his black ass.

The hillside pulsed in pandemonium. The lights lured paunchy paparazzi. Rampart Patrol and Rampart Detectives showed. I gave a statement. I said I hit the lights to flush some hobnobbing homos. Exodus—let my people go!

Cops prowled the ravine. Miguel described the suspect. He had a monster migraine. My *cabeza*, oh, fuck.

Donna had the best view. She built a likeness with a sketch artist and an Identikit guy. Said suspect: white male, skinny. Bad zits, fat fangs for teeth.

Suspect: unknown. Victim: one white male wrapped in the wrecks. We walked down. Donna stuck close. We looked for lurking witnesses. We saw none.

Nine cars piled at the ravine ledge. No eyewits at all. They ran. They swam. They grappled garbage and floated on cardboard flotillas.

We found the purple Pontiac. The death car was lavished like Liberace. White interior/tuck & roll/lavender love balls.

The dead man covered the backseat, ass upward. K-Y crawled out his crack. A cop lifted his head. Shattered teeth and big-bore bullets flew.

A cop scoped out Miguel. "You look like Luis Figueroa."

Miguel said, "He's my daddy."

A cop said, "Fucking fruit snuff."

A cop said, "They're all named Lance or Jason. Every fruit snuff vic I ever worked."

Donna said, "Ten bucks that he's got another name. Come on, put up."

A cop extracted the stiff's wallet. A cop riffed sleeves. Bingo—
California driver's license/Randall J. Kirst.

The cop paid Donna off. I lounged in her eyes. Hurricane bea-
cons beamed.

A loudspeaker blared. "It's a wrap! LAPD says we can't shoot
until this mess gets cleared up!"

I looked at Donna. Donna looked at me. I said, "I'll drive
you . . ."

Donna said, "I'll drive myself."

I L O I T E R E D at the Academy. Miguel tried the "I'll drive you
home" bit. Donna flipped him off. A tech crew brought a winch
in. They hauled fruitmobiles off the ravine. The Rampart geeks
wrote a bulletin. The gist:

Randall J. Kirst, HOMOcide victim. Sodden fruits wanted!
Reclaim your keester kayaks at LAPD impound! Submit to fruit
snuff interviews! Insincere apologies for the work of Detective
Rick Jenson!

I lounged in the bar. The print guys worked outside. They
smeared the purple Pontiac. I found some Donna Donahue head
shots. They voodoo-vapped me. A notion nudged my head.

"Witness needs protection! LAPD guards her! Round-the-
clock watch!"

Yeah, but:

Miguel Figueroa saw him, too.

Yeah, but:

The fuck pad had *five* bedrooms.

Yeah, but:

Rampart had the case. Their jurisdiction/their job.

Yeah, but:

Russ Kuster had clout. Rampart owed Russ favors. I witnessed
the snuff.

Good odds. I grabbed the Donna shots and rolled.

THE HILLTOP HUNGARIAN RESTAURANT:

A strudel structure on the Cahuenga Pass. A goulash gulag, the shits. A hut for homesick Hungies and Russ Kuster's preferred brooding pit.

I drove over and walked in. Russ was snout deep in schnapps. Six couples slurped slivovitz. An accordion clown played for chump change.

Russ saw me. He pulled out a bar stool. I straddled it.

"Tell me you found the fuck pad."

"I found the fuck pad."

"Tell me there's not some catastrophic fuck-up to mark your first day at Hollywood Homicide."

"Welllll, there's this . . ."

Russ grinned. "Rampart dicks called me. You passed your test. You felt the need to tell me you fucked up yourself."

I unclenched. I whipped out the Donna shots. I spread them on the bar.

Eyeball alert—Russ looked, lingered, leched.

"Tell me she's the sole witness and she's afraid for her life. She saw too much. The killer wants to nullify her before she testifies. She *needs* a room at our fuck pad, and she'll be properly grateful."

I said, "No."

"No?"

"No, there's a second wit, a male, and she'll smell a shuck in six seconds."

Russ lit a cigarette. "The male's a fag, right? He doesn't play into the scene."

I shook my head. "He's no fag."

"What are you talking about? He's an actor, right?"

"He's an exception. Trust me on—"

"O.K., we've got the dish and the world's only non-fag actor, and a fruit snuff in Rampart that they only nominally care about. We want . . . what's her name?"

I said, "Donna Donahue."

"Right, as a guest, so you need me to call Rampart and get us assigned to the case."

The accordion went off-key. Bela Marko strapped it on. Bela was Russ's batshit bête noir and meshugina misdemeanant. Bela played bad squeeze box. Bela stole waiters' tips. Bela dined-and-dashed. Bela sold weed in the parking lot. Russ kicked his ass regularly.

Bela kicked off some screechy anthem. Bela waved the squeeze box man's cup. Bela table-hopped.

Table one: the cold shoulder. Table two: a quarter and a dime. Table three: half a chewed breadstick. Table four—a dyke duo— two kicks in the nuts.

Bela shook the bellows. Bela dropped the squeeze box. Bela stumbled outside clutching his nuts.

Russ laughed. Russ sipped schnapps. Russ said, "Donna Donahue is mine."

I shook my head. "My case, right? Come on, I'm a rookie. It's a nowhere fruit snuff."

Russ nodded. "You're right. Nobody else will want it. Now, look in the mirror."

I did. I saw myself. I saw Russ. I looked away. Russ jerked my head back.

"Look at us. You look like a harness bull with bad sunscreen. I look like William Holden in *Sunset Boulevard*. You want the case, you want to take Donna Donahue around and show her mug books and show her Taco Tom's and the place where you capped Huey Muhammad 6X, fine. When she comes home to the safe house, I'll be there with bourbon and Brahms."

I stood up. Russ said, "Be sure to tell her you planted that throw-down piece on Huey."

I LIKE TO sleep with dogs and muse on women. Cross-species warmth promotes insight and empathetic vibes. Donna Donahue deserved the sensitive Rick Jenson. A six-dog night would calcify my callow and callous side. Yeah, I waxed Huey X and the Garcia brothers. I *dug* it—but I didn't *love* it. Donna had to grok the moral split.

Dog Night was a ritual.

I bagged my F-car. I drove by Sombrero King and bought six oki pastrami burritos. I got on my two-way. I gave them Donna's name. They kicked back:

Donahue, Donna Welles. Brown/hazel, 5'6", 113, DOB: 3/13/56.

Good stats. 27 to my 31. Good Westside address.

The food and dogs consecrated life. The ride roused the dead.

I went by Carlos and Gower. I felt Ian Campbell's ghost. I heard bagpipes. I smelled onion fumes and cordite. I went by the Hollywood Sears. Robert Cote fell there. I saw arterial blood gush. I heard morphine syrettes snap.

I hooked over to the shelter and hauled out the chow. Growls and bays echoed inside. I unlocked the door, hit the lights, and kounted K-9's. Six was right—the pit bull, the Dogo, the bull terrier, an Airedale, the Aussie shepherd, and Reggie the Rhodesian Ridgeback.

Food first.

I fed individually. It prevented dogfights and canine chaos. Yum, yum—fried pastrami, fried cabbage, fried tortillas. The fart index would soar tonight.

Dave stashed blankets near the dog crates. I laid six out on the floor. I kept six for covers. I grabbed a pillow and tossed it down in my middle spot. The dogs piled on. We all stretched out. The Airedale and pit hemmed me in. We burrowed under the covers.

I said, "What's shakin', you big-dick motherfuckers?" I answered for them—my voice/their imagined responses.

"I want a beach pad." "Fuck that—I want a Bel-Air crib owned by some hebe in the movie biz. He's got six juicy daughters to penetrate with my air-to-ground Airedale missile." "Fuck that shit. I want to live at the Pacific Dining Car. I could roam the floor, sniff crotches, and score steak at will."

The dogs started to snooze. Their warmth engulfed me. I lay still and laid out my lament.

"There's an actress. She's got kaleidoscope-flecked hazel eyes. She's got a sturdy sense of herself, doesn't fall for cheap lines, and outdoes me in the looks department. I'll bet she comes from money. She's *the* woman. I want her, whatever it costs, whatever it takes. Dig that, you big-dick motherfuckers!"

No dog yipped or barked to affirm my pro-love prologue. The bull terrier cut a fart.

Donna: my man-oh-man metaphysic and priapic précis.

She grew up nonplussed by her beauty. She was jazzed and vexed by boys in pursuit. She got the actor's gestalt: assume varied identities and cherish your cheap leap at the moon. Learn your core. Hold it close. Don't buy that courage-as-ruthlessness shit that defines Hollywood. Know this: It's just yuks and fucks and a dubious place to appease appetites. Levy the love tools the Good Lord gave you. See through Roguish Russ Kuster and Maladroit Miguel. Find THE MAN. He waxed the Garcia Brothers. He capped Huey X. He took bad lives and saved good lives. He wants to know you.

Donna, sleep now.

I WOKE UP at dawn. I changed clothes. I brushed fur off my suit. The ridgeback eyeballed my crotch. I wondered how Donna viewed size. I turned on the radio. Whamm-o, straight off: "And the LAPD's Hollywood detective squad—not Rampart's—will investigate last night's homicide in the shadow of a movie shoot on the grounds of the L.A. Police Academy. Detective Russell Kuster said, "We're adept at solving faggot snuff—I mean the murders of people of alternative lifestyles. We're on the job."

Job *me*, dickbreath—Donna Donahue is *mine*!

I WALKED THROUGH the squadroom. I got a catcall cacophony. Fuck—Russ blew the word on our "rivalry."

I met my partner—"Phone Book" Tom Ludlow. He said, "Let's roust queers until we get one to confess. All those guys got father and guilt complexes. You sweet-talk them, I'll do the heavy work."

I laffed. He picked up his Yellow Pages. Dig the dried bloodstains. Dig the spit stains—Tom probably French-kissed it.

I said, "Later, Tom. I'm driving a witness around today."

A cop yelled, "Rhino's in love!" A cop yelled, "Rhino sucks Chihuahua dick!"

Russ called me over. I straddled his spare chair. Russ slipped me his Canoe cologne. Subtle pimps and furloughed Marines preferred it. I splashed it on.

Russ said, "Nobody on my squad smells like a 3-way with Lassie and Rin Tin Tin. Now, moving along, here's your day. First, you go by the Wilshire Sheraton. Slatkin's giving a seminar there. You find him and tell him to get the best trusties available and spiff the fuck pad, while he forensics to his heart's delight—then you reinterview Donna, show her some mug books, and talk her into the pad."

I said, "I'm on it now."

"Tell her Huey X was on a rampage. You diverted it. Tell her you subscribe to *Ms.* magazine. All the liberals and carpet munchers read it."

THE SHERATON— Dogman Dave blasting full.

A small banquet room. Cops at long tables. Coffee urns/donuts/hard bagels.

Dave hogged the mike and lectern. Dave waved the pointer

Knife murderer Stephen Nash stabbed a boy
twenty-eight times and bragged, "I'd never killed
a kid before. I wanted to see how it felt." *(Los Angeles
Times Collection, Department of Special Collections,
Charles E. Young Research Library, UCLA)*

stick. Dig the cat on the screen: Stephen Nash/'50s lust killer/
fruit-snuff artiste supreme.

Big, burly, curly-haired, gap-toothed. Monstrous shit-eating
grin.

Dave soliloquized. "For sheer viciousness and braggadocio,
Nash stands alone. He was a proudly affirmed homosexual in the
mid-1950s. He killed out of both a psychopathic resentment and
for the sheer fact that killing sexually aroused him. His exact death
toll remains unknown. There's the three in the Bay Area, the gay

hairdresser in Long Beach, and the 10-year-old boy under the Santa Monica pier. Nash's killing spree ended in November '56. He hinted at more killings, but never named names, and five victims since his summer '54 parole from San Quentin seems like a low number."

I bit a bagel. A tooth cracked. I tossed it away.

Dave said, "There's a rumor that's floated around for years, that during a portion of his free time in '54 and '55, he was befriended by an actor who took amateur movies of 'colorful' L.A. characters, along with tape recordings of some of their ramblings. Don't laugh—I know some of you scoff at my psychic shit—but I've seen a big, white Spanish house in conjunction with all this."

A cop yelled, "It's Reggie the Ridgeback's house."

A cop yelled, "No, it's that Airedale's pad."

Dave grinned. Dave said, "Reggie's your collective daddy." Dave flipped the whole room off.

I walked up to the stage. A woman cop yelled, "Stephen Nash is my type! I could turn him straight!"

Dave said, "Gas chamber. August 19th, '59."

I flipped the mike off. Dave and I huddled.

I said, "Russ wants the clean-up today. If you really want to score some points with him, scrounge some water beds and a sound system."

Dave snapped his fingers. "Roger that. That clown at Appliance King's dealing Quaaludes. I'll talk to the D.A."

I yawned—fucking Reggie slept *on* me. A sleep deficit loomed.

Dave said, "That cologne stinks. Russ is trying to fuck you up with Donna."

"Does the whole world know?"

"Yeah. It'll probably be in *Variety* tomorrow."

DONNA SAID, "It's a shuck."

I said, "Nix. You're a material witness. The killer saw you. You need round-the-clock protection."

We stood outside the Academy. The crew set up shots. Donna
wore faded jeans and a beige turtleneck. She looked like Exeter or
Andover or some swank school with no jigs.

I said, "Miss Donahue, this is no shit. These fruit-snuff geeks
get off on icing women, too. I read it in *Ms.* magazine. And, I
have it on good authority that before I dropped Huey Muhammad, he was on his way to kill a woman."

Donna smiled. "I'd prefer the Beverly Wilshire, but I'll settle
for the Biltmore or New Otani downtown."

I rhino-revamped my pitch. "Miss Donahue, the LAPD is
undergoing severe budget cuts, but we do have at our disposal a
five-bedroom house in Hollywood, inhabited by hardened detectives 24 hours a day, and you are graciously invited to stay there
under our protection."

Donna laughed. Rhino-revise that—Donna roared.

"I've got two cop cousins. I'm conversant with the term 'fuck
pad.' A policeman named Kuster was here an hour ago. He leered
at me sidelong while he lured Miguel into the so-called safe
house with the promise of God knows what kind of goodies, most
likely female."

I crashed. I crumpled. I withered and whimpered and went
rhino-recumbent.

"Shit, you're my damsel in jeopardy."

Donna smiled—incipient/preemptive/*almost*.

"It's 'damsel in *distress.*' "

"O.K."

Hazel eyes hammered me. "Did I catch a Freudian slip there?"

"What do you mean?"

"You said 'my,' not 'our,' meaning the rest of the horndogs."

I rhino-revived. "Shit, I just want to be around you while I've
got the chance."

Donna smiled—regal/resplendent/*real*.

"O.K., I'll stay."

Don't sweat now/don't sway now/don't swoon now—

A grip yelled, "Hey, Jenson. Some guy named Ludlow called. You're supposed to meet him at the impound ASAP."

THE IMPOUND IMPOSED IMPERIOUS—six long Jap-town blocks. The poof Pontiac posed by the fence. Tom Ludlow leaned against it. He hugged his phone book/teddy bear.

I pulled in and parked. Tom pulled his hip flask. Aaaaaah— Old Crow and Sprite—Breakfast of Psycho Vietnam Vets!

I said, "Did it ever occur to you that you're a remorseless alcoholic psychopath?"

Tom belched. "Yeah, it did. I got that way 'cause my new partner sleeps with grungy-ass dogs."

Touché.

"Do you always carry that phone book?"

"Yeah."

"Do you ever read it?"

Tom picked his nose. "I read the names of the women, then I call them up, say nasty things, and try to make dates with them."

I laffed. I scanned the impound. It was the Audi Auschwitz, the Buick Bergen-Belsen, the Dodge Dart Dachau.

A tech man walked up. Frappé Freddy—no smile/no jive.

He pulled a master key. He unlocked the Pontiac's trunk. He let the door pop.

I looked in. I inventoried:

K-Y jelly, one tube, 1/2 squeezed. Boy-banger books: *Cock It to Me, Shlong, For Those Who Think Hung*.

Stamped on back: Porno Vista Boox/Selma Ave/Hollywood.

Loose twenty-dollar bills. Bank-inked. Dried ink coating the trunk.

Tom said, "I don't get it."

I did.

The killer wants butthole. The vic's got bank cash. The killer's

clueless: The vic 211'd a bank. He stores the gelt in his trunk.
They're pouring the pork. The killer loops back for lubricant. He
sees bankrolls. He pops one. Ink jets spray. He's packing a piece.
Rock it—Rhino lites the lites and pops windows. The killer shoots
the vic. The killer beats feet. Donna eyeballs his ass.

I nudged Tom. "Call the Feds and Central Robbery. Get the
stats on 211's going back a week."

Tom slapped his phone book. "Hey, *I'm* the senior partner, and
I got some important calls to make."

"I'll give you a call. It's a freebie, because we're partners now."

Tom grabbed his pen. I said, "Carol F. Brochard. 213-886-
1902."

"Who is she?"

"My ex-wife."

"Wow!"

"She's a nympho. She pulls trains for spooks. She's a real mud
shark."

Tom went ugggh. The tech guy said, "I'll scrape an ink sample
and get the numbers to Dave Slatkin. He'll match it to the dye
batch."

I said, "Thanks." Tom Ludlow ran to a phone.

DIG IT:

The Hollywood Fuck Pad.

I walked into the macho-maimed maelstrom. Dig what I saw:

Trusties hauling disco balls. Appliance King coolies lugging
water beds. Detective "Condom Cal" Coleman walking the
room-to-room rubber route. The biddy landlady—replete with
Camels and oxygen tank.

There's Dave Slatkin. He's checking out a wall crack.

I said, "What—"

Dave cut in. "That impound clown called. Some shitbird
clouted the Hollywood Federal at Santa Monica and Cole four
days ago, and I made the ink comparison off a fax slide. There's a

surveillance photo of the guy stomping a bank guard, and he matches the late Randall J. Kirst. SID took his prints at the morgue, and guess what? They matched a latent on the teller's ledge."

I leaned on the wall. "We solve a 211, but come up short on the snuff. Kirst was a horny motherfucker. He drives around with his stash in the trunk on a pork run."

Dave squinted at wall flecks. "Or it's a lovers-thieves' altercation."

I shook my head. "They'd have gotten a motel room."

"You mean a pork pit like this one?"

I looked around. Trusties rolled TVs on dollies. Va-va-voom—fuck flix in every room.

I said, "What's Russ doing?"

"Canvassing, borrowing guys and hitting the fruit bars near the Academy. He's got Ludlow leaning on registered sex offenders."

"Ouch."

"Yeah, ouch, but it works."

I heard growls, sobs, shivers, and oh shits. It sounded like Migraine Miguel. I figured I'd console his ass and divert him from Donna.

I walked upstairs. Miguel rolled his head on a wall beam.

I said, "Bad one?"

"Yeah, with accompanying pix—you know, recurring shit."

I leaned in the doorway. "Tell me."

Miguel said, "Recurring since age 1, in 1950-fucking -6, where the same big pervo guy is chasing me through my house, with my mother chasing him, bashing LP records over his head. Headache, nightmare, day flash, the fucking trinity."

Miguel looked up. Fresh-dry eyes/no twitches/no temple throbs.

I said, "How do you handle it?"

"The Collins way, man. Fantasy and vodka."

Grunts graveled next door. Triple X/staged sex/some zit-backed cat with a monster curved shlong.

■

I drove by the station. I left Donna messages at her pad and the set. Porno Vista Boox/Selma near Highland/probable surveillance film.

I checked the squadroom. Phone Book Tom held sway.

Six interrogation booths. One pervert per. Tom in booth 4.

He swung like Ted Williams. The hip pop, the crisp follow-through. The suspect was cuffed to a chair. He ducked 40%. Tom batted .600.

Teeth dribbled. Pages riffled. Blood dripped.

I walked out. Rhino reg #6: phone-book jobs on rape-os and child molesters only.

SELMA: A DRAG-QUEEN drag off Sunset. Homo from the get-go. Prostie boys and chicken-hawk Charlies. Porno book bins and backseat fellatio. Lice like Lassie and burned-rear-end rubber. Malignant microbes like Mount Matterhorn.

And Donna Donahue—right by the bookstore—a bliss blast in LAPD blue.

I double-parked and *jumped* out. Donna said, "I didn't have time to change, but it bought us some time here."

"Say what?"

"I impersonated a cop. The bookstore guy's cueing up his surveillance film from two days before the robbery. We can stand in a stall in back and watch."

I walked in first. The clerk ignored me. The clerk salaciously salaamed to Donna. He pointed us down "Dildo Drive"—a mobile-mounted, salami-slung corridor. Packaged porno reposed on racks and shimmied off shelves. It was a donkey-dick demi-monde and Beaver Boulevard.

We ducked dildos. We made the booth. Donna doused the lights. I tapped a projector switch. Black-and-white film rolled.

We saw pan shots. We saw ID numbers. We saw Sad-Sack Sidneys slap sandals in slime.

Donna said, "I already checked the credit-card receipts. Nothing from Randall J. Kirst."

I nodded. "Nobody—not even turd burglers—want credit-card receipts from the fucking Porno Vista."

Donna said, "Right. We're looking for two men making purchases together—the victim and the killer I saw."

Police smarts in forty-eight hours—add breeding and brains. I said, "What kind of work does your family do?"

Donna laffed. "They manufacture toilet seats."

I yukked. My gut distended. I hyper-humped it back in.

Film rolled. We saw dykes buy dildos. We saw kollege kids buy *Beaverrama, Beaveroo, Beaver Den, Beaver Bash, Beaverooski,* and *Beaver Bitches.* We saw flits flip through *The Greek Way, Greg Goes Greek, Greek Freaks, More Is More, The Hard and the Hung,* and *The Hungest Among Us.* I laffed. Donna laffed. We bumped hips for kicks. Donna's gunbelt clattered.

Moby Dick's Greek Delite, Moby Dick's Athens Adventure, Moby Dick Meets Vaseline Vic. We yukked. We howled. We bumped hips. Donna yelled, *"Now!"*

I punched Stop. The frame froze. The clerk ran back. The clerk ogled Donna.

I poked him. The clerk said, "That's the dead guy from the TV news on the left. The other guy is Chickie or Chuckie Farhood. From his height, I'd say it's Chickie. Chickie's queer, but tough. Chuckie's a chubby chaser that likes fat chicks. He runs fat out-call whores out of the counterculture rags. And I mean *fat.* Real quarter-tonners with cheese, and—"

Donna poked him. "Get to it."

"Okay, Chuckie lives at the Versailles on 6th and Saint Andrews. Chickie steals cars and sleeps in them, and you didn't get this from Burt D. Lelchuk. I'm a clean man in a dirty business."

THE VERSAILLES/6th and Saint Andrews—Koreatown, *aaah sooo*.

We rolled south. Complexions combined and palate-popped yellow. Crime stats crawled low. K-people kept to themselves. I was Rickshaw Rick here. Dig the signs—all Korean—no coons with Olde English 800.

We hit the address. Fuck it—let Donna roll, too.

We checked the mailbox bank. Donna tapped 106—"Farhood." A K-lady said, "Velly fat woman, no can climb stairs."

We walked to 106. Donna knocked. I heard TV noise. A woman yelled, "I'm in bed! I can't get out! I'm too heavy!"

I heard a coughing fit. I heard "The door's open."

Donna turned the knob. We walked in. Wig the walls: photophased by 8-by-10 testaments—monuments to morbid obesity.

Six hundred-pounder pix. Eight yards, the Big Ten. Donna looked around and down. I prayed for aerobics in heaven.

A cracked door. That voice: "I'm in here."

Donna pushed the door open. The bed: an endomorph endeavor—big/wide/bolted down. On it: a nude woman, horribly fat.

I said, "Police officers. We're here to—"

Donna yelled, "Gun!"

Instinct: I hit the floor. Actor's instinct: Donna piled on me.

I pulled my piece.

I dropped it.

I saw the gun. I saw the shooter: a mini-man *under* Fat Mama.

He fired. Two shots went wide. Donna pulled her gun. Donna fired. Fuck—empty actor's prop.

Fat Mama reached under a pillow. Fuck—it's a .44 Mag. Mini-Man shot over my head. I rolled. I dumped Donna. She pulled off my ankle piece. Velcro snapped. Fat Mama aimed and fired. A wall section blew out.

Donna stood up.

Donna walked to the bed.

She aimed. She shot Fat Mama in the head. She shot Fat Mama in her fatty mass. Fat Mama buckled. Mini-Man got exposed. Donna shot him four times in the face.

THINGS WENT SLO-MO.

I called Russ. Russ called Wilshire dicks. The Wilshire guys brought extra throw-down guns. I gave a statement. It was *my* gun. I assumed credit/blame per guidelines. Russ called the shooting board a lockdown. Donna wasn't even there.

Russ brought her Ativan and scotch. She snarfed it. We stood in the hallway. We hugged and stood head-to-head.

Donna said, "Say something nice to me."

I said, "You know who you are now."

SHE WOULDN'T GIVE up her uniform. It was bloodstained. It was dirty. She wouldn't go home and change. She wouldn't visit the set. She wouldn't scrounge fresh threads.

The pills and booze zorched her. She stared out her window. She stared at people. She said, "Brave new fucking world."

I said, "You saved my life." I called her "Partner." She said, "Brave new fucking world."

Dusk hit. I drove to the fuck pad. Donna fell asleep. I wedged a bulletproof vest under her head.

I walked inside. Russ was playing Bruckner for the heathens. Symphony 7/movement 2. Lyrical shit/music for honors.

Full house.

Cops in Jockey shorts/women in robes. Couples standing in hallways. Couples staying up to see Donna — you could plain tell.

Dave brushed blood from wall cracks. I said, "Where's Miguel?"

Dave coughed. "He saw some detail on the wall, you know, some nightmare shit. He went to his mother's place."

Russ said, "Your girl's something. She's too much woman for me."

Bruckner soared. It was an elegy for a century dead. Donna walked up and stood in the doorway. She got a wild locomotive ovation. The sound deafened her. She bowed. Blood dripped off her badge. She said, "Brave new fucking world."

WE DROVE WEST. A light rain hit. Russ's cocktail wore off. She said, "Let's go see Miguel. I worry about him sometimes."

"Where does he live?"

"Rosie's place. Roxbury north of Sunset. Big, white Spanish place."

"You want to talk about it?"

"No. I want to say hi, and get under some covers with you and see if I can cry with some more pills and scotch."

I drove to Beverly Hills. Donna showed me the pad: big/Spanish adobe/George Gershwin's ex-crib.

We parked and knocked. Rosemary Collins answered. She saw us. She saw a cop and an actress. She did mental math. She went, "Sssshhhh. Miguel's had a rough one, too."

We walked inside. We just made it. The rain went haywire. Donna exercised Hollywood etiquette.

She hit a bathroom. She popped the medicine chest. She popped some prescription shit. She found a liquor sideboard. She guzzled straight scotch.

Rosie winked at me. She was big and fat now. She'd gone down behind every appetite.

I said, "Where's Miguel?"

She walked downstairs. Donna stagger-followed her. I came up last. Rosie said, "Old Luis's archives are down here. He made these doco films in the '50s."

Film cans on chairs. Film cans on shelves. Film cans stacked shelf to ceiling.

There's Miguel:

Passed out in cop blue. Gone behind Belvedere vodka.

I tossed a blanket on him. Rosie tucked his feet under it.

I said, "Can we stay here tonight?"

Rosie said, "Sure. Third bedroom on the left upstairs. I'll run Donna through a shower."

Donna stumbled to a bathroom. I found a bathroom and stripped. I saw bullet-graze marks on my cheek and shoulder. Dry blood flaked off.

I showered and found a robe. I stretched out on the bed. Rosie walked Donna in. Donna's robe dwarfed her.

Rosie killed the lights and shut the door. Donna snuggled into me. The darkness felt right.

Donna said, "Can we make love in the morning? I'm too wrecked now."

I said, "Sure. It's my best time."

The bed dropped a thousand yards and settled back up with us in it. A sync settled in—her heartbeat, my breath.

2.

"Brave new fucking world."

Her first morning muse. I woke with a chart-busting chubby. Delightful, delirious—Dangerous Donna now.

I'd notched next-door nightmares. Luis Figueroa's voice. The partial pop of a self-described killer. Film-sprocket click. Luis called the cat "Steve." Faded fuzz sounds.

I mapped some mental math. Mid-'50s. Luis's home movies. Dave Slatkin's pet perv Stephen Nash. Dave's vision: the sparkling Spanish house—Rosie's Roost?

Donna nudged me. "I *said* 'Brave new fucking world.' "

My chubby chugged out and up. Piss-deflate it or pave new penile paths with Donna—quick call.

I said, "It's our world now." Donna leaned in. I kissed her neck.

I kissed her cleavage clung to Rosie's robe. She pulled my head up. She kissed my bullet bites. Our lips latched and launched the world's longest kiss.

I swirled in it. I tasted my morning breath. I mowed medicinal scotch off her tongue. We held the kiss. We ripped off our robes. I dropped into Donna delirium. She rhino-reciprocated. We tasted each other all over. We flared freckles and tweaked toes and centered on our center parts. We savored our scents there. She pulled me in. It lasted ten seconds or ten hours. It was all eyes-closed climax and breathing one breath and one hard holding until I thought our bones would break.

■

We rerobed and coursed through the casa. Donna rapped with Rosie. I nudged Miguel next door.

He fiddled with film cans and cataloged cassettes. I said, "Luis knew some wild characters."

Miguel lit a cigarette. "Delusional types. He'd give them a few bucks and get their shit down on film. It was his variation on the—you know—study the surreal to learn the real. It's sort of like Donna yesterday. She wasted two freaks, so now she can play a cop better."

I laffed. "Can I see those films you were watching last night?"

"No, you may not. You banged Donna this morning, so I'm jealous. When the jealousy wears off, I'll let you see them."

I said, "Fair enough."

Miguel blew smoke rings in my face. "Enjoy it while you can, man. Donna goes through men like Rosie goes through Häagen-Dazs."

I coughed away smoke. Donna yelled, "Rick, the living room! We're on TV!"

Miguel said, "Get me some creeps I can off, Jenson. Donna's got the upper hand on life experience now."

I fast-walked to the living room. Rosie wore a muumuu. Donna wore bloodstained LAPD blue. She was the statuesque still point of Stanislavsky.

Russ Kuster talked from the tube. "Officer Jenson's slaying of Charles "Chuckie" Farhood and his female accomplice Melissa "Mama Cass" Cassavailian was entirely within LAPD shooting policy, and I am sure he will be exonerated at today's shooting board."

A quick cut. A handsome newsman: "Miss Suzie Park Kim of the Versailles Apartments has a different story to tell."

A quick cut. A korpulent Korean diesel dyke filled the screen.

"No, no, no! I see TV actress in uniform with policeman! She killed Chuckie and Mama Cass! I see her on *Hawaii Five-O*! Donna something! She stone fox—yum, yum!"

Donna grabbed me. "I should pack and run. Chuckie's brother's got a bullet with my name." I grabbed her back. I smelled her hair. I caught Alberto VO5 and our lovemaking sweat.

"I've got the shooting board. You stay here and watchdog Miguel. He's torqued on his dad's old films. I'll be back later."

Donna nodded. Rosie said, "Come on, baby. Häagen-Dazs and bonded bourbon. Breakfast of champions."

RUSS MET ME at Parker Center. Room 463—Internal Affairs.

I said, "Update me."

Russ ratched earwax with a paper clip. "The dead guy's Chuckie Farhood. He's the heterosexual chubby chaser. Chickie's the fruit, and here's his MO. The late Randall J. Kirst and Chickie were part-time fuck-film actors, and Chickie 459's pharmacies, steals dope, and sleeps in cars that he steals. He's a swish psychopath. He goes to straight and fag porno theaters, takes pixes off the screen with a high-speed camera, and sells them to porno bookstores. That's all shit we coerced out of that clown at Porno Villa."

I said, "He must have a darkroom somewhere."

Russ said, "Correct." He handed me some Chickie Farhood mugs. I said, "Stolen car reports—"

Russ cut in. "We've got six teams from West Traffic checking stolen-car reports and canvassing for wits, and six SID teams and a rover van to dust for prints. We've got a meeting at Central Vice in two hours. You and Tom Ludlow are to hit the fag bars and porno theaters, anywhere Chickie can 'work' and hide out. We've got 12 teams total, and Chickie hit a Rite Aid pharmacy last night. Left three latents and stole a fuckload of Seconal, Amytal, and Tuinal. What that means, I don't know."

I scratched my balls. "Suicide attempt?"

"Maybe. Before the meeting, go by the fuck pad and talk to Slatkin. Our resident genius is freaking out about something."

I scratched my nose. I smelled Donna.

"I'll hit the pad, then go by the Versailles and chill out that Korean bitch. She's flapping her mouth about Donna."

Russ shook his head. "Low priority, especially if Chickie's on a suicide run."

"Russ, shit, she's—"

"*No*. And if you see that fucked-up snitch of mine, Chuy Nieves, put some hurt on him. He's been telling street creeps I gave him up to the Sheriff's on a hot-prowl job."

I hitched up my rhino-horn gunbelt. "What about Donna?"

Russ sighed. "The last I heard, Donna could take care of herself."

THE SHOOTING BOARD— precisely pro forma.

Wasp cop kills pornopreneur and Mama Cass. Wasp cop's bullets waste welfare wench and *ex*-caped *ex*-con with felonious faigelah brother. Suzie Park Kim's musings—meshugina.

The board deliberated. I sat alone. I poked my skin for Donna scent-sightings. I found arm and ankle aromas—aaaah, the Stanislavsky-stopping studdess!

The board returned. Unanimous decision: killings in police policy.

Deadly Donna—Manslaughter Two mandated to mush.

I INSUBORDINATELY ITINERIZED. Koreatown kame first—gag fat Suzie fast.

I daydreamed per Donna. I called up some caution. *Don't propose until next week.*

Chuy Nieves notched into my noggin. He was Kuster's kustom snitch. He hot-prowled UCLA dorms. He flashed his herpes-hammered hamster at comely coeds. He got screeches and screams back. Russ caught him. Russ made him his sniveling snitch. Now he rebelled. Now he screamed for a "screen test."

I got to the Versailles. I checked out the adjacent alley. Fuck—Doomonic Donna and Sick Suzie captured in catfight configuration.

Donna in bloodstained blue. Suzie in a mauve muumuu.

They yelled. They yodeled. They yipped. I ran back. Suzie tried to beat on Donna and caress her concurrent. I interceded. Suzie belly-bumped me. I flew. Donna caught me. Sick Suzie mouthed off.

"I saw you shoot Chuckie and Mama Cass! Man was here—he show me picture of you—movie reference book—Donna something. Man Chuckie's brother. He show me picture. I munch your socks off, yum, yum."

Chickie—back for revenge—gone now.

I started to lecture Donna. "I told you to stay at Rosie's. You can't go around impersonating a cop all the—"

Shots. Big-bore right to left, over the alley fence, ring-a-ding ricochets. Bam—the dyke socks one in her eye socket. She goes down dead. Her flab flares and flattens. Fuck—it's a 6.8 earthquake.

Donna jumps up. Donna fires over the fence. Fuck—fake uniform/live bullets.

I vaulted the fence. My rhino horn hung up on a fence post. I

got impaled upside down. Donna shoved my ass. I de-impaled
and dumped to earth on my derrière. Donna fired at fleeing Farhood. Her shots went wild. They pinged pavement and skimmed
skyward. I proned out and fired a full clip. I fanned Farhood's
hair. I narrowly notched his Nikes. I blew the full clip.

Donna jumped the fence. I said, "Real bullets?"

"Miguel convinced me. He called it Stanislavsky plus."

I CALLED IN the 187. Russ Kuster arrived. Wilshire dicks followed. I described the scene. I omitted Donna's gun. The cops
eyeballed Donna and asked for autographs. Donna wrote "Brave
new fucking world" and "Love, Donna" on their ticket books.

We gave formal statements and humped to Hollyweird. We
argued per Donna's props: blue suit and flesh-flaring bullets.
Donna said, "Hollow points. I'm a feminist. I want to kill this
cocksucker in the name of oppressed women worldwide."

We drove on. We headed to the fuck pad. I saw Chuy Nieves at
Sunset and El Centro.

I braced the brakes. I careened from the car. I chased Chuy.
Chuy chugged slow—methedrine malignancy and three packs a
day. I waggled his wetback ass. I cuffed him. I dragged him to the
car. I tossed him in the backseat.

Donna said, "As a liberal, I should protest."

I said, "*Former* liberal. Now dig on the 'screen test.' "

I punched the gas. I hit 60. I hit the brakes. Chuy hit the front-
seat/backseat mesh. It was crisscross/crosshatched metal. It left
tic-tac-toe tattoos.

I hit the gas. I hit the lights and siren. I hit 80-plus. Chuy hit the
mesh. His nose broke. I hit the gas. I hit 70. Chuy mashed the mesh
headfirst. Dig his hip haircut: hatch marks scraping his scalp.

I stopped the car. I got out. I hauled Chuy out. I dumped him
in the gutter. I said, "Don't talk out of school about Russ Kuster."

I got back in the car. I said, "Please don't say 'Brave new fucking world.' "

Donna said, "Let's get a motel room, watch fuck flicks, and make love."

"When Chickie's dead or captured."

"You're going to waste his faggot ass, aren't you?"

I said, "Donna, there's never been a woman like you."

WE HIT the fuck pad. There's Dave Slatkin on the porch. He's shivering, shaking, all shook up.

We parked and walked over. I said, "Tell me."

Dave shook and shimmied. "The house is evil. I found blood mixed with polio vaccine and cranial fluid in a wall crack. I went by the Hollywood library. Three little boys disappeared from the polio clinic at Queen of Angels in April '56."

Chills churned through me. "You're thinking Stephen Nash."

Dave nodded. "We've got to bring in scent dogs and dig up the yard."

I whispered. "We've got to get Farhood first. Be realistic. Nash is dead, the kids are dead."

Donna whispered to me. "The man-in-the-street shit. Doesn't Miguel have something like—"

I shushed her. "Dave, go back to the shelter and chill out with the dogs. There's a meeting at Central Vice. I'll cover for you."

Dave shivered. "I keep seeing that big white Spanish house north of Sunset."

I CALLED a cab for Donna. I told her to go back to Rosie's and watchdog Miguel. *Go through his old man's film cans. Be careful. I'll explain later.*

We kissed good-bye on a shitty Hollywood side street. My whole life was one big blur.

CENTRAL VICE. Parker Center—Room 506.

Yours Truly at the lectern. My plastic rhino horn perched near the mike. I updated, I preached, I assigned.

Twenty-four cops listened. Detectives, SID men, clue clowns. Russ gave me a fact sheet. I riffed off of it.

Forty-two fruits claimed their cars. None knew Randall J. Kirst or the Farhood brothers. A few bun buddies said they'd "seen them around" and no more. I gave the Valley porn theaters and bars to eleven two-man teams. The names drew laughs: Dee-Lux Dicks, Fort Dicks, the Ramrod, the Manhole, the Colonoscopy Club, the Boy Toy, Boys R Us, Locker Room Larry's, Lance's Lancer Room, Leather Leo's Love Nest, and Ten-Inch Tommy's.

I ended with a slide show and a macho-maimed musing. The slide featured bare-chest mugs of Chickie Farhood. Bad zits— Mount Matterhorn pustules and blasting-cap blackheads. The whole room went ugggh. My musing: "He's got pharmacy downers. He's armed and dangerous. Take him out the second you see him."

I PAIRED WITH Phone Book Tom. We hit West Hollyweird. Tom traded his phone book for a beavertail sap. We hit Pussycat theaters. We lingered for the straight fuck-and-suck action. We talked to cashiers. They'd "seen Chickie around"—"the cat with the zits, right?" We shined penlights in patrons' faces. We caught guys slamming the ham. We caught a policewoman doing deep throat in *Sharon Shags Sherman Oaks*. Tom made a note to call her.

We hit fruit bars—Jason's Jamboree, Lariat Lee's, Rudy's RUMPus Room. We got one lead: Patrons called Chickie "Zits" and "Pus." One fag called him "Date-Rape Dave." Chickie tried to slip him some Rohypnol. Tom howled. He started calling *me* "Rohypnol Rick." He said it's the only way I'd get laid. We hit more straight theaters. We saw John Holmes do an ad for the Donkey Dan Dick Extender. It involved pulleys and possible prostate problems. I made a note to call Donna about it.

We walked back out to our F-car. The radio blared. I picked up. West Traffic found Chickie's car in Griffith Park.

THERE IT WAS: a '79 Toyota cum '56 NASH.

Parked on a bluff. Cityside view. Egregiously exhibitionistic.

Choppers chugged overhead. Russ and two bluesuits blockaded the car.

Tom and I got out. Dig the infernal interior:

Demonic dashboard: duct-taped Stephen Nash news pix and clips. Nash gnashing his nublike teeth. Nash ghoulishly giggling. " 'I'm King of Killers,' Boy Slasher Sez." Nash braggingly brandishing lead pipe and knife. Nash blinking back flashbulb flare. Nash knife-wielding and pipe-posing. "King of Killers stabs boy 28 times under pier. Brags 'I'd never killed a kid before. I wanted to see how it felt.' "

A canvass crew crawled into the hills. I checked the backseat. Foto Fiend Farhood created a cruel-ass collage.

Stephen Nash with flared fly. John Holmes's jumbo Johnson jumping out. Political paste-up: Devil Dick Nixon gobbling his gonads.

Russ said, "He left it here for us to spot. SID got his latents off the dashboard. The car got clouted two days ago at Ted's Ranch Market. He won't come back. He's too hip. We've got six canvassing crews tracking stolen cars within a four-mile radius. He had to steal some fresh wheels."

Tom banged his phone book against his leg. Dried blood dropped off the pages.

I said, "Tips?"

Russ said, "Percy's Perch. It's a fruit bar on Ventura. The barman said he's got information. You and Tom go over and brace him."

I saw an 8-track tape secured in a sound system. I hit the ignition. Tom tapped some dashboard dials. HIS voice, fogged by '56 fuzz:

"I'm the King of the Killers! I'll go to my death like any malevolent monarch! I'm the monster of mass-production killing!"

———

PERCY'S PERCH:

A poof palace in palate-popping purple and pink. Nancy boys in niggered-out Naugahyde booths.

The barman was a sweaty swish in spangled spandex. He saw us and steered us to a back room.

No introductions. Spandex Spanky spit it out.

"Chickie has AIDS. He's slipping guys that date-rape drug and deliberately giving them the virus."

He popped a cassette in a console TV. Spliced footage screed the screen. There's Harrison "the Hunk" Ford in *Star Wars*. There's Sylvester "Steroid" Stallone in *Rocky*. There's Chickie Farhood made up as Stephen Nash. It's a fantastic faux cluster fuck.

The swish said, "Chickie shoots the stuff off regular movie screens and splices himself in. God forgive us, but there's a market for such blasphemy."

We walked back to the bar proper. I saw a cadre of cadaverous Calvins downing daiquiris and massive martinis. Spanky said, "Chickie's victims. They've got four months between them to live."

I said, "Let's kill him."

Tom fanned his phone book. "I got no problem with that."

I DUMPED TOM at the fuck pad. I rhino-rolled to Roxbury Drive.

There's Rosie. There's Donna. There's Miguel bombed on Belvedere.

Donna took me aside. "Rosie got tanked and explained Miguel's visions. Stephen Nash tried to attack him. Rosie chased him and beat him with a stack of 78 records. She shattered sixteen copies of 'You Belong to Me.' "

"Did you go through the old film cans?"

Stephen Nash starts his last ride. *(Los Angeles Times Collection, Department of Special Collections, Charles E. Young Research Library, UCLA)*

Donna nodded. "I found it and cued it up. *Brace yourself.*"

We walked to the next room. A screen covered one wall. I doused the lights. Donna ran the projector. Stephen Nash gnawed at the camera.

"I snatched the three snotty-pants from the polio joint and beat their heads against the wall of this rooming house where I was staying. I cornholed them postmortem and buried them out back. It was April. I figured the fuzz would get me sooner or later. I found me the ugliest bitch I could find and fucked her blind. I put a big banana on her stomach and made like she was a boy. She had pimples all over. I heard she popped twins right when they sent me to death row."

Offscreen: Luis Figueroa's voice. "I find this hard to believe."

Nash: gap-toothed/floppy-mouthed/curly-haired/beady-eyed/*baaaaaaad*.

I believed every word.

The room lights flicked on. I saw Miguel walk in. He said, "I remember him now. I haven't had a migraine since Donna showed me the film."

I said, "Rosie saved your life."

Miguel nodded. "I'm going to buy her all the Häagen-Dazs in Beverly Hills and a case of Wild Turkey."

I kissed tears off Donna's cheeks. She said, "Can we make love now?"

WE FOUND a room. The bed belonged to two baying beagles. We booted them. They chose two chaise lounges and watched.

Percy's Perch. Pimple-piled killers. Camera-eyed K-9's. Brave new fucking world.

We dusted dog dander off the covers and climbed on. Donna wore static-stark cashmere now. She peeled off a pink turtleneck shift. Shiver-sparks sparked spangled light.

I shucked my shirt and pants—threadbare third-world threads. Donna hauled off my "Home of the Whopper" shorts. Naked in a nanosecond—heaven in a hound dog's hutch.

I remember the one long kiss. I remember blue veins synced to her heartbeat. Her breasts tasted like *essence de Donna* and sharp shower soap. Her mouth meandered and made me moan. Lip locks and licks made me pitch to her pivot-spot.

We fitted finally. Her call—I was orphaned in her orbit and didn't know where I was. Beagles bayed. It lasted ten years or ten seconds. Our climax was a climb up the pyramids and a ten-planet pirouette down.

DONNA STIRRED FIRST. "Miguel and I have missed six shooting schedules. We might get fired."

I said, "Chickie's all over the media. We'll get him soon."

"I don't want it to end. How do you go back to guest shots and dates with actors after something like this?"

I kissed her neck. "You don't. You stay with me."

Donna shook her head. "I'm a move-on-but-always-live-in-L.A. kind of girl."

I shook my head. "It's not a life sentence. You've been through too much to be who you were."

Donna smiled. "I feel like an adventuress. I came to Hollywood, I was Andover and Wesleyan, it was grins and giggles, and now I'll see Stephen Nash the moment I wake up for the rest of my life."

"You're right. And I'll pick up the phone and call you when I'm scared or bored, and we'll meet for coffee and talk around the wild shit of fall '83 and how it changed us."

I cupped her breasts. I felt a *ka-tick* murmur under the right.

"You're saying you can't be subordinate to any man."

Donna squeezed my hand on her heart. "And I imagine it'll last until I'm 47 or -8 and I'm afraid of being alone."

I shook my head. "You'll have a grave and terrible beauty then. You'll get the face you earn, and Stephen Nash and me and Chuckie and Mama Cass will be part of it."

Donna burrowed into my chest. It hit me then—the cop part. *Chickie clouted a Rite Aid. He stole Seconal, Amytal, Tuinal. He did not steal demonic date-rape Rohypnol.*

Donna said, "I love you. I'll never just walk from all of this."

I said, "I love you, and I don't think I'll ever love anyone more."

Donna touched my lips. "Rick, don't say that. You're 31 years old."

"I'll rephrase it, then. I've got a kick-ass will and volition, and I'll never let myself love anyone more."

LUIS'S HIP HACIENDA. A kooky kasa in Coldwater Canyon. Wild warped wood whipped out at raucous right angles.

We pulled up and parked. Miguel said, "Typical actor's pad. Build as you go, between residual checks. The cocksucker starts out with *Hamlet* and ends up with *Count Borga, Vampire* for scale."

Donna mock-swatted him. "It's the world we chose, and we'll be lucky to do as well as he did."

"The cocksucker cheated on my mom during their honeymoon, then bird-dogged half of my bitches."

Donna mock-swatted him—harder. "Women are not 'bitches.'"

Miguel said, "Excuse me. 'Chicks.'"

Donna nudged me. "Can I kill him?"

I laffed. "If you'll marry me as part of the cover-up, yeah."

Donna said, "I'll consider it."

Miguel flipped off the kasa. "Hey, Luis, eat shit and die, you old cocksucker."

The old cocksucker cold-cocked my headlights. I braked and missed him. He was Miguel fifty years hence. Balder, Disney-esque Dumbo ears, blackhead-blotted beak. Garb: madcap madras golf shorts and an "I Choked Linda Lovelace" T-shirt.

We got out of the car. Father and son embraced. Papa pulled a pint of Padrone from his waistband. Miguel took two gulps. Donna declined. I took two—aaaaah!

They saltily soliloquized in Spanish. Luis talked fast. Miguel talked slow. I heard "*mujer magnifica*" "*chinga su madre*," "*Count Borga—dinero grande.*"

Miguel turned the talk *a ingles*. "Stephen Nash? *Hoto sicótico.* TV news, that killer. Come on, Daddy, speak English."

Luis whipped it out. Luis pissed in the driveway. His dick was divertingly donkeyesque.

Luis said, "It pays to advertise."

Donna said, "For those in the market."

Luis stumbled up his steps. The living room was a dump. We followed. Dave Slatkin lamented from a wall TV.

"We dug up the remains of the three children at the backyard location today, utilizing dogs from the LAPD's animal shelter. The boys had been missing from the polio ward since April 1956. Their broken pelvises denote a posterior-based sexual attack."

Ronald Reagan replaced Dave. Luis pounded Padrone. I badged him. "LAPD. Here or downtown."

Luis slipped on a crown and robe. Dig the nametags attached: "Property of the *Count Borga, Vampire* set."

Miguel grabbed a phone book. Miguel patted it. Miguel cracked the crown off Luis's head.

Dig the joltingly Jack Webb-like *Dragnet* drawl:

"Give us the straight dope, Pancho. You worm-eating wetbacks get no truck with my partners and me."

Donna grabbed the phone book. Donna hit Luis in the head.

"That's for whipping it out and hitting on me on *Hawaii Five-O.*"

Hollywood—man-o-Manischewitz!!!!

Luis humbly hurled Latin. I'm priapically Protestant—it was gravel Greek to me. Miguel said, "Sssh. It's the prelude to confession."

We all stood stock-still. The count chugged Padrone and chanted "nam-myoho-renge-kyo." We waited. He tossed the jug at the TV. The TV shattered. He corrosively confessed.

"It was '54. I'd lost it. I had no more self to transmit to the screen. I met Steve Nash. We got in a fender bender. He recognized me. We talked. He'd just robbed a liquor store. He was a heist man. He carried a knife and a pipe. He proudly stated that he was a butt banger, but I'd be safe because I wasn't his type. I fell into his sway. We smoked reefer and ate Benzedrex Inhaler wads together. I drove while he robbed stores. He never spent money. I held his stash, and I've still got it. He ate dog food exclusively. He drank Thunderbird wine. I thought he was real, *and* false and reinvented, and I believed roughly half of what he said. He fucked filthy winos in our poolhouse. It drove Rosie crazy. He used to joke with you, Miguelito. It drove Rosie crazy. Once she broke a stack of records over his head. He meant you no harm, *mi hijo*, I swear it."

The count picked his nose. The count took a deep stage breath.

Donna patted her phone book. "Wrap it up, Chico. *Rapidamente*, or I'll yank your green card."

The count went contemplative.

"I thought he was schizophrenic or the world's greatest actor. His all-dog-food diet netted me $108,995, all of which is in that top cupboard. He told me he killed three polio-afflicted children, and I never believed him. Then they found that boy under the Santa Monica pier. I wept when he went to the gas chamber. He was evil, but his genius meshed with mine, and together we will reach our zenith as I portray *Count Borga, Vampire*."

I said, "You're a fucked-up cat, Luis."

Donna hammered his head with the phone book, two-handed.

Miguel grabbed the drawer gross with greenbacks. He said, "*Yo te amo*, Papa, you cocksucker."

IT WAS LATE. We were tired and hungry. Loose lettuce lolled in my trunk. I called Kuster on my 2-way. Chickie Farhood—still at large. Massive manhunt. Habitual haunts held down. Homicide men at known homo huts. Camouflaged cops trawling the Swish Alps.

We drove southeast. The Pacific Dining Car—"Open All Nite." We hit Highland southbound. We saw shelter lights shimmer. We pulled up and walked in.

Bull terriers barked. Bloodhounds bayed. Airedales went aoooo! Reggie the Ridgeback rammed his snout under Donna's skirt.

Jane Slatkin was asleep. Three-dog night. Litter-mate Labs.

Dave sat on the floor. Donna shoved Reggie off. He sniffed Miguel's crotch and snickered.

I said, "He's still out there."

Dave nodded. "The big white house was the Collins pad, right?"

Miguel said, "Right. You're a fucking psychic genius, man. Want to go to the Dining Car?"

Dave shook his head. I said, "Stephen Nash ate an all-dog-food diet."

"Proving there's some good in all people."

Donna scratched Reggie's ridge. He almond-eyed her with *looooove*. Dave said, "I had a certified vision. There *is* an afterlife, and dogs run heaven. Jesus, Buddha, and all those other cats are just shills to keep squares walking the straight-and-narrow."

Reggie snout-skimmed Donna's skirt. Donna dodged him. She said, "*Jesus, and this is all real.*"

WE HOGGED a booth at the Car. We pounced on porterhouse, tore into T-bone, fattened our fangs on filet mignon. Donna said she'd adopt Reggie. Miguel said he'd adopt the two bull terriers. We piled into pecan pie. Donna held my hand in her lap. We yawned in unison. Our pads were too far to tango to. Let's roll to the Hollywood fuck pad.

Donna said, "What did your dad do with his Oscar for *Hamlet*? I didn't see it at his dump."

Miguel laffed. "He hocked it to Schwab's pharmacy for phenobarbital and booze."

I said, "Maybe he'll mount a comeback with *Count Borga*."

Miguel said, "Nix. It's a grade-Z turkey headed straight for TV."

A waiter walked over. Donna pointed to some steak scraps. "Will you wrap this up for my dog?"

WE DROVE to the pad. It was dark and dank quiet. No window lights, normal TV or fuck-flick flares. No laughing or lip-smacking of late-nite libidos.

We walked in. I hit the living-room lights. It was too tidy—no dropped drawers or gunbelts shed for the sheets.

Donna yawned. "I'm going up to the roof. I want to look at the lights and extend this whole adventure."

Miguel said, "I'll go with you."

They walked upstairs. I eyeballed the stairways and landings. No kitchen lights. No de rigueur disarray.

Donna and Miguel hit the roof—I heard gravel grab. I walked upstairs. No hall lights. No sconces skimming light. No bathroom lights, no light-lit walkways to the johns.

Five bedroom doors—identically shut.

My neck hairs nipped and nudged me. I opened one door. I hit the wall light.

There's Condom Cal Coleman and a mulatto meter maid snoring. They passed out dressed. There's a nightstand. There's a Jim Beam jug. There's a red capsule popped and white powder residue.

The Rite Aid 459. The stolen barbiturates—

I tiptoed. I opened doors. I got insidious instant replays. Snores. Clothed couples. Barely broken bottle seals and popped-pill residue.

I ran upstairs. The roof door was open. There's Donna and Miguel by the south ledge, grooving and grokking the view.

I pulled my piece. The door slammed back. It hit my nose. It tore my teeth. I dropped my gun. It fell down the stairs. It sheared a shot accidental.

I stumbled. I staggered. I saw the Antichrist: Chickie Farhood made up as Stephen Nash.

I pulled my throw-down. Chickie caught it and kicked it away. He slammed the door. My fingers got fucked. Three thread-dangled off the knucklebones.

Gravel ground, grabbed, crackled, and crunched. I saw Donna and Miguel.

They grabbed Chickie. They pulled his hair. Donna gouged his eyes. Miguel kicked him and stuffed gravel in his mouth. Donna ripped an eye out. Chickie screamed. Miguel lashed a belt around his neck. Four hands tightened and pulled.

I saw Chickie scream. I saw Chickie thrash, spasm, and spit gravel. I saw the ledge. I saw Donna step on his face and make him eat mica-flecked grounds. I saw Miguel lift his legs and throw him off the building.

◾

The shooting board cleared me. One call to Kuster—case clapboard-closed. Donna drove me to Cedars of Lebanon. The ER docs saved my fingers.

I badged the night nurse. Donna slept in my hospital bed with me. The morphine drip made for mad nightmares—all Stephen Nash.

They released me next noon. We all met at Hollywood Homicide: me, Donna, Dave, Russ, Miguel.

We agreed. The house was evil. It had to burn. The Nash stash would fix the landlady—some swank oldster's crib for life.

Chuy Nieves had a firebug brother. Street name: Matchhead Manuel. Russ said he'd call him.

We watched it burn. We sat across the street and drank canned daiquiris. I held hands with Donna. The fuck pad ignited. Firemen showed. The roof caved in. Kitsch house to kindling in twelve minutes flat.

I walked Donna to her car. We kissed. She said, "We were fucked by this and made by this, and I'll never love anyone more than you, and I'll go through men and cut them loose because

I'm an actress with appetites and nothing in my life will ever be this goddamn motherfucking real."

I brushed soot from her hair. "I'll remember every moment. That'll see me through."

She got in her car. She threaded past fire engines. She drove west on Hollywood Boulevard.

I died in a futile gunfight. Others fell before me.

Russ Kuster died 10/9/90. It happened at the Hilltop Hungarian. Bela Marko was drunk. He had a laser gun. He aimed it at customers. Russ told him to stop. Marko refused. Marko shot Russ. Russ shot Marko. They killed each other. It took six seconds flat.

Donna attended the funeral. We held hands. We wept at the eulogy.

Dave and I rose within LAPD. The big one—downtown Homicide. Donna and Miguel became TV stars and did feature work. Donna never married. I'd see her on the street sometimes. We'd hold each other and whisper-talk for an hour at a crack. People thought we were nuts. We embraced for two hours in a rainstorm once in Beverly Hills.

I never married. Everything Donna said outside the burned-down house proved true.

I lived to age 96. Donna's still alive. She's got a recurring role on a nighttime soap job. The show's about as good as Count Borga, Vampire.

Here's how I died.

I was in a mall in Orange County. I was old and frail. I still carried a gun. A very old Mexican cat walked up to me. He had tic-tac-toe scars. I remembered immediately: Chuy Nieves/the screen test.

Chuy had a big Glock. I had a big Browning. We blew each other away instantaneously. The papers called it the "Oldsters' O.K. Corral."

Dogs run heaven. Donna's generations of Reggie Ridge-backs call the shots. There's lots of clouds and a fuckload of dogs. The food's good. You get to have sex with people you really love. You get to relive your earth life and hit a Pause button. I always go back to fall '83.

I miss Donna. I want to get hammered by those hurricane-hurled hazel eyes up close once again. There's only one catch. I never want her to die.

Hot-Prowl Rape-O

Heaven's forever. *Time trips on and traps you. Time cordons you corporeal. Time circumscribes your surfeit of earthly events. Time immobilizes the immortal and makes them look back.*

Donna. Me. A long jump: '83 to '04, time-trippingly.

It had to happen. The fitful laws of physics mandated more of us. Our vibes ran vampiric. They recklessly reconnected. They spun out and sparked in our spiritus mundi and nuclear-napalmed L.A.

Donna and me. Lashed to the language that pops on these pages. Allegorized in alliteration and bound back boldfaced like this:

Hush-Hush 2000, October 2004 issue.
SCANDAL KINGPIN GETCHELL DEAD!
FUNERAL BODES AS STONE GASSER!
By Gary Getchell
Yeah, he died of AIDS—but he was no skin-flute hootin' tutti-frutti! Daniel Arthur Getchell—the skank-scamming, scandal-skimming, scopophile king—was a heroin-hooking

junkie with a 40-year monkey on his back. Danny the G. was a mensch. He neighborly noodled out his needles and got malignant microbes back. He landed in a secret AIDS ward at Cedars-Sinai. It was fat with faigelahs he outed in *Hush-Hush*. They homo-humped Danny. Dolorous dozens of gay Getchellphobics stormed the hospital. Danny the G. got the gate. He survived this turd-burglar tyranny and hid out at home. He was tenderly tended by magnificent mama-san Megan More, cable-flick floozy supreme. He died September 12. Ms. More said he went out with "dystopian DTs." He "alliterated alluringly" to the end. He spritzed the linguini-like lassos of language that have invasively influenced bad-ass bop-talkers worldwide. Ms. More dug Danny G.'s death spiel. It was "wild shit by James Joyce and Iceberg Slim, Danny's two favorite authors."

Danny Getchell took over *Hush-Hush* magazine in 1955. He rode out lynch-mob-like libel suits. He was L.A.'s litigation-licking truth-trumpeter and mendacity-mauling musketeer. He fragged fruits. He nailed nymphomaniacs. He print-pronged corrupt cops and dollar-driven D.A.s. He punched out pork-barrel politicos. He banged behind-the-scenes in the '58 California election. He immortalized his work in the Mephistophelian memoir *The Trouble I Cause*.

D. the G. ran *Hush-Hush* up to 1999. I wrapped the reins then. I dropped my nowheresville name of Irv Moskowitz and took the moniker "Gary Getchell." I follow Danny's metasta-sizing mandate. I traffic the truth triumphantly.

I've got Danny the G.'s secret dirt files. They're furtively fail-safed and hidden *Hush-Hush*. They barbarously berate and insidiously indict. They pummel political correctness. They priapically prick predators and frappé the frail. They knock Danny's no-good nemesis, the LAPD.

The LAPD hassled Danny from '55 up. Danny grew a hard-on to hurt them back and sucked up to certain fractious factions within. I've got that hopping hard-on now. It's pounding in my pants. I don't like the new Chief, Joe Tierney. The mischievous mick from filthy Philly gores my goat. He's a headline hurdler and media mauler from the get-go. I don't dig his command staff. Take Captain Linus "the Laundry-man" Lauter. The Feds are looking at Linus lingeringly. His son, Leotis Lauter, runs a Southside dope cartel. The Feds think Linus launders Leotis's long green. Linus belongs to the 4-A Club: He's African-American *and* Affirmative Action. *J'accuse*—Jolting Joe Tierney's afraid to suspend him while the Feds *coon*duct their biz.

I've inherited Danny G.'s moral mandate. I'll be there at Forest Lawn next week. A rent-a-rabbi will soliloquize. He'll tip topical and irradiate the Iraqis. The crowd will be huge and Dannyesque diverse. Dig the details on my public-access TV show, and dig me at hush-hush.com. Don't send flowers or waste your bread on mementoes. Send your money directly to me. I'm broke, and I need garlands of good Getchellite gelt.

Remember, dear reader, you heard it here first: off the record, on the Q.T., and *very Hush-Hush*.

Los Angeles Times, September 22, 2004.
RESIDENTIAL BURGLARIES IN BEL-AIR AND HOLMBY HILLS
By Miles Corwin

A house burglar has struck six times in upscale West Los Angeles neighborhoods over the past eight weeks, a LAPD spokesperson has told the *Times*. All the homes were occupied at the moments of entry, which detectives consider a crucial aspect of the burglar's modus operandi.

Captain Bill Dumais, the commander of the detective unit at the West Los Angeles Station, said, "The burglar enters his target homes through half-open windows or doors with easily picked locks. He temporarily sedates pet dogs with mild pre-scription sleeping pills stuck in pieces of raw meat, which leads me to believe he's an animal lover who doesn't like to hurt pets. He's not so gentle with humans, though. He finds them, usually asleep, or rousing at the sound of his entry, and shoots them with a tranquilizer gun. He uses a powerful tranquilizing substance that sedates the people from six to ten hours."

Captain Dumais went on to discuss burglary precedents and the West L.A. burglar's probable motives. "We call burglars who break into residences with people inside them 'hot-prowl men,' " he said. "They tend to get aroused by the prospect of interaction with the people, and they often graduate to physical assault, rape, and even murder."

Does this burglar possess that potential? Captain Dumais thinks he does. "So far, the burglar has been stealing only small trinkets," the captain said. "It appears that he's not out for saleable items, so it's our belief that he's a fetishist looking for souvenirs to commemorate his break-ins."

And the LAPD's plans for apprehension?

"Plans are in the works," Captain Dumais said. "We want to catch this guy before he hurts someone for keeps."

1.

Donna Standard Time stung me. The squadroom was dead. I decided to desk-dally and dream.

I moved the unit TV over. We used it to magnify mug shots and match fingerprints. It was computer-compatible and sturdy state-of-the-art. Dave Slatkin wired a voom-voltage VCR in.

Hospital Hearts—Donna does doofus TV. She's an on-call oncologist with a loser love life. The series flailed, flatlined, tipped, and tanked.

I settled in. I dug on my desk detritus and mused on my murder mandate.

There's my PC. It features fine-tuned Fed software. There's my rhino-horn paperweight. There's my fetishistic photo spray, plied under Plexiglas. A dozen Donna-look-alike girlfriends—failed flings from '83 up. There's Stephanie Gorman, DOD 8-5-65/

unsolved—the case that I clamor to clear. Snuffed at home/West L.A./botched rape-sex job.

LAPD Homicide, Cold Case Squad. Dave Slatkin, D3 in charge. Six detectives. Mildew-musty murder files to read, review, reject, peruse, and pursue. Divinely deigned DNA—our most clever clue-clearance tool.

Three years as a unit. Serial killers caught. Rape-os wrapped up and courtroom castrated. The cutting-edge culling of old file data and karmic comeuppance.

I loved the work. I loved the Donna-dalliance downtime. I popped *Hospital Hearts* in the VCR and sailed the sound off.

There's Donna. She's wearing wicked white. She's telling a sickly citizen he's got the Big C. *Fuck that*—she's saying she loves me!

The Donna scene denoumened. A comatose commercial commenced. I shut my eyes and dreamed.

I was 52. She was 48. It was 21 years since *then*. We never married. We serialized separate sex. We mired ourselves in molten and moping monogamy. I carried a flaring flame and a tumescent torch.

Donna was rich. Donna won two Emmys. Donna lived in Holmby Hills. I was middle-class. I'd shot two wetbacks and three jigaboos. I lived in Chino Hills.

Donna had dogs—generations of Reggie Ridgebacks. I had in-place informants. Dig: parking-lot punks, coffee-house confidants, maître d's, *molto bene*. They saw Donna and buzzed me toward her. I showed up dippy and disingenuous. Donna dug on the game and saw through the shuck.

I opened my eyes. Dog-food dramaturgy drilled me. I scanned the walls. I saw old LAPD pix.

Black Dahlia shots. Onion Field shots. My favorite fiend—the doomonic Donald Keith Bashor.

It's '55. Don's a hot-prowl hunk and one strapping studly. He whips through the Westlake Park District. He B&Es women's pads. He steals cash only. It's always late nite. The women sleep on.

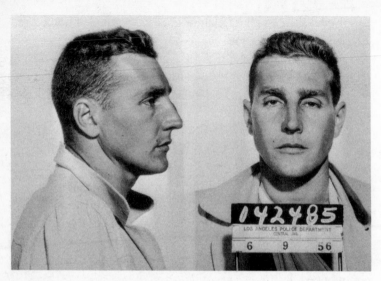

Donald Keith Bashor was sentenced to die for the murders of two women victims of burglary forays. *(Los Angeles Times Collection, Department of Special Collections, Charles E. Young Research Library, UCLA)*

Until 2/16/55 —

Don caroms down Carondelet Street. Don pops a pad packed with nurses. Don pops out with three purses.

Don nets ninety scoots. Don dumps the purses. Don catwalks down Carondelet. Don taps 271 South. Karil Graham's door's ajar.

He enters. She wakes up. She screams. He beats her dead with a pipe. He loots her purse. He considers a postmortem rape. The blood turns him off.

He skates on the Graham snuff. He sidles out to South Pasadena. He hot-prowls there. He waits fourteen months. He whips back to Westlake Park.

He hot-prowls. He steals. He tools off his turf. He rapes an Echo Park woman. He wiggles back to Westlake. It's 5/56. He hot-prowls a pad on West 5th Street.

Laura Lindsay screams. He beats her dead with a hammer.

Demon Don kept it up. Geography is destiny. Westlake wigged wicked magic on him. LAPD ran rolling stakeouts. Said stakeouts snagged Demon Don.

June '56—it's over. October '57—Don fries at Big Q.

Demon Don dug under my skin. He stuck as the Stephanie

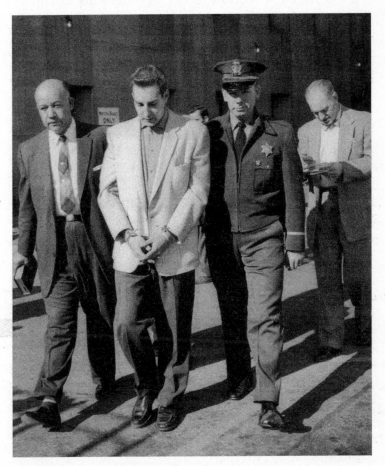

Donald Bashor, flanked by Senior Deputy George Coenen, left, and Sheriff's Sergeant Howard Earle, starts on the trip to San Quentin Prison. *(Los Angeles Times Collection, Department of Special Collections, Charles E. Young Research Library, UCLA)*

Gorman paradigm. Your prowl pads. You think you come for cash. You *really* seek sexual succor. You've got an urge to unleash the unknown. Every pad gores your gonads. Your adrenaline's addressed. Every woman's a witch wired to take you where you *have* to go.

I checked the screen. Donna was back. Her hazel eyes hit me hard as hybrids of la Gorman's. I fast-forwarded. Donna dunned a baleful boyfriend for lasting love. I tossed out the text. I licentiously lip-read. Donna expressed explicit love for *me*.

Two print techs walked in. I popped out the cassette. Donna Standard Time, *adieu*.

I beamed up at Bashor. Dave Slatkin beatified the beast and correlated him to the current hot-prowl man. Dave made the man as moon-mad. He was long-term lunar-looped. He slinked to sliver moons and sharp shadows. The man bopped Bashor-like. Dave figured he'd rape and kill soon.

The squadroom filled up. There's my partner, Tim Marti. He's a heavy-handed hard-charger and a thrill-seeking throwback. He priapically predates the Rodney King/so-PC/no-beavertail-sap-slapping days. There's Dave. He's dog-hair-dusted and dog-food-flecked. He's still got that dog shelter. He's breeding brindle pits now.

I was bored. I was restless. DST re-resurrected. Stephanie Gorman caught Donna dust and coopted the ride.

Identikit internment. Sizzling symbiology. Stephanie and Donna as one.

I punched up the program. My computer popped and pixilated two faces. There's Stephanie at 16. There's Donna at 48. Slow now—let's mix-and-match faces.

Four bright hazel eyes. Stephanie's summer tan. Donna's soft paleness.

I free-form Frankensteined for an hour. The now and the then got jungled up and jangled. I thought of Russ Kuster. I thought of fall '83 and the Jenson-Donahue dead. Stephanie—freeze-frame frissoned at youth forever.

It hit me:

Danny Getchell was dead. He snitched for me. He bid me to bop-talk. I owed him some flowers.

MY DEBT: One boss bouquet. Narco Division's: floral flotillas. Danny handed them wholesale hopheads and mucho meth dealers. They heaped him heroin back.

I elevatored down. The Narco bullpen: doom-deep in depression.

Twenty-plus desks. "Laundryman" Linus Lauter's cops lolling listlessly.

I looked at them. They looked at me. They tapped their toes and popped on their PCs. They booted up beaver-shot bashes. They socked in solitaire. They Internet-ignored me.

I whistled. "Flowers for Danny G. Who wants to contribute?"

Some guys flipped me off. Most guys depressive-deadpanned me. Bill Berchem tapped his toupee and twirled one finger. Bob Mosher picked his nose and snagged snot my way.

Division-deep depression. One Fed-fucked captain. The trickle-down trap. Cops headed for Subpoena City.

I scanned the squadroom. The freeze frappéed me. I checked the chalkboard. I saw Gary Getchell's loathsome likeness. Gary's gobbling a big dick. Gary's got shivs shoved in him. A caustic caption read, "Die, motherfucker!!!!!"

I said, "Gary G. isn't Danny G. Come on, Danny did us all solid."

Cal Eggers walked up. Call it: Linus Lauter's less-than-listless lieutenant. Sixtyish. Still a stud. Still a fast-track finagler.

He urged me outside. We walked. We caught some corridor schmooze space. I said, "Danny G. didn't burn Lauter, the Feds did. Gary's rattling cages in *Hush-Hush*, and so what?"

Eggers whipped out his wallet and fanned five fifties. I grabbed gratefully.

"Thanks, Lieutenant."

"Come on, Rhino, it's 'Cal' to D2s and up. You know I'm clean and on the Captain's List, and Linus Lauter's a dumb jungle bunny who bought a six-million-dollar house, *cash*, on a captain 2's salary. Tell me I'm not happy he's going to burn, and since I'm a recent transfer in, tell me I don't have a shot at the command."

I smiled smug. "It's a good summation."

Eggers winked. "You glommed Danny G. dope when you worked Hollywood Homicide. You're not afraid that your name's in a file that hump Gary's got?"

I shook my head. "It's a he-said/he-said scenario. Danny's dead, and I've won the Medal of Valor."

Eggers shook his head. "You're a fucking eccentric. You're a fifty-plus bachelor who wears rhino-horn regalia. You capped three spooks and two wetbacks in a reasonably distinguished police career, but the balance of public opinion has tipped away from us. Look down the fucking hallway."

I did it. I didn't dig the drift.

Bulletin-board brouhaha. Diversity classes: malevolent and mandatory. Pernicious postings: the Federal Consent Decree/stiff strictures/Radically Reform Your Wicked White Man's Ways. Civilian lawsuit updates: ultimatums from shyster lawyers/cleverly cloaked class-action shit. Call it cold: baton-bopping back-alley justice, *adios*. Viva malignant multiculturalism and coerced *coon*sensus.

I yawned. "Yeah, I know the precedents. O.J., Rodney King, the '92 riots. Payback time for the great L.A. unwashed. You know how I see the Lauter thing playing in? He catches a bullet for being a cop, and dodges one for being a jig. His kid, Leotis, is a piece of shit, so that tips the balance against him."

Eggers cracked his knuckles. "You saw the squadroom. Middle-

aged white men up the ying-yang. They'll all get tarred with the
Linus brush, their careers will flatline, their retirement job
prospects will tank, and every fucking man is thinking, 'Danny G.
could keep his mouth shut, but the fuck wrote everything down.
Will that sick little shit Gary use his files?' "

I shrugged. I wanted to short-shrift this shit. *Hush-Hush* was
non-mainstream media. Both Getchells were scum scamsters. A
noxious Narco probe—yes. Linchpins Linus and Leotis—yes.
Fed subpoenas for *Hush-Hush* files—not likely.

My hackles hopped. Eggers felt hinky. I got instantly itchy. My
bald head buzzed.

I said, "You're tweaking me. You want an outsider's damage
assessment. Okay, here it is. Linus and Leotis go down, but nobody
else does. Yeah, your guys bought snitches from Danny Getchell,
and yeah, he wrote it down. So what? It ends there. Danny's dead,
and Gary G.'s a secondhand, compromised informant."

Eggers bowed. My tweak take—touché!

"Yes, I wanted an outside opinion, and you confirmed what I
thought myself. There's that, and the fact that I always enjoy talking to the guy who had ten minutes with Donna Donahue."

I laffed. "It went fast. Ten minutes twenty years ago, and I'm
fucked forever."

Eggers laffed. "I worked the Rampart DB then. I know the
whole story."

"No, you don't. And Donna and I aren't telling."

"*Cherchez la femme.* I've always gone by that."

"I've got two women. I *cherchez* more than most."

2.

Cherchez this:

Beverlywood. A delightful demimonde near Beverly Hills.
Peaceful and pastoral. A kalm Kosher Kanyon.

Hillsboro and Sawyer—Stephanie Gorman's house still
standing.

I parked across the street. The sky tipped toxic tan to bleached blue. The red-rimmed sun set. I dug on the dark.

She died in daylight. *Ma chère* Stephanie.

It's 8/5/65. There's a hellacious heat wave. Stephanie goes to summer school—Hamilton High sessions.

She carpools home. She's alone. Her mom's at their tennis club. Dad and sis work downtown.

There's two doors in. It's a horrific hot-prowl variation.

The back gate. The backyard. The sliding door in. The front door. The possible unlocked status.

He brought mason's cord. He brought a small pistol. He hit Stephanie. He dragged her. They made the front bedroom. He tied her to a daybed. He stripped her.

She broke free. She screamed and ran. He shot and killed her.

The investigation clicks. The Watts Riot runs roughshod and reroutes it. Career confessors cop out and lie themselves loose. Cops ream rape-os. Cops whip on wienie waggers. Cops hurl hurt on hot-prowl hyenas.

Nothing. Zero, zilch, bupkes, bust, goose egg, gornish.

Thirty-plus years pass. Dave S. reads the file. Tim Marti reads the file. I read the file, *cherchez-la-femmingly*. We fall for Stephanie. She's a lost daughter shared. She's *my* daughter with Donna D.

We pry up print cards. We cough up comparison prints—family, fuzz, friends. We winch a wild-card print. We feed it to the Feds. We get a hit.

The guy's a minor miscreant. He racked up a receiving charge, post-Stephanie. He's kool, kalm, and kosher—before and since.

We blast a background check. We crawl up every known crack and crevice. *We know he did not know the Gormans.* Check this, Chuck—what's your fucking print doing there?

Dave and Tim braced the guy. He guy gassed with them. Cops, huh? How can I help you?

Dave said, "Stephanie Gorman." Tim said, "She was murdered." The guy said, "Oh, yeah, the little dead twist."

Oh, shit—he's coming on callous, ink him innocent.

Dave dug in. Tim tore in. *Tell us what you know.*

I was across the street. I was boning my best buddy's bitch. He got his schlong shot off in Korea. The twist's sister ran over. She was shit-your-pants scared and screaming. My buddy was a quack herb doc. The sister yelped for help. I went over for groovy grins and giggles. Bummer—the little twist was Deadsville.

Call my buddy. Talk to his wife. I poured her the pork for twenty-six years. They'll vouch and verify my story.

We did it. The No-Dick Doctor confirmed it—call him *il cornuto*. The wayward wife was one wicked wench. She waxed wild at eighty. Our suspect "gave it to me from 1:00 p.m. on. Man-o-Manischewitz, what a schvantz! He was hung like a nigger!"

One suspect suspended. One case closed—for now.

Open-file status. No semen from '65. No way to DNA-match.

I couldn't let it go. I read and reread the file. I combed for connections. I looked for leads and linkage. Nothing nudged me. No brain broils, no synaptic sizzles. I cultivated communion. Stephanie Standard Time stung me. I parked by her pad odd evenings.

A breeze brought leaves up. Clouds climbed past the moon. Window lights leaped inside the house. I shaped shadows as Stephanie.

My cell phone rang. I hit the Talk button.

"This is Jenson."

"Hi. It's Rob. You know, from the Starbucks on Beverly Drive."

"Oh, shit. Is she . . . ?"

"Yeah, you fucking horndog. She's on a big-ass mocha, so I think you've got time."

SHE WORE a serge skirt and a coral cashmere coat. Her hazel eyes hopped.

I sat down. She popped her paperback in her purse.

"I would have gotten this to go, but I saw that kid pick up the phone."

I mainlined some mocha. Too thick and sweet—ugh.

"He's a valued LAPD informant."

Donna laffed. "Are you coercing him or paying him?"

"Both. He honked a vice cop at the Wiltern, and I bought him out of jail. That, plus ten bucks a sighting."

Donna said, "I could go to the Coffee Bean. It's just across the street."

"No go. I've got all the shift managers bribed. That, plus the—"

"—the valet park guys, all—"

"—of whom are fucking coercible wetbacks."

Donna laffed. I mooched more of her mocha. I held her hands for a heartbeat. I straightened one stocking seam.

"You can't lose me. Not for more than six months at a time. We're both L.A. lifers, and I know this place too well."

Donna looked around. I looked around. Our eyes tapped table to table. Beverly Hillsites beamed back, blasé—so what if you're Donna Donahue.

I said, "Who are you doing these days?"

Donna said, "A screenwriter. He's handsome and much younger than me. I control things. It's an indoor relationship, and the age gap embarrasses me. I don't like to be seen with him."

I slapped my knees. My suitcoat slid, my holster hitched, my badge beamed, my gun glistened. Jaded eyes jabbed me—who's that cop with Donna Donahue.

"I was seeing a deputy D.A., who just happened to look like you. We had bad sex twice, and she states her agenda. She wants to get married, move to Portland, and adopt an Iraqi war-refugee baby. I got out then."

Donna laffed. She held *my* hands for a heartbeat. She notched up my necktie knot.

"That burglar hit a block over from me. I thought, 'Shit, let's be prepared,' so I called Tom Ludlow. He sold me some guns."

Fuck—Phone Book Tom. Still at Hollywood Homicide, still a phone-book freak.

"Throw-down guns, right? Unregistered pieces?"

"Right."

I shook my head. "You're bored. You're reliving '83. 'Brave new fucking world' and all that."

Donna drained her drink. "I get bored and think about it. Last week my agent sent me a script. I'm supposed to be a cop moonlighting as a serial killer. I'm killing my ex-boyfriends' wives, and having a high old time mutilating the bodies. How do you tell someone you can't take the job because you killed three people in 1983, and certain things scare you and certain things own you?"

My pulse pulled to 120. My blood-pressure pressed. Dangerous Donna—radical redux.

"What did you do with the guns?"

"I booby-trapped the house."

"Will you show me?"

"Of course."

■

Chez Donna: a sharp chateau off L.A. Country Club. Nestled by the north course—some Holmby Hills hutch.

Tall turrets, big bay windows. Fucking football-field footage. Heavy housage for one woman and a randy ridgeback.

We two-car-caravaned over. We parked in the porte cochere. Donna let us in. The horny hound hurtled high and humped me.

He locked my leg. He pawed my pubes. He bit at my belt. HIV-test me—the fag dog drew blood.

Donna tossed him a treat. Reggie Ridgeback relented. We thrown-down-gun-toured the pad.

One mighty Magnum—couch-cushion concealed. One fat

.45—thrown under a throw rug. One revolver—rigged by Ridge-back Reggie's dog bed.

The downstairs: designered-out and Donnaesque. Fine fabrics offset by oil paintings. A rapturous Renoir. A magnificent Monet. A clever Klee. Furtive firepower amidst all.

Dangerous Donna, *mon dieu!*

We walked upstairs. Reggie Ridgeback crept and crotch-sniffed me. Dig the master-bedroom Browning. Dig the guest-room Ruger pump. Dig the Derringer hung in the shower stall, à la soap-on-a-rope.

French provincial trappings—tricked-out wood and wall beams. Pop art by pederastic modern masters. Hard-hitting hollow-point ammo and deer-stopping double-aught buck.

Devil-horned Donna—neo-noir succubus!

We bopped out to the balcony. Reggie crotch-crept between us. The night air made me snap, crackle, pop.

Golf-course view—one vibrant vista, one plumb line south-east. I felt Stephanie starting up.

We laid lounge chairs adjacent. We sat down. We laced hands loose. Reggie registered his cue and vamoosed.

Donna said, "You're thinking about the girl."

I stared Stephanie's way. I heard cars whoop down Wilshire. I orbed into Stephanie's orbit.

"She's older than us, but she'll always be younger. And I was thinking of both of you."

Donna squeezed my hand. "Everything's foreplay and yearn-ing with you. You only want what you can't have."

A mist meandered in. The golf course metamorphosed into moors.

"I figured something out about us. It takes in '83 and wraps things up."

Donna said, "Tell me."

I said, "We've downscaled our expectations on the things that most people live for, so we can live in a world of possibility."

Donna stared southeast. Her gaze got moor-mired up.

"There's times I want things to go bad, just so I can go there again."

"For instance?"

"My Web site's been getting too many hits. There's been a lot of nasty questions on my old boyfriends, and intimations that I'm a dyke, because I never married."

I smiled. "You could marry me."

Donna smiled. "That would effectively quash *all* sense of possibility."

The moor mist rose. The moon moved into it.

"There's more. I've been getting e-mail requests for my panties, which is not unprecedented, but—"

I cut in. "Why not? And if you start selling them, let me know."

Donna laffed. "I made a cop flick with an actress named Megan More. She's primarily a soft-core porno star, and she made a pass at me. She's sold her panties on the Internet, and she told me it's quite profitable."

Dig it! Pounce on that pounding possibility!

I invade the Internet. I shore up my shorts. I buttress the bulges and rack them retail. Rhino Rick Jenson—rhino-horn raider!

Donna poked me. "Here's the semi-spooky part. The e-mails and the panty requests both come from public-library computers, so there's no way I can tell the pathetic asshole or assholes to fuck off."

Reggie walked up. I raked his ridge. I made him mew *molto bene*.

"One set of assholes in a twenty-year career isn't so bad."

"Two, actually. I've been getting love-hate notes in the mail, on and off, for years. He loves it when I show skin, he hates it when I show skin. He's a skin sicko."

I raked Reggie. "If you're scared, I could sleep on the couch."

"For the next thirty years?"

"Why not?"

Donna said, "Speak, Reggie." Reggie flashed his fangs and growled gravel gruff.

I got the point. Possibility meant abstinence. I had a wishful woody. She had a killer K-9, boocoo guns and guts.

The moor mist moved in. Reggie mewed at the moon.

3.

Dystopian Disneyland—Danny Getchell's wigged-out wake!

Myriad mourners and morbid scene makers. Legions of L.A. losers festooning Forest Lawn.

Hopheads and hermaphrodites. Porno film stars and Gen-X actors genuflecting. Nihilistic college kids digging on dead Danny. An anarchic assembly of perverts, punks, and free-wheeling freaks.

Anti-Danny pickets: quixotic queers high on homo hegemony. Narco cops poised on the periphery—bad Bill Berchem and beefy Bob Mosher.

Forest Lawn—capped to capacity. Green grass broiled brown—700 soiled souls smack in a *baaad* smog alert.

I stood with Tim Marti. We lugged our loopy floral flotilla. Tim pointed out pertinent personas bellied up to the bier.

"The guy with the earlocks is a rabbi with a kiddy-raper jacket. He made a little girl nosh his kosher salami at some Holocaust gig. The stacked blonde is Megan More. She's on these late-night T&A flicks. My kid Brandon sneaks down to watch her and belt his hog all the fucking time. The skinny guy is Gary Getchell, aka 'Scurvy' Irv Moskowitz. He's the so-called editor-in-chief of *Hush-Hush*, but his full-time gig is caddy at Bel-Air Country Club. He's a wienie wagger. He likes to flash nuns. I popped him when I worked West L.A. Vice."

I laffed lewd. I looked at the losers. The rabbi rang me wrong. He vibed skin-pop junkie. His neck was needle-notched. Call the faux Getchell caddy-clad and fully fucked up. He wore gatorskin golf shoes and seersucker shorts. His shirt showed off patterned penguins. Dig his yellow yarmulke—the full-fucked finishing touch.

I laffed loud. I leched on Megan More. She was a skyscraping skin-flick goddess. She soared six feet plus. She was wispy white and tantalizing tan—a bravura Brünnhilde de-luxe.

Tim tapped me. "I saw Berchem and Mosher taking pictures. You think—"

"I think they're putting heat on Gary Getchell, for no good fucking cause. Maybe he's got a Narco file, maybe he doesn't. Maybe Danny G. had shit on Linus Lauter, maybe he didn't—"

"—but in *any* case, *Hush-Hush 2000* is a fucking joke. The circulation's low four figures, it's a mimeograph job, the only people who read it are movie- and music-biz hipsters, and the only reason it survives is that the ACLU protects it from libel suits pro bono."

The rabbi reached for a microphone. The *craaaazy* crowd pressed up. I saw bleary and bloodshot eyes. I smelled righteous reefer. A sea of sick souls surrounded us. I flung our floral flotilla. It banged Danny G.'s bier.

Berchem and Mosher moved in. They mingled and moseyed by Megan More. They missed Tim and me. They bopped by the bier. They carried cameras. Said cameras clicked.

They shot Megan More. They shot Megan More and the mourners she talked to. Click/click/click—Megan More and Minox minicam pix.

I shrugged. Tim shrugged. It vibed hinky shit.

The rabbi mauled the microphone and licked his lips. The rabbi davened and delivered.

Danny G. was a marvelous mensch and a sharpshooting shtarker. He wasn't a schmendrick, a schlemiel, or a schlimazel. He was one magnificent motherfucker.

The rabbi ratcheted it up. Some klezmer clowns joined in. Jazz Judaism jumped. Tim and I splitsvilled.

THE FUNERAL GORED my gourd. Residual reefer smoke smacked me. It was a cool contact high. I drove home to Donnafy and contain it.

The buzz dipped and diminuendoed. I got restless and re-Donnafied. I got the urge to merge. Let's *real-life* re-Donnafy before your sex drive cessates.

I called Donna. I came on breezy and brazen. Those panty printouts perturb me. Please let me look.

Donna bought it. I'm going out—I'll put the printouts on my doorstep. Thanks, Rick—you rock.

I hit Holmby Hills. I picked up the printouts. I chugged back to Chino Hills. I put on some righteous Rachmaninoff—Rick and Donna, *you* Rach.

The Opus 32 Preludes—preternaturally precious *and* priapic. Sex seldom seen/lilting loss/heavy heartbreak—the Rick-loves-Donna précis.

I studied the printouts. Bim—silly shit. Bam—similar shit. Bip—sent from West L.A. libraries. Call it cold: silly and similar shit *sent by the same sender.*

Let's seek a second opinion.

I called Dave Slatkin. Dave said, Sure—let's see the shit. I'm busy right now. I'm going out to Bel-Air, to sit in on a hot-prowl stakeout.

The hot-prowl guy is lunar-phased—I *know* it. His last vic caught two trank darts. He almost died. The geek will kill sooner or later.

I stressed my printouts—Donna danger and pervo potential. A Freaky Freddy in the Panty Pantheon. A Sick Sidney and a morbid masturbator.

Dave laughed me off. Yeah, I'll read the shit. Find me on the stakeout. And get real, Rhino—you're just Donna-diddled right now.

Ouch—

I started to hang up. Dave said, Oh, and call Chief Tierney's office—he's got an errand for you.

I hung up. I relived the call and re-ouched. Dave Slatkin slams me. Dave instigates my inventory. Be real, Rhino Rick. You're Donna-diddled. You're a Donna doofus and a Donna dunce. You Donna-dallied in 1983. You're a Donna determinist. You're Donnafied and Donnafried behind the hellbound heat and monster meshugas of that moment.

Yeah, and it's solemnly sad—but it's so fucking *goooooooooood*.

I propped up the printouts. I underscored ugly outtakes. Dig the pandemic pantyphile:

"Dear Donna: I'm a handsome & well-hung collector of women's undergarments, which I catalog & keep behind glass at my bachelor pad in Malibu. Would you e-mail me about the availability of such items & how much they would cost?"

"Dear Donna: I would like to purchase your panties to fill out my collection, but I can't do it unless you answer my e-mails, which so far you haven't done. Are you too busy to connect with your fans, or are you just terminally stuck up?"

"Dear Bitch: You've got a last chance to redeem yourself by selling me your panties at discount prices. Don't hesitate! Do it today!"

I skimmed skanky cybernotes. Nasty nuggets stood out:

"I think it's twisted that you've never married. Are you some kind of muff muncher or rug merchant?"

"I know you've been thru lots of men. Who was the biggest & the best?"

"I want to douse your panties with Chanel #5 & take them to school with me, because they remind me of my mom."

Maybe one deadly Donnaphobe. Maybe a kook kavalcade. Maybe one passive putz.

I got out my notepad. I wrote:

"Panty man—frustration/violence of language escalating. Does he know of panty-selling-actress precedents? Megan More told Donna she sold *her* stuff."

?????—let's seek a second opinion. Brace Brandon Marti—Tim's tumescent teen.

I buzzed Tim's pad. Brandon picked up.

"Uh, yeah?"

"It's me, kid."

"Oh, hi, Uncle Rhino."

I cleared my throat. "I need help with something. I know you're a guy in the know."

Brandon said, "Uh, sure. What do you . . . ?"

"I'll talk turkey, kid. You're red-blooded, but you've got no *real* outlet, if you catch my drift. You've got to know where to find all the porno babes on the Internet. You know, their Web sites."

The little lech laffed. "My dad said you had this martyr thing going. He said you couldn't see past this actress chick who did you, like twenty years ago."

Double-aught ouch.

"Brandon, come—"

"Well, there's Jenna Jamison, and Seka, and Summer Storm, and Porsche Poon, and . . . shit, I don't know . . . mostly they're just . . . *chicks*."

Sterile stuff. Deep-down depressive. Downscale Donnaphobia and teenage ennui.

"Thanks, Brandon. You were a big help."

"You're welcome. Oh, and my dad just handed me a note. It says, 'Get a life.' "

I WALKED WEB SITES. I juked Jenna Jamison. I sought Summer Storm and Seka. I popped Porsche Poon's page.

Skin pix and news notes. Pathetic fan postings. No panties for sale.

Let's move mainstream. Let's mine movie stars.

I Web-walked. I hopped home pages. I hit salty Sandy Bullock and nasty Nicole K. Dig: pathetic postings and news notes. No panties for sale.

I moved my mouse. I hit Megan More — the "official" Web site.

Panties proffered — $29.95 per. News notes. Pathetic postings — whoa, wait, what's this?

The pathetic poster: Big Bob at bigbob.com. Paragraphs of pathos, then this:

> I tapped into this guy Jack Jen-kin's website. He offered this
> so-called 'Master's Thesis' on Megan, for sale at $16.95. I read
> it, and it's nothing but a bunch of blasphemous lies. I urge all
> Megan fans to boycott this clown.

I boycotted Big Bob's boycott. I moved my mouse. I jumped Jack Jen-kin's Web site. I got this:

> *The Transformation of Megan More,* 168PP, $16.95. The
> Truth About the Soft-Core Sensation. Visa, MC, Amex,
> Discover: Punch in number & exp. date after cue. Prepaid
> money-order purchases to: Jack Jen-kin, 1284 S. Berendo #14,
> L.A. 90018.

Interesting. Insinuating. A kool Koreatown address.

I moved my mouse. I caught cues. I ordered the book overnite. I sat back. I pondered pantyphile pathos and *me.*

Odds on Donna danger: 10 to 1 against. The reality: Rhino Rick battles boredom and entrenched ennui.

There it is: that Stephanie stasis/that Donna disjuncture. Unfathomable crimes/unattainable women — and *me.*

I sat there. I salaamed into sadness. I set truth traps and snared *me.* You don't prize the prosaic. Opportunity owns you. You foreswore family for possibility.

It was dinnertime. I had no warm woman, no kid cacophony. I marked my moment: Porno-site printouts. Filthy fetishism as opportunity.

I wanted more deep Donna moments. Danger would mandate them. My primordial prayer was for peril to paralyze her and free me. Donna for love. Stephanie to stamp me as figurehead father and father-obsessee.

It was 10:00 p.m. Donna was diverted with dog and lucky lover. Stephanie was still stamped DEAD.

Possibility. Cop conundrum as communion. Stephanie's house called to me.

4.

Jolting Joe Tierney—all hail the Chief!

He sized me up silent. He eyeball engaged me. His gaze cut to the quick.

I called his office. I made the meet. I sat steady now. Junkyard Joe Tierney—you malevolent mick.

He said, "The rhino regalia works for the most part. I like the tie bar and the belt buckle, but the rhino-patterned tie has to go."

The chair chafed my ass. The office offended. The pictures piqued me.

Joe T. and the Pope—a Polack pals pose. Joe T. and that boss babe Mother Teresa. Joe T. and Hillary Clinton—dyked-out like bull-dagger Biff.

I said, "Thanks, Chief. I'll take you with me the next time I go shopping at Costco."

Tierney yukked. "You know, this is not the righteous right-wing white man's LAPD you grew up in."

I yukked. "Yeah, call me lucky. I got to waste three spooks and two wetbacks pre-Rodney King."

"You've got panáche, Rhino. I'll give you that. And you're smart enough to know that the Department can't handle more bad publicity right now. We've got civilian litigation up the ying-yang, we're hamstrung by the Consent Decree, and our officers are afraid to make arrests, because every street creep they jack up is thinking lawsuit."

I yukked and yawned. I was tapped out and tired. I stayed up late at Stephanie's.

"Did you call me in for a valid reason, or did you just want to critique my wardrobe?"

Tierney tapped his teeth. Booze breath blew my way. One malign mick/one power-lunch lush.

"All right, let's get to it. You knew Danny Getchell. You gave him dope for information, which was a common practice in those days. Your mistake was giving dope to a guy who kept files and wrote everything down. Now, Danny's dead, but Gary Getchell's alive, and he doesn't like our chum Captain Lauter. He's mentioned him in one *Hush-Hush* piece, and he may be thinking he can milk Narco Division in upcoming pieces that will gravely embarrass the Department as a whole. Your job is to dissuade him."

I seethed silent. Hold for the humping. Thrill to the threat.

I held hard. Junkyard Joe mowed out martini fumes and maimed me.

"I wouldn't want to press departmental charges on you for indiscretions that came to light via *Hush-Hush*. So, you and Tom Ludlow lean on Gary Getchell and tell him to lay off Captain Lauter *and* the LAPD. Tell him we're sacrosanct, tell him never to use his files against us, and make your point with some pain."

MUSCLE JOB—MAN-O-MAN! Coercive copwork calls!

I humped to Hollywood Station. Phone Book Tom stood outside. We bopped to Bel-Air CC.

Tom trumpeted trouble. He waved a Westside book and wafted obscenities. He still stiffed dirty phone calls. He still "nabbed nymphos" and "bagged bitches" that way. He still got vivid Vietnam flashbacks. Said flashbacks floored him. He dug the noxious nostalgia and draconian dramaturgy. Aaah, youth! Tender times of torture and vivisected VC!

We hit Bel-Air. I saw unmarked cop cars undulate up Udine Way. Dig the full daytime rehearsal for the fiend who fends by night. Beautiful Bel-Air: prime turf for the hot-prowl *bandido*. Rolling stakeouts tapped for tonite.

There's the country club. There's the caddy parking lot. Dig that dinged-up Dodge Dart. Dig that calcified Cadi*black* and that lake-piped Lin*coon* Coon*tinental.

There's a vandalized van. It's flame-painted and flat-tired. The windshield's cracked and crushed. The back door's bent free.

There's Gary Getchell inside. There's a mimeograph machine. He's packaging items—perchance panties?

We parked and popped over. Getchell piled panties and plied them in plastic baggies. Dig the van's wild wall pix—all vintage *Hush-Hush*.

Marilyn Monroe: Mandingo-esque miscegenist! Ava Gardner's dusky delights! Johnnie Ray's men's room misadventure! Hunky homo Rock Hudson!

Getchell said, "Fuzz, huh? This feels like grief I don't need."

Tom tapped his phone book. The binding: busted loose from overuse. The page ends: bristly brown from blood.

I said, "Don't use the files. That means no Lauter and no LAPD."

Getchell guffawed. He picked up a panty package. He twirled it Tom's way.

"Ten bucks a sniff. What do you say, caveman? Megan won't mind, and it just might tighten up your wig."

I signaled Tom. Tom torqued his phone book. One bonaroo backhand—Getchell's snout snapped.

His nose dripped and bipped blood on plastic. Dig the panty-package stains.

I said, "Don't use the files. No Lauter, no LAPD."

Getchell popped a panty pack. Getchell hooked out a hanky-panty and blew his beak.

"Last call. Two sniffs for fifteen snoots. You cats are way out on the sex-violence nexus. Come on, two sniffs *for ten*. That's my last offer."

I signaled Tom. Tom torqued his phone book. One fine forehand—Getchell got thwapped.

I said, "Don't use the files. No Lauter, no LAPD. Say yes and we're gone."

Getchell groaned and grimaced. Getchell tugged a tooth loose. Dig the devastated dentistry.

"Here's my final offer. The Megan More Premier DVD Collection, plus two sniffs apiece, for ten scoots. Come on, I'm taking it up the shit chute on this."

I signaled Tom. Tom torqued his phone book. One overboard overhand—Getchell flew and flattened out on the floor.

He coughed. More blood blossomed. More teeth tore free.

I said, "Don't use the files. Come on, Gary. I'm not enjoying this."

Getchell got up. He stood stern and stared at me.

"I know about you and that actress cooze. Fall '83. Does that sound familiar? I hate that cooze, 'cause a friend of mine does, but there's this avenging angel out there."

A cold curtain caught and contained me. It held me and hurt me and bloomed like blood.

I grabbed the phone book. I backhanded bad and forehanded fierce and underhanded *ugggggly*. Getchell banged the walls. The van rocked and rolled. Phone Book Tom pulled me free.

NIX THAT NEXUS. Say *sí* to sex. Violence—voice a *nyet*.

I moped through a muscle-job menopause. I felt fucked up and fit for shit. I was apocalyptic *and* apologetic. Post-panty depression hit me.

I dropped off Tom L. I drove by Stephanie's pad. I salved my soiled soul and heard my cell phone sizzle.

Conflicting calls. Donna's at the Hamburger Hamlet, Donna's chilled out at Chia Brasserie.

I hooked by the Hamlet. A Donna look-alike lapped lager in a leatherette booth. I chugged by Chia. Charlie Chink said, "Miss Donahue get food to go."

Dusk. Deign me Donna-deprived, down in the dumps and digging on diversion. I drove to the hot-prowl stakeout.

Bel-Air again. Regal Roscomere Road. Piles of palm trees and sparkling Spanish mansions. Two unmarked units parked at perimeter posts. West L.A. cops couched in one. Dave Slatkin and a piebald pit bull piled in another.

I parked behind the pitmobile. I joined Dave and the dog. Said dog: all lapping love for LAPD and all malicious muscle. Dave: dander-dusted and deep in dog-lover delight.

We settled in. We sipped corrosive coffee. We shot the shit.

We agreed: Fuck the Lauter/Narco/Getchell file fantasia. Linus laundered Leotis's dope cash. Linus fathered Leotis—loin linkage went deep. Joe Tierney—our new Chief—fearful of the Feds. I said this deal hops hinky—weird shit shears this way and that. Dave said it meant fuck-all. Fuck it and forget it, and feast on this:

Tim found a file box. Dig—it's detritus on Stephanie. The box: back at Parker Center. Tim found it in an old file bank. It was crammed into a crevicelike crawl space.

We resettled in. We racked our seats back recumbent. Pancho the pit bull surveilled the street. Dave hoped the hot-prowl man was a boogie. Pancho craved dark meat.

The night was dead dark. Dave dug it. Listen—this lout's lunar-tuned.

Dave dug in. Dave profiled the prick.

He's a full-fledged fiend. He's Donald Keith Bashor made millennial. Bashor righteously rape-o'd one woman. Bashor almost rape-o'd Karil Graham in death. Our guy's female-fucked. He's out to instigate an image. His hot prowls: preludes to rape. He's looking for *the* woman.

I agreed. I added: And he's brazen. You can't drive through Bel-Air or Holmby Hills and not bid big-time suspicion. Dave agreed. Dave added: He walks. It's why he's lunar-tuned. He's down on darkness.

I agreed. I added: He parks south and sidles up silent. South of Wilshire equals Holmby Hills, south of Sunset equals Bel-Air. Dave agreed. Dave added: He could go to ground on golf courses. L.A. Country Club/Holmby Hills, Bel-Air CC/Bel-Air.

Our talk tapped out. We yawned. Pancho snored and snoozed in my lap. I slipped into sleep. Dreams drifted through.

Stephanie. Donna. Time suspended surreal. Gary Getchell, beat on and bold: "I hate that cooze, 'cause a friend of mind does, but there's this avenging angel out there." Angels rigged as ridgebacks—choice cherubs with coarse coats and dog faces. Megan More lez-leering at Donna.

I dream-droned. I slid in and out of sleep. Pancho panted beside me. I made him my mascot. I framed the front seat as my marriage bed with Donna. Dig the mastiff metamorphosis—pit bull Pancho as Reggie Ridgeback.

Our radio rumbled. Static stammered and stuck. I woke up woozy. Dave jerked and woke up—

"2-A-44, hit your brights!"

Dave caught the key. The engine engaged. I lit the low beams and brought on the brights. Right there—midnite made broad daylight.

A Spanish manse laid to our left. A large lady screaming. Light behind her—2-A-43's brights.

The woman scree-scree-screamed. She stumbled down the steps. She dug at a dart in her neck. Man down in the doorway— *her* man in matching pj's. He's two-dart devastated: one dart in each eyeball. He looks dart-defiled dead.

Two cops coming up—2-A-43—on foot *faaaast*. That large lady on her lawn, screaming. It's all front-lit-framed with back lights bouncing.

I pulled my piece. Dave pulled his piece. Pancho piled out the window. We lurched into the light. A car cut in front of us. It ran in reverse. I caught a brief blip: sixty-plus white man, grinning.

We fired. We hit the car. Ricochets resounded. The other cops fired. They hit the car. Ricochets racked up and reverbed.

Pancho ran. The car ran in reverse. Pancho dived in the driver's side window. The hot-prowl hump raised his trank gun. Pam—Pancho picked up a dart.

We chased the car. We fired. Four fuckers on foot, one reverse rocket ship. The car careened backward. It banged backyard fences and tore through trellis posts. We ran. We reloaded. We ran and shot at the reverse rocket. We ran and ran out of ammo. The car barged through backyards and disappeared in the dark.

THE FUCK RELANDSCAPED eight backyards. The fuck fucking *ex*-caped.

A SWAT team swung through. They door-knocked and bopped through backyards. No Hot-Prowl Harvey extant. Choppers churned overhead. Their belly lights burned. No Hot-Prowl Harry hiding. No 60-plus sickos seen.

Pancho lived. One dart to the duodenum—no damage there. Dave kissed and caressed him and came on with dog treats. I posited Pancho for LAPD honors. The SWAT cops agreed.

The two-dart man died. Toxic shock tore through his system. His wife stood strong. She stuttered out a statement.

She heard hinky noises. She woke up. There's Hot-Prowl Hal in her bedroom. He's got his hot-prowl hamster out. He's siphoning said python in her lingerie drawer.

She shrieks. Hot-Prowl Humphrey darts her. Her hubby wakes up. Hot-Prowl double-darts him.

A lab crew hit the house. They ladled up the lingerie and located some jizz. DNA testable—yeah! Dip it through the DNA database and hold your hot-prowl breath.

The crew crawled entry points. They found fresh dirt by a dinged door lock. The crew crept backyards. They walked down to the west Bel-Air gate. Similar dirt—in scuff patterns on the sidewalk.

Dave and I talked. The 2-A-43 guys talked. All hands agreed:

We couldn't eyeball-ID the hot-prowl hellhound. No way to cut a composite. No way to initiate an Identikit pic.

We all popped to Parker Center. We mowed through mug books and looked for likenesses. One sixtyish sicknik—nothing popped out.

Dawn. The Chief of Detectives arrives and anoints us. Hey, Jenson and Slatkin. Grab Tim Marti and work this hot-prowl homicide.

Dave dug it. Dave was an emphatic empiricist and a dedicated Donald Keith Bashor-phile. His take: Our guy was older. He might be hot-prowl hip to his bad Bashor-like roots. He'd killed now. He masturbated moments before. He fucked the fuzz on his getaway. His essential escalation Bashor-boded: rape and rape-kill!!!!!

Tim showed. His take: Let's track the tranquilizers. Tim dug the dichotomy: powerful potions for humans, benign benzo-diazepines for dogs. Dave disagreed—it's too tough to track. There's street stuff and privately prescribed. Our Bashoresque best bet: more rolling stakes.

I yawned. All this hot-prowl hurly-burly bored me. I only prized its proximity to Donna.

I wanted back in her bed—flat-on or fleeting. Evil e-mails and panty precedents might tweak her toward me. The Hot-Prowl Hymie—clamoring close by—might help.

I wanted to hide in the heart of her hearth.

5.

I hooked home. I racked up some rest. I refitted my head and dipped out to my doorstep.

No Megan More master's thesis. No fucking FedEx, no UPS, no Overnight Express.

The hot-prowl job boded—back-to-work big. Donna Standard Time torqued me more. The master's man lived in Koreatown. I could cruise out and run back to Robbery-Homicide.

The day unrolled ugly. Smog smeared the L.A. basin and hid the Hollywood Hills. The air was lash-your-lungs carcinogenic. The sky was tamale tan. Koreatown was heat-hazed and Seoul-ful. Pico Boulevard bustled. It was a slant-eyed sluice and a last line of demarcation. The L.A. Congo came on south of there.

I poured down Pico and bipped up Berendo. The master's man's pad stood straight ahead. It's a ten-story tenement walk-up. It's stark stucco and smells of bracing broiled eel and kimchi.

I parked and lolled through the lobby. Listless layabouts eye-balled me. They tipped tallboys of Schlitz malt liquor. They oozed absentee attitude. They were slick slants and Cheerless Charlie Chinks.

I moseyed to the mail slots. Jack Jen-kin—up in unit #14.

The elevator churned and chugged. The vents vibrated. Sexy scents siphoned through. I made monkey meat and pulled pork cooked in kimchi.

The elevator stopped. I stepped out and hopped down the hall-way. There's #14.

Whoa, wait, what's this—

Stink crawled out a door crack. Bugs batted the baseboard and dinged the doorway within. Buzz, buzz, bap, bap—insects inflamed, distressed, and disturbed.

I got out a credit card. I dug at the doorjamb. Tumblers tipped. The door popped.

Fumes flew up and fucked me full. I braced my breakfast back down. I shivered. I shut the door. I shook off bug battalions. Said bugs buzzed back to a hallway. I followed the fumes and stared at the stiff.

One maggot-mauled male Korean. Deep dead and decomped. Laid out on a lavender rug. One big-bore head wound.

There's the gun. It's by the body. It's a fat .44 Mag. The wound was wide. Maggots mamboed out a cranial crack.

I knelt down. I noticed neck wounds. Bright bruises and tight torture cuts. The stink stung me. I pinched my nostrils. I hooked my ham-and-egg McMuffin back.

There's the note. It's tacked to the wall. It's plied in plain view.

"I cannot go on. I love Megan More more than life itself, but she does not love me. Good-bye, Megan. I'll see you where the angels sing."

Hinky handwriting. Heaps of hesitation marks. Vibrating vowels. Crawling consonants coerced. Torture to instigate information. Murder made suicide.

I pored through the pad. I pinched my nose and pulled up peremptory details. I stared at staged shit and staved off the stink.

The kitchen. A mainline maggot migration. Full sink. Dirty dishes. Maggot-maimed chunks of chuck steak. Call it cool: The killer caught Jen-kin here and juked him.

The bedroom. Megan More on white walls. Cheap cheese-cake/snappy snapshots/no dust underneath. Call it cold: put-up pix. Prime props to suicide-sync.

I dumped desk drawers. I reached under rugs. I bombed through bookshelves. No Megan More master's thesis.

I jacked on Jen-kin's computer. I mouse-moved and tapped in "Megan More." I mapped in Megan More–ish cue words. No Megan More master's thesis or minutiae scrolled up.

I walked back to the hallway. Maggots julienned Jack Jen-kin and marched down his mouth. The door dipped open. A slant-eye slithered and slid and crept through the crack. The door closed and clicked. I rhino-ran up.

I ran out. I heaved down the hall. I saw Chuck the Chink reach a fire door and stop short. I jumped him. I heaped on the hurt. I smashed his face. He dented the door. I booted him in the balls. He wiggled and whimpered. I grabbed his greasy hair and hauled him back to the pad.

I shut the door. He saw the gore-dead gook and the maggot majorettes. He screamed. I rang up the reaction. Unfaked fear/ unlikely killer/don't make him for Murder One yet.

The smell smacked him. His yellow skin grew green. He projectile-puked. I dodged food flecks. He brought up broiled eel cooked in kimchi.

I dragged him to the kitchen. I stood him by the sink. I coursed on some cold water. I dunked him and doused him and saw his skin grow back from gray-green.

He sputtered. He shook and shaked. I patted his pockets. I pulled out pills. He possessed Percodan sans prescription. I knew he knew *something*. I knew he'd snitch.

I pulled my beavertail sap. I patted my palms. I let him hear the weight whip.

"You know something. You know something happened here, so you thought you'd check it out. Come clean, and you walk. Fuck with me and I pop you for the perks."

He shuddered. I patted my palms. I sap-slapped the side of my legs.

He shook. He moved away from a maggot mound. His voice vibratoed. He sounded off soprano. He came on like a queer and a quiff.

"Four days ago, maybe. I see narcs who bust me. They follow Jack. They get him in lobby and bring him up here. Then I hear screams."

I poked him hard. I bounced my beavertail on my knees. He shivered. Shakedown Rick scared him.

"Who were the narcs? You know their names, because they popped you."

The gook gulped. "Berchem and Mosher. They bad. They plant dope on me."

Flashbacks floored me. Lauter. His hinky hard-on for *Hush-Hush*. Megan More with Gary Getchell. The funeral. Berchem and Mosher. Surreptitious surveillance. Two goons taking Megan More pix.

I walked to a wall phone. I called the Cold Case Unit. Dave picked up.

"Slatkin."

I said, "It's me. I need you to do something, no questions asked."

"Well . . . O.K."

Maggots tripped up my trouser legs. I beavertail-beat them and drove them down.

"There's a homicide. It's Narco and Lauter-connected. Cal Eggers is probably the only up-and-up guy in the division. I need you to call Tierney and get his O.K. to pull Eggers and hold him."

Dave said, "O.K., but this sounds—"

I hung up. I passed the punk his pills. He ran out. I cultivated connections.

Narco goons. Linus and Leotis Lauter. Gary G. Megan More. Jack Jen-kin—the maggot-munched Meganphile.

Nyet—nothing clicked conclusive.

I walked to the door. I saw a panty pile atop a TV. I was sailing on the sex-violence nexus. I stopped and took three good sniffs.

COOL CAL EGGERS—couched in a cat box—an 8 by 12 interview room.

We watched through a 2-way. The mirror made Cal wiggle and weave. He was drip-dry and freon frosty. He vibed no guilt.

I thought so. Ditto Dave and Tim. We watched. We waited. We killed the air-conditioning and hitched up the heat. Cool Cal kept his coat on—you can't sweat me.

Dave talked to Tierney. The mad mick sent a SID team out. They reconnoitered and ran through room 14. The pad—professionally print-wiped. The suicide note—a felonious fake. The maggot multitude made the man a full four days dead. The queer called it correct. Bill Berchem and Bob Mosher—not there at Narco—"out in the field."

Cal wiggled and weaved. Cal winked at the mirror. We shared a look and walked in.

We chose chairs. We tilted them tableside. Cal slid his seat closer in.

I said, "It's about Narco, and maybe Captain Lauter."

Cal said, "You're putting me to sleep."

Tim said, "Nobody thinks you're dirty."

Cal said, "Wake me when it's over."

Dave said, "You weren't in the unit when Lauter pulled those stunts with his son."

Cal said, "Hit me with some new stuff I haven't read in *Hush-Hush*."

Tim tapped the table. "Bill Berchem and Bob Mosher. An actress named Megan More, and a dead slant named Jack Jen-kin."

Cal craned his neck. Cal cracked his knuckles. Cal said, "Oh, shit."

Dave drummed the table. "You've got interdepartmental immunity. That's straight from Tierney. Beyond that, it's chilled. We're giving Jen-kin to the media as a suicide. We'll make it stick."

Cal called up some chutzpah. "Tell Tierney to jump me to captain and I'll give up Berchem and Mosher. Tell him I want a done deal."

I slid out my cell phone. Tim tapped Tierney's number. Tierney took the call two rings in. Dave coughed up Cal's chutzpah sotto voce. Tierney yelled, "Fuck it, O.K.!"

I filched my phone back. Cal shot me a shit-eater grin.

"So, Linus Lauter craves white lady and white snatch. He gets jacked on coke every night, sees Megan More on TV, and gets a jones. He contacts her through her Web site and gets a sick thing going with her. He thought he was seducing her, but she was seducing him. She knew the late Danny Getchell, she knew Linus was a cop who did snitch deals with him, she pumped him for information and got the word on his money-laundering deals *before* the Feds and the fucking *L.A. Times* did. Linus learned she was tight with *Gary* Getchell, and that she was going to leak shit on his deals and their affair to Gary, and he'd publish it in *Hush-Hush*."

Megan More—miscegenist mama. Multicultural malfeasance *coon*fidential.

Now cut to Koreatown, now jump to Jack Jen-kin.

I said, "The homicide, Cal. The pad at 12th and Berendo."

Cal coughed. "I got this from Linus. He's wacked on coke and spilling all this paranoia. It seems that Megan More did Berchem, Mosher, *and* him, so now you've got three motivated fuckers out to get her. They heard about the gook's 'Master's Thesis,' learned that he'd sold practically zilch copies, but that it was full of so-called embarrassing shit. So, Linus tells me that Berchem and Mosher were going out to lean on the gook, and I guess things got out of hand."

A flashback flamed me. Gary Getchell, per Donna D.:

"I hate that cooze, 'cause a friend of mine does, but there's this avenging angel out there."

"Avenging angel" Megan More—maybe. Lez-leched on Donna—her motive, maybe.

Captain Cal stood up. Tim said, "We've got to grab Berchem and Mosher."

Dave said, "I'll tell Tierney what we've got, but *we're* on the hot-prowl case."

Connections clicked and stopped stillborn. The Donna Diaspora, the Hot-Prowl Holocaust—shit shoved itself at me.

Cal said, "Rhino looks distracted. Want to bet he's thinking about a certain actress?"

Dave said, "Yeah, I know that look."

Tim said, "My kid's a Megan More fan. This shit will fucking destroy him."

I PLAYED HOT-PROWL hooky. Those connections clicked too close to Donna. I hopped by Holmby Hills. She was home. I rhino-riffed on contained coincidence. Donna dug my morbid Megan More tale. I said, let's find her. She said, I'll go.

I called R&I. They ran Megan More for rap sheets. Bam— Megan More, minor misdemeanant. Four Beverly Hills beefs. Heavy hooking at high-line hotels.

I called the DMV. I dunned them for Megan More's address. They delivered: 8542 Charleville, Beverly Hills.

We rolled. Lack of sleep slapped me. An anxious undercurrent uncoiled underneath. My Donna deprivation diminished. That sex-violence nexus tipped to sex straight.

We found the pad: a prime provincial four-flat. We parked and dipped up to the door. Four rings, two knocks—no answer. Donna diddled the doorknob. The door popped in.

The living room: bleak, blank-walled, and bereft of furnishings. The kitchen: cleaned out completely. The bathroom and bedroom: bug-sprayed, Lysol-lapped, and furniture-free.

Donna dumped a clothes hamper. Soiled panties sailed out. Premium price tags were clipped to the crotch.

Donna said, "Ugh."

I still stood on that nexus. I stopped and took three good sniffs.

THE BHPD BODED. I felt rhino-revived and ready to rock. Those sniffs snared me. Sex scents as mainline meth.

We hit the cop shop. Cops recognized Donna. They winged out wolf whistles and lighthearted leers. A clerk clued us: The Vice guy's Vic Vartanian. Find him by the files. He's hard to miss.

We walked back. Cops caught sight of Donna. They called out TV titles. Donna called back, curtsied, and came on cute. There's

Vice cop Vic. He's fucking with a file stack. He's swarthy and sweaty and acne-addled. Blackheads bloomed on his big beak.

He saw us. He scoped my belt badge. Donna dinged him. He salaamed, sucked in his gut, and slapped himself dandruff-free.

He said, "So?"

I said, "Megan More. Ring a bell? I thought you might have a sheet on her."

"I do. Crime reports, dispo reports, known haunts, the whole shmear. That said, I got to say I got something better."

I whipped to his wavelength. Call him coy. Praise him and say pretty please.

Donna tapped me telepathic. "Could we see your paperwork, Detective? It would be a big help."

Vic V. veered to a file bank. He draped over the drawers and pulled paper. He came back with some cardboard-bound sheets.

"Some clown wrote a half-assed book about Megan. I bought a copy to squeeze her with, if she ever tried hooking in my jurisdiction again."

Chills churned through me. It was one wild nexus nudge. Donna held a hand out. Vic tossed her the text.

"You can sit at my desk and read it. You might enjoy it especially, Ms. Donahue."

TORRID TEXT. The Mephistophelian Megan More Movie. Megan, crazed on crack-cocaine and fulsome full disclosure. Megan's mea culpa and *Mein Kampf*. Jack Jen-kin—her barroom bard and bothersome Boswell. Her un-Christian Korean konfessor.

We read together. We sat chair to chair, cheek to cheek. Donna's scents soared and socked me. Honeysuckle hair and sandalwood soap and full-bore pheromones. All our lopsided love Meganized and poured back onto the page.

Dig:

MEGAN MORE WAS A MAN!!!!! He was born a big-dick

bohunk in Billings, Montana. Mikhail Metrovich was his name. He looped to L.A., age eighteen. His shvantz topped the tape at sixteen sizzling inches. Mikhail male-prostied. He called himself Mighty Man, Mikey Man, Magnum Man. He serviced surly studio studs and tamed them with his tapeworm-long appendage. They took his tapeworm in to their tonsils. They bounced as bottoms to his top. He mulched men at MGM, he popped poofs at Paramount, he cornholed cats at Columbia. Fruits freed themselves and climbed from the closet to cloister with him. He outed outrageous numbers. His clients cliqued up and shared notes. Paranoia ran pandemic. These Hollywood hellions hated themselves. Mikhail turned studio studs into quivering queers and simpering sissies. Their self-hatred sizzled. They vowed revenge.

The studio studettes got some gelt and hired an A-rab assassin. The cat was a cold camel-fucker. He had terrorist ties. He was movie-mad and one mean Muslim. He said, "You give me role as action hero, and I cut off his dick. Better to maim than to kill."

The unctuous studio un-studs underwrote his plan. Khalid Khareem cornered Mikhail and cut off his dick. The studio stupes commissioned a script. Catch this: Khalid Khareem as Israeli agent Israel Bonds. Soon to star in *Jerusalem Jihad* and *Tel Aviv Terror.*

THEN—SEPTEMBER 11!!!!!

A dragnet dragged in Khalid Khareem. The Feds found him and filleted him and fucked him fundamental. He got the big bone to hop heavenward and hail Allah. He sat in his cell. He mauled his wrists with a mattress spring. He hurtled to heaven or hell.

Mikhail viciously vowed revenge. He set sail on the sex-violence nexus. He decided to disguise himself as a woman. He stormed to Stockholm. He hooked down hormone shots. Surgeons altered his Adam's apple and shaved his big bones bare. He caught cutting-edge technology. Doctors plowed him the best plumbing. He became a woman—intractably indistinguishable.

SHE shot back to Hollywood. She sought soft-core porn gigs and got them. She met Danny Getchell. She met Gary G. They dug the amazing Amazon. She urged them to dig dirt on the studio stupettes. They sucked up to the soaring sorceress and agreed. She continued as their consort. She hid her boldly big-dicked and positively pestilent past. She became a lascivious lipstick lezzie. She laid siege to lezbo nitespots. She munched muff in Malibu and boffed bush in Bel-Air. She took on TV roles. She met Donna Donahue on *Murder Most Gently*. She shot her crazy crush Donna's way. Donna said, "Back off, Butch—it's not my scene." Megan More moped off miffed and bid Donna bye-bye, bereft.

BUT:

The rejection rankled and reawakened her. She refined and reinvented her revenge. The studio gonifs gelded her. She made them whimper womanlike. They begged for her beef torpedo. They suffered postcoital remorse and regret en masse. They made her a for-real woman. She'd woman-whip them and coldly castrate them and wrap up her revenge.

The manuscript ended. The climactic cliffhanger: no more demon details on revenge.

I tingled. I looked at Donna. Her hurricane-hurled hazel eyes hit me.

She said, "Brave new fucking world."

I said, "Yes. It's that time again."

WE NABBED THE known-haunt list. We knew Megan More lit out on the lam. We mapped out our meshugina mission. We crazy crisscrossed L.A.

We ducked by dyke dens. We hit Linda's Little Log Cabin, Biff's Boiler Room, Mary's Munchbox, and Florence's Flame. Fuck—no murderous man-woman Megan More, ratched up on revenge.

We hit Helen's Hideout, Claire's Clam Club, Brenda's Brig, and Sapphic Sal's. No six-foot succubus, no mogul-mauled monster within.

We hit June's Jungle Room. Wacs and Waves and Marine Corps mamas moved in on fawnlike femmes. We hit Shondrika's Shangri-La. Mau-Mau music metastasized. Soul sisters slow-danced and slipped tongues. No white wench Megan More here.

We popped to Pacific Palisades. We nailed a non sequitur. Megan made time at Guru Guraji's Ashanti Ashram.

Wow—a whitewashed old adobe. Two floors flared around a calm courtyard. Fountains and floating flamingos. Parrots perched in palm trees. A trumped-up tropical scene.

A paved parking lot. Non sequitur number 2: *Mucho* movie vans. What's this—Sam's Sound, Lee's Lighting, Ken's Camera.

I parked by a purple Pontiac. The plates read "PRN STR." Donna said, "I'm getting this feeling."

We beat feet to the building. We perused the perimeter. We wrapped our reconnaissance to the back. We watched window light leap. We heard salacious sex noise. It was nihilistic and nasty and amplified apocalyptically.

We barged in a back door. We heaved down a hallway. We slid side doors ajar and perv-peeped the cracks. We saw lurid lighting and big boom mikes and cameras catching close-ups. We saw full-bore fucking and filthy fellating and groovy group gropes. We saw ashramites in turquoise turbans. They laid lights and moved mikes and hauled Handycams.

We dipped doors. We saw double-digit dicks and bravura breasts augmented out to *here*. We saw daisy chains and dalmatian dogs doing women. We lunged to the last left-hand door. Donna dipped it deep. There's Megan More lez-locked and loving it lewd.

It's a four-on-one fever. It's torrid tongue-kissing and beavers bushwhacked. It's major muff miscegenation. There's Nettie Negress, Lola Latina, Charlotte the Chinkess. It's a mountainous Megan More cluster fuck.

I barged in. The scene got me sex-sizzling and hopping homophobic. I was apoplectically ambivalent and turgidly turned on.

I lashed down light poles. I brought down boom mikes. I tripped tripods and crashed cameras—*kerrack!* Turquoise turban-heads tore out, tearful. The climactic cluster fuck climbed off the mattress. The multicultural mound made for the hallway. Only Megan More held back.

The room was rhino-wrecked. Capsized cameras, mangled mikes, laid-out lighting. There's a pulverizing postsex silence. There's Megan, there's Donna, there's me.

Donna shut the door. I heard a post-roust rampage outside. The porno parasites poured down the hallway. Vans vamoosed outside.

Megan moved off the mattress. Megan got into a mauve muumuu. Megan said, "Hi, Donna dear."

Donna deadpanned her. I said, "LAPD."

The horrible he-she harrumphed. "Your Rodney King number did not go unnoticed. I've been dealing with you fascists for years."

I said, "Like Captain Lauter?" Donna said, "Why did you run?"

Megan mewed at me. "Making erotic films is not illegal. The ashram people can sue LAPD."

I rhino-raked her. "They won't. They'll blow their 'alternate lifestyle' clout if they do."

Megan moped to the mattress. She fluttered, flounced, and flung herself down. She sulked sissified. She boded borderline bored.

"Tell me why I should talk to you. Give me one good reason."

Donna dinged her. "I've got a good shot at a series next season. I'll make sure you get work."

Megan milked the moment. "Oooh, dearest, that's wonderful. Can I do love scenes with you?"

Donna flipped her-him the finger. Get bent and butt out, Butch!

I said, "We read Jack Jen-kin's manuscript. Jack's dead, by the way. Your old Narco pals chilled him."

Megan mewed. Megan muttered. Megan made the sign of the cross.

Donna said, "Lay it all out. I'll be needing a female sidekick."

The "female" flattered and floored the hip he-she. Megan lolled back and laid her legs out. *Goooooood* gams—some certified surgeon's art.

"O.K., so I ran. I saw these Narco cops I fucked at Danny Getchell's funeral. Believe me, this girl knows when it's time to cut her losses."

He-she boned Bill Berchem and Bob Mosher. She gender-bent them bad. It french-fried and freaked them out.

I said, "Keep going."

Megan tossed her tresses. Her blondness bloomed—some cool colorist's art.

"So I fucked those guys *and* Linus Lauter. They used to tap all my Web sites, and somehow they got ahold of Jack Jen-kin's thesis. Weeeeel, you can just guess how it made them feel. They dallied with a former man, they couldn't live with it, so I guess they had to pressure Jack to get his copies back. Something happened, and Jack wound up dead."

I said, "How did Jack get his background shit on you? You know, the stuff he put in his thesis."

Megan simpered. Silk tones—some thorough throat surgeon's art.

"He was friends with one of the doctors in Stockholm. The doctor spilled everything he knew on me. All the stuff I told my shrink pre-op, everything."

Donna drilled the he-she. *Ouch*—those hazel eyes *hurt*.

"You hit on me. I shut you down, and I've got a hunch this ties in to your 'revenge.'"

"It does, dearie. I made up my mind to screw those silly studio savages by beating them down at the box office. I was going to fuck every name actress in the business. You know, performers are deeply decentered, and they'll all fuck men, women, and beasts.

You see, I'm really *straight*. I *looooove* women, which is why I hit on you. That sixteen-inch shlong of mine was a terrible burden. It was why I turned lez. I wanted to love women woman to woman."

I whooped. Woman to woman—whoa! Donna did a double-take and slid slack-jawed.

The succubus went sulky. She pouted, poofter-style.

"So I decided to fuck all these actresses, and Gary Getchell was going to film it, and I was going to threaten to show the films publicly, and blackmail the studio boys. 'Here's your biggest stars jungled up with a soft-core porno queen. How do you think that will affect your box office in Topeka and Des Moines?' "

Donna said, "Let me guess. You've got a film of you fucking Linus Lauter. It's your wedge against those cops."

Megan patted a purple purse. "I've got the cassette right here. You're no dummy, Donna dear."

I brought out my beavertail. I sap-slapped my legs. The business end flopped phallic-like. Donna doe-eyed dug on it.

I said, "Where does Gary G. keep his dirt files?"

Megan said, "I don't know."

Donna said, "You must hate me."

Megan coughed into a hankie. Purloined pubic hairs spun in her spit.

"No, darling. I *looooove* you."

"Are you this 'avenging angel' that Gary Getchell told Rick about?"

"No, no, no. I *loooooove* you. But Gary was talking up this 'bounty' on you. He said he knew a psycho who had 'this big Donna Donahue plan.' Really, that's all he said, and I'd *never* hurt you."

Annihilating angels. Film fucks and lip-locked lezzies. Bounty-bait Donna. Details dug at me.

Looks lanced the room. Megan to Donna to—

The door cracked and crashed. The door hooked off its hinges. Bill Berchem and Bob Mosher barged in.

Looks *lashed* the room. Eyeballs socked in their sockets. Bad Bill and Big Bob to Donna, Megan, me.

Megan pulled her purse. The suddenness startled and stunned. Three guns hopped off holsters: Berchem, Mosher, me.

Donna ducked. Shades of '83—Donna dove and dug out my ankle piece.

Berchem blasted Megan. Bam—a cartridge caught her carotid. Short-range shootout/the room 12 by 12/four guns out and arcing, fuck me—

Mosher fired. Mosher missed me. I fired back, I rang a ricochet—one bip off his bulletproof vest. Megan blew blood on her muumuu. Berchem capped her hairline-high. Her bleached blond wig sailed off by the seams.

I fired at Berchem—four feet between us—the punk panicked and pantywaist-screamed.

My gun jammed. A jacked round jumped from the breach. Donna rolled right. Donna got behind Berchem. Donna braced her arm on an arc light and arced a shot upwards. Berchem's brains zinged.

Mosher fired down. Donna ducked. I jumped in and body-blocked him. I smacked him, gouged his gun hand, and smothered his aim. He hooked his head back. His mouth went wide. He showed his teeth and bored in to bite me.

Donna got between us. Donna tapped his teeth with a 2-inch barrel and popped him point-blank.

His teeth shattered and shrapnelized. Bloody bridgework bristled Donna. Dental detritus dinged me.

Check the charnel house. Three dead. Megan's *morte* in her muumuu. The Narco cops are wrapped to the River Styx—*finito* at Donna's feet.

I grabbed a wall phone. I mauled my memory. I lined up Linus Lauter's home number. I dialed it delirious. I heard a pickup click.

I heard "Hello." It was Linus L. I greased my greeting.

It's all over. Your boys bought it. They killed the Korean. You fag-fucked a he-she. It's caught on cassette—vivid VCR shit—don't wait for the DVD.

I knew he'd do it. He race-mixed radical. He gender-bent for bootie. He couldn't ignore the ignominy.

I heard the hammer hitch.

I heard the cylinder slip.

I heard the muzzle roar that meant Meet Your Maker.

I dropped the phone. Donna grabbed me. We held each other a whole half-minute. Her heart never missed a beat.

6.

We hid by her hearth. We fooled with the fireplace. We cranked a big blaze and upped the AC.

Then to now. Twenty-one years. Four fucked hours at Parker Center. Joe Tierney's tantrum. Two cops shot dead. Linus Lauter's suicide—horrific hara-kiri.

The sex-violence nexus. Official obfuscation. The Berchem–Mosher–Megan More "suicide pact." Witnesses bought and bullied at Ashanti Ashram. Leotis Lauter's precise press release:

The LAPD did my dad in. Ditto Bill Berchem and Bob Mosher. They racked up their relatives—don't rag the suicide scenario, don't risk your pension pack.

The media—quelled by quid pro quo. Try to trust Tierney—he'll pay you back.

The sex-violence nexus. Say *sí* to sex, violence vividly *yes*.

The nexus nabbed us new. The charnel house challenged us. It was our final fait accompli.

We laid logs in the fireplace. Reggie Ridgeback reclined nearby. His amber eyes orbited our way.

Cashmere cushions and comforter. A tantalizing temperature. Lit logs and a glorious glow.

My brave bride again. Another cross-fire christening. Our moment to memorize and test time with.

We climbed from our clothes. Embers eddied and shot shadows across us. My memory guided me. I called up every curve and surface and kissed her there.

Then to now naked. Curves and constellations. The memory map of her spark points, now spin with her sighs.

We traded curve caresses and kisses. Flame shadows shifted and showed us where to kiss this and that. It felt timeless merged with urgent, imperative and aimless, make me arch and sigh, breathe my breaths and do that.

The hearth heat made us glisten. We tasted sweet swirls of sweat. Our kisses went *right there*. Her taste was her taste all fresh and twenty years back. I wanted to stay there and breathe it and live it. She made me stop. She kissed *me* there and made me move inside.

It was timeless merged with urgent, all imperative-momentous, this nexus NOW harnessed hot. The hearth heat held us. The flames died and darkened. I kissed sweat from her hazel eyes as new memory mapped.

D A W N. The fire fizzled out and fanned to enduring embers. Reggie wrapped between us.

Donna slept on. Her head rested on Reggie's ridge. I watched her veins vibrate. I counted the cadence of her heartbeat. I saw her breasts bracing brown fur.

I watched. I wondered how much time she'd give me. Hearth heat and homicide held us. Hold for more horror. Hope for more heat to hold us—or pray for prosaic times to teach us to live sans intrigue.

Donna slept. I watched my witch woman and wondered. My righteous right brain broiled. I got crisp and creative. I recultivated connections.

Megan More—no "avenging angel." Megan More's ripe-panty racket. Donna's panty pursuer. Library love-hate e-mails, all anonymous. Megan More: Gary Getchell's panty pal. Megan, vile-verbatim: "Gary was talking up this 'bounty' on you. He said he knew a psycho who had 'this big Donna Donahue plan.' "

Connections cultivated. Cut to:

The Hot-Prowl Hoagy. His niggardly nominal thefts. His hot-prowl hits. Their prime proximity—to Bel-Air and L.A. Country Clubs.

Dave Slatkin said he's ripe for rape. Donna's Holmby Hills house—hard by L.A. CC. Gary Getchell: Bel-Air caddy. The hot-prowl homicide—hard by Bel-Air CC. Dirt on the hot-prowl hump's shoes.

I called Dave. I watched Donna and whispered. The dirt, Dave—did the lab latch on to a make?

Yeah. Dig—the dirt came from Bel-Air Country Club. Hot-Prowl Herb *ex*-caped on foot.

Cold-call it: the hot-prowl harridan's a caddy. It's a tantalizing target obfuscation. He's only out to get Donna D.

He's Donna-diddled and Donna-driven and Donna-determined. He's a Donna doofus and a Donna dunce, just like me. He's me made malignant. He's my Donna doppelgänger.

I woke Donna up. I cued her into my connections. She mentioned her "on-and-off" fan notes. They ladled love-hate. "He loved it when I showed skin, he hated it when I showed skin. He's a skin sicko."

The *old* notes, the *new* e-mail notes. The pathetic panty requests. One sender or two?

Some note nexus—maybe.

Donna dug out the old notes. Donna explained the dates.

They ran to the run of *Biloxi Beach*—her boffo '80s show. They ran out and restarted per her feature film work. The notes flew and flurried. A gulf-wide gap stretched. Then the panty-putz e-mails began.

Donna offered up the old notes. She pack-rat-possessed them still. I read racy and repetitive text. Hot-prowl references repeated.

"I want to get inside the house of your love."

"I want to steal inside your secret places."

"I can get inside anyplace. I've done it. I killed a girl once, long ago."

Sixteen sick notes. Bland block printing. Scary and skin-obsessed. One note nexus nabbed me bad. The return address—charted as Chino Prison. The addressee pseudonymed as Sal Skinman. Sad sentiments—Donna dunned for love—scary skin ruminations. Say he's censor-scared. Bet your booty he's in for burglary.

Scary skin-talk overall. "I killed a girl once"—good grief.

Donna watched me nail notes. Donna was nexus-nonplussed. Donna danced on my dime now. Homicide and hearth-hunger. Donna could handle herself.

I cruised to my car. I brought back my evidence kit. I compared the evil e-mails to the skin-scary notes. I tapped textual styles. I saw simple similarities. The same sender—maybe, maybe not.

I forged on forensic. I fingerprinted Donna. I tipped her tips on print paper. I noodled out some ninhydrin. I sprayed the sixteen sick notes. I latched up two latent prints.

I culled comparison points. I caught ten per print. I compared points to Donna's. Bingo—no repeated ridges, no similar swirls.

His prints—the skin man's and probable hot-prowl hyena's. Call it collusive. Call it combined-case combustion. Rick loves Donna. Donna loves Rick. It's our brave new world brought on back.

WE POPPED to Parker Center. We briefed Dave and Tim. We broiled to bring Hot-Prowl Hymie down. We clamored for climactic closure.

Dave took the prints. He promised to feed them to the Fed system fast. We caught a commotion down the corridor.

There's Leotis Lauter. He's one jacked-up jungle bunny. He's jumping all over Joe Tierney. The mad mick's mollifying Mrs. Linus Lauter. She's Aunt Jemima-ish. She's jumping too.

There's Cal Eggers. He's a newly coined captain. He's laying the law to Leotis. You're a dope dealer. You're indictment-indebted. We're dead deep in suicides—get your blasphemous black ass the fuck out of here.

I ducked into an empty office. Donna ducked with me. I called Deputy D.A. Daisy Delgado and cataloged our combined case. I asked for grand jury subpoenas. Let's detain degenerate caddies. Let's call in all caddies from Bel-Air and L.A. CCs.

Daisy agreed. Daisy promised prompt paper—two hours tops. Tim tapped me. I've got that box of Gorman paperwork—you can kill time with that.

Tim brought a big box up. Donna delved in. She saw poignant portraits—Stephanie vivid and vibrant, alight and alive at fifteen. Tears took her over—*sa chère* Stephanie.

I pulled old paper. I found field reports. I went through wienie waggers whipped and reluctantly released. I saw pud`pounders and parolees pounced on. I saw rape-os rounded up. I saw child molesters charged with tangential crimes. I saw bisexual brunsers bruised and ripped from rubber-hose techniques. I saw—whoa, whoa, whoa—*wait.*

The date: 9/12/65. One innocuous and innocent piece of paper.

Field report. Reinterview. Stephanie's dad states:

It's late 7/65. One week before my daughter's death. I had some yard work done. I hired Hillcrest caddies.

Hillcrest—hard by Hillsboro and Sawyer. Hillcrest—one hop to L.A. and Bel-Air CCs. One follow-up field report. Four caddy names caught. Four rap sheets run. Four Mickey Mouse misde-meanants made.

1. Alan Aadland, DOB 3/4/46. One reefer roust. One joy-ride job.

2. Richard Donatich, DOB 8/19/44. Popped for Peeping Tom. Caught cunnilingizing his sister.

3. Harvey "Huck" Horan, DOB 12/16/40. Boocoo booze busts.

4. Sol "Wino" Weinberger, DOB 6/2/37. Obscene phone-call fuck, ladies' room loiterer, boss barbiturate *bandido*.

I got goose bumps. My hackles hacked. I showed the shit to Donna. She got the shakes, too.

The scurvy skin man's note. "I killed a girl once, long ago." The current hot-prowl hoo-ha. The country-club cacophony. A time machine torqued back to *this*.

I ripped through reports. Nothing juked me. No fucking follow-ups. No exonerations expressed.

The cops might have polled the punks and aligned alibis. The cops might have polygraphed or pounded them punklike. It dangled like a dead end. Still, it stung me.

Daisy Delgado called. The subpoenas—serviced and servable now. Nice—but that sting still stung me. I called Hillcrest CC. I got the caddy shack. The caddy master said he went waaaay back. I named my names. He right-on responded.

Aadland—AIDS-dead—he freelanced as a fruit hustler. Donatich—dead from Dilaudid-coke combos. Horan—hit by a bus on Beverly Boulevard. "Wino"—winding up his caddy career at beautiful Bel-Air CC.

Caddies.

Culminations/coincidence/connections—

Dave walked in. "The Feds kicked back on your prints. The guy's a 67-year-old white male. His name's Solomon Weinberger."

Heaven hurled itself on me. Donna hugged me hard. Hail the hot-prowl man with *Hush-Hush* hosannahs!

Wino for Stephanie—thirty-nine years later.

7.

Bel-Air bid us. We winged to the Wino Weinberger Walpurgisnacht.

Tim toted a shotgun. I brought my Browning .9 and a big Beretta. Donna brought brains and a wild will to whip Wino with.

Dave did backup. He ripped R&I and glommed a Wino mug shot. He made up a four-man mug card—the sixty-plus Wino and four similar sixtyish cops. The plan: Work the West L.A. libraries. Engage an e-mail alert. Track the panty postulant. Confirm Wino as the panty punk *and* hot-prowl hump.

We ran up Roscomere. We bombed up Bellagio. We pulled into the club parking lot. We tripped into a traffic jam—a cop-car kaleidoscope.

Black-and-whites, unmarkeds, coroner's canoes—all snared up snout to snout.

We ran. We cut through the caddy shack. We caught the cart cottage. We gonifed a golf cart and coursed out on the course. We followed fleet-foot figures. We traipsed after truck tracks. We hit a big barnlike maintenance shack.

Bluesuits blocked the entrance. I badged them and bullied us through. I saw Bill Dumais, West L.A. dicks. I saw a starched stiff and junkyard Jesus.

It's Gary Getchell. He's crucifix-crisp. He's stiff on a stack of manure sacks.

He's nicked with neck notches—tough torture cuts. He's blood-blistered and mutilated maroon. He's wearing golf togs. He's pincushion-pricked with two dozen trank darts.

Dumais saw Tim and me. Golfers and gofers and coroner's cats saw Donna. They dug her more than the dead man. They dunned her for autographs.

Dumais dipped over. The big barn vibrated with voice overlap. I orbed outside. I saw fractious factions fixated on the action inside.

Eyes right—there's two Narco cops. Eyes left—there's Captain Cal Eggers. Loop left again—there's Leotis Lauter. He's looking *coon*cerned and *coon*temptuous. He's boogie bodyguarded. He's couched with four cool coon commandos.

Dumais said, "It looks like we've got two scenarios. The torture shit looks a couple of days old, but the coroner says he caught the trank shots within the past few hours. The maintenance boss says Getchell hung out and wrote his scandal shit here. I figure the killer found him alone, darted him, and walked off the course unseen."

Tim walked over. "You think he was tortured for file information?"

Dumais looked around. Eyes right—Narco cops. Eyes left—Leotis and his *coon*vocation.

"I figure it's Leotis or some rogue Narco guys, and they're both pissed off at that shit at the ashram and Linus's suicide."

Tim said, "They tortured Getchell for file skinny, before they learned that Linus offed himself."

I agreed. Dumais agreed. I tiptoed tall. I eyeball-orbed. Caddies/connections/convergence. Where's the Wino man?

The crowd crammed up to the barn. Bluesuits barricaded them out. Donna signed autographs. I saw a cat with a "Caddy Master" name tag. I cornered him.

He said, "Some scene, huh?"

I said, "Where's Wino Weinberger? We're old friends."

The caddy master cackled. "Try Skid Row. I heard Wino's on a toot down there."

Autograph hounds hurtled by—six blissful bluesuits. Their autographed field forms read, "Brave new fucking world *again*—Love, Donna D."

WINO:

Let's find him. Let's fuck him. Let's stomp him for Stephanie. Let's scour Skid Row.

The caddy master kicked loose his address: The Viceroy Hotel, East 5th Street. It was skanky and scummy and scurvy down there. We slipped east and slid into slumland.

Sidewalk cities. Hophead Hoovervilles. Crackheads camped out in cardboard-box billets. Loonies looped on Listerine. Wiggling wineheads and jake-legged juicers made mad by Muscatel.

We hit the hotel. The lobby was lice-laced linoleum. Wine stains and bloodstains blistered the cracks. Palsied pensioners toked Tokay shored in short-dog bottles. We shook them down. They jitter-jumped and Tokay-toked and palsy-punked-out. They gave up Wino—room 218.

We walked up. Horror hallways hooked ahead. We crunched crack pipes and shattered short dogs. We sidled through Syringe City and Hypodermic Hell. Floor debris flew. Our shoes caught needles coated with virus-vapped blood.

There's 218. The lock looks loose. Let's let ourselves in.

Donna ditzed the doorknob. I jiggled the jamb. The door swung in.

No Wino. Nobody. Sicko City socked in 12 by 12.

A sink. A made-up Murphy bed. A lice-lined linoleum floor. Crabs hopping head-high and Wino-Walpurgisnachted walls.

Craaaazy crime fotos. Filched archival shots. Major-case madness, all glossy-glared.

Mesmerized Mansonites. Bleary Black Dahlia pix. Stark Stephen Nash shots.

Photo-fucked fiends. Demonic Donald Keith Bashor. Sirhan Sirhan surrounded by Sheriff's deputies. Freaky Fred Stroble, ax-assassin of a little girl, gassed circa '53. Our Stephanie, strapped to a gurney, all shorn up in a sheet.

Crime—Weegeeish and Wino-warped. Infernally interspersed with quixotically quantified SKIN.

Actresses—all alive in 8-by-10 fotos. Bikini babes and halter-hot honeys. Red-headed Rita Hayworth. Red-tinted and divinely deigned Donna Donahue. Freckle-fraught Nicole Kidman. Titian-topped Julianne Moore.

Random redheads right below—costars culled and cultivated

off TV. Riotous red hair—august auburn straight to strawberry. Strict strumpet-type women. Fortyish foxes. Choice chignon-tressed aristocrats.

Donna said, "Holy shit." That nexus nudged me. Pile on the panties—I need some sniffs.

Footfalls fell behind us. I whipped and wheeled around. Wino walked in.

He saw us. He stood startled. He started to run.

I chased him. I tackled him. I laid him out on linoleum. He sheared his shins on shattered glass. He gave up then.

WE RACKED HIM to his room radiator. My handcuffs hitched him up firm. He beady-eye-bored into Donna. Her presence pronged him.

He panted. He salivated. He drooled Draculean. His trouser trout jumped in his jeans.

I found a phone book. Donna dug out my beavertail. We stood stern over him.

Donna said, "You sent me notes, didn't you? On and off for years."

Wino wiggled. The cuffs cut his wrists.

"You got it, baby. I'm a note man and a breather. I tried to get your phone number, but no fucking soap. You'd have got a real taste of me then."

I said, "What about e-mails? Some sicko was e-mailing Ms. Donahue. He was asking her to send him her panties."

Wino went outraged. "I don't feature that panty shit! I'm a note man and a breather! I don't fuck with no computers. Give me a pay phone any day."

Donna bent the beavertail. The lead weight whipped within.

"What about ladies' rooms? You dig that action, don't you?"

Wino snorted and snickered. "I like to sniff toilet seats once in a blue moon, I'll give you that. But basically I'm a specialist. I'm a note man and a breather. I'm a fucking virtuoso, and I'm fucking proud of it."

I said, "What's with the redheads? All Donna's got is a little tint."

Wino winked. "Dig this. My mom was a redhead, and I never got over it. I got a thing for red gash, and that is no fucking shit. Donna looks like my mom. You don't got to be fucking Sigmund Freud to figure out this shit."

I fingered my phone book. The pages rolled and riffed.

"Have you been hot-prowling lately? There's been some jobs in West L.A."

Wino rolled his wrists. He got ratchet-ripped.

"I ain't pull no 459s since the '70s. I found my calling then. I'm a note man and a breather, and I'm fucking proud of it."

I said, "You admit those notes to Ms. Donahue?"

"Yeah, you know I do. I'm a note man of long standing, and I'm fucking proud of—"

"You did some time at Chino, right? You sent Ms. Donahue a note from there."

"That's right. I'm a note man, the best in the west."

"Were you in for burglary?"

"Fuck, no. I was pushing yellow jackets to high-school kids, out of the Mar Vista Bowl. I quit that burglary shit in the '70s."

Donna said, "And you deny sending me e-mails?"

Wino snickered, sneered, and stuck out his tongue. Wino licked his lips loathsome and leered.

"I'm a note man and a breather. That's my twenty-year MO. Don't try to hang no other shit on me, because I ain't buying it."

I said, "You quit sending Ms. Donahue notes. Why?"

"She's stale bread, that's why! She never shows no more skin! I'm a skin man! I go squirrel shit if I don't get no skin!"

Donna looked at me. I saw her nip toward the nexus. Her hazel eyes hit me and *hurt*.

She sapped Wino. She beavertail-bashed him. The weight whipped and leather lashed skin. She hooked him a new hairline. The cut dug deep. Blood blew down to his chin.

Wino went wild. "Baby, I dig it! You're turning me on, 'cause I've got this guilt thing! Ask all the old cops! I confessed to the best in the west!"

I caught a cue. "You said you killed a girl once. You put it in one of the notes you sent Ms. Donahue."

Wino hooked his head. The hairline cut coursed backward. He tongue-torqued lizardlike and licked the blood off his lips.

"I never killed no girl. I said it to get back at the bitch. I wanted to scare her. She wasn't giving me no skin. I'm a skin man. I need my skin!"

I fingered my phone book. I fought the urge to fuck him up *faaaast*.

"What's with the confessing? Tell us about that."

Wino wrist-rolled. The radiator rocked.

"I go back to the Dahlia. I was 9 then. I copped to all the big snuffs. You name it, I copped to it. Bashor, the Stephen Nash jobs, the Manson shit, all of that. It was my thing back in the old days, before I got this boner for skin."

I looked at him. His boner bounced. He grimaced and jizzed up his jeans.

Donna said, "Ugh." Wino exhaled ecstatic. It cued me in for the kill.

"Did you murder Stephanie Gorman?"

Wino laffed. Wino leered. Wino said, "What if I did?"

I said it slow. *"Did you kill Stephanie Gorman?"*

Wino wiggled. Wino winked. Wino said, "What if I did?"

I hit him. I beat him binding-side-outward. I hit him heavy. I rammed him repeated. I pounded and popped him and pulled back abrupt. He pissed his pants and poured out postnasal drip.

"Did you kill—"

"No! I did some yard work for her old man! I copped to the snuff,

but I couldn't milk it for three hots and a cot, and the fuzz cut me loose!"

I looked at Donna. She said, *"Rick, no more, please."*

Wino rolled his wrists. The radiator ripped free. Pipes popped loose. Steam stung me.

I checked the closet. Clothes—but no trank gun, no tranquilizers, no benzodiazepines. I slid out my cell phone. I dialed Dave Slatkin.

He picked up. "Slatkin."

I said, "The mug runs. What did you get?"

Dave coughed. Dogs barked in the background. I heard Pancho panting. I heard bull mastiffs bay.

"No hits on Wino, and that's at all six libraries. I had some mugs in with Wino, and a couple of librarians said Cal Eggers looked most like the guy. Is that a fucking hoot?"

I laffed. I looked at Donna. Wino whipped his head. Blood blipped onto her blouse and skirt. Blood skimmed her skin.

Wino said, "I'm a skin man. I'm a note man and a breather. I dig red gash, and so fucking what?"

I pulled up a chair. It was straight-backed and slatted. I sat down. I flexed my forearms. I snapped the slats off.

Wino rolled his wrists and resoiled himself. I said it sotto voce: *"Did you kill Stephanie?"*

Wino went calm. Wino said, "I caddied at Hillcrest that day. It was a big tournament. They'll have records. I was on the course when the Gorman kid got it."

Donna dug out her cell phone. I heard her hit Information. I heard her ask for Hillcrest. I heard her hit the listing and get the first tee.

She whispered. "Weinberger" and "August 5th, '65" wound back to me. Wino watched me. I laid out a lapsed Lutheran prayer: LET IT BE HIM.

Time ticked by. Donna said, "He's checking records." I shut my eyes and saw Stephanie. Tick, tick, tick—two minutes topped.

Donna said, "Thanks." The phone fizzed off. I opened my eyes. I still saw Stephanie.

"It's not him, Rick. He was on the golf course from 1:10 to 6:20." *Auf Wiedersehen, adieu, adios—shalom*, Stephanie.

I uncuffed Wino. Donna perused her purse and took out two twenties. Cut-rate reparation—she tossed them on the bed.

We walked out. We crunched crack-pipe glass and short-dog shards. Wino screamed, "I'm a skin man, and I need my skin!"

8.

The stink, the stain, the malevolent malodor—wash Wino off of us.

Donna's house had a huge hot tub. We boiled out his bad-ness and talked our terror tactics through. Donna copped to faux-feminist rectitude and rage. Whipping-boy Wino—the genus of genderized crime. I copped to venal violence vetted by Stephanie. I skirted the skin-madness issue. It hit home hard. Panties paralyzed me. I memorialized *my* mom. *She* was a righteous redhead, too.

Dave called. I told him Wino went south. The old note man/the e-mail hot-prowler—served up as two separate freaks. Dave said he'd reinstate the rolling stakeouts. He said he made Leotis Lauter for the Gary Getchell snuff. The dart death—deep diversion—let's hurl heat on hot-prowl now.

Plus:

The West L.A. dicks dug up some eyeball wits. Leotis Lauter loitered outside Gary Getchell's pad three days ago. Two rasty-assed Rastafarians reconnoitered with him. The pad: pored through and randomly ransacked. Odds on no files found. Found today: torched paper files in Leotis L.'s fireplace.

I debated Dave. Leotis Lauter—dope dealer—not a deep diverter. The hot-prowl hump—good for Gary.

We argued. We agreed—I had two days off—call it downtime to dally with Donna.

We dallied. We hearth-hid. We made love and feasted on fireplace food. We cooked kabobs and flame-fried burgers. Reggie Ridgeback scrounged scraps.

We dallied. We did ourselves up as a dog pack. We slipped into slumber. We *dozzzzed.*

Wino witch-hunted me. I Oedipaled awful. Titian-tressed trespassers trudged and traipsed through. My mom materialized. She mumbled rebukes. I'm lost in her lingerie drawer.

I heard something. It rang wrong. My reverie—wrecked.

I opened my eyes. There's Cal Eggers. Cal's got a trank gun. The hearth flames flare—Cal's caught in the light.

My synapses snapped. The libraries. The mug runs. Cal's coincidental pics. *He's the hump they ID'd.*

He fired. I rolled onto Reggie. I disturbed Donna. My weight whipped her awake.

The dart popped onto a pillow. Reggie reared up. I rolled right and picked up a poker. It ran red with heat.

Donna rolled. Donna ran. Donna dug through couch cushions. Reggie rammed Cal's crotch and tore in with his teeth.

Cal screamed. I poker-popped and brand-broiled him. I nailed his neck. I scalded skin. He dropped his trank gun and pulled a *real* piece.

Big bore. A nasty nickel-plated piece.

He screamed at me. He fired. I lurched left and made him miss. Reggie bit through his balls and castrated him. I saw his sac sawed through and his scrotum scrunched up in dog teeth.

Cal screamed. Cal ran toward Donna. She tossed couch cushions. She threw up a throw rug. She made the Magnum. She found the fat .45.

Cal fired. He missed Donna. Bullets ripped the Renoir and mowed down the Monet. Both paintings dropped off the wall. Reggie mewed through a mouthful of mangled balls. Donna two-handed aimed.

She caught Cal low. She laid down leg shots. Four hit hard. Cal caromed off a couch edge and careened.

He fell flat. He dropped his gun. I rolled right and ran up to him.

His leg wounds coursed copious. His pelvic wound pulsated and poured blood. He was close to the clouds. He was staring at the River Styx. I said, "*Dying declaration.* Give it up, *please.*"

He coughed. Bloody phlegm flew. He found a firm voice. He spoke to Donna, not me.

"You . . . were the one. I had this thing for you since '83. I was working Rampart then. I was working up to get you . . . but I didn't know if I could do it . . . I always had a hot-prowl jones . . . I tried to buy out of the obsession . . . e-mails, panties . . . I took my cue from Megan More . . . Oh, Donna, at least I didn't rape you . . . oh, Donna . . . oh, shit."

The fuck was fading fast. I said, "There's more, Cal. Come on, all of it."

Donna knelt beside me. She sent scents of sandalwood soap and gunshot residue. Reggie regurgitated. Male genitalia flew.

Cal coughed. "I was in with Gary G., independent of Megan. I . . . fed him Narco dope, more than Danny G. did . . . I wanted to take over the division when Linus Lauter got moved out . . . Gary knew I had this thing for you, Donna. I was the 'avenging angel' . . . Leotis and his niggers tortured Gary . . . I was afraid he'd rat me if they fucked him up again . . . so I snuffed him."

Reggie bayed. Cal coughed. His eyes said, "Oh, you kid." He coughed blood, blanched, and died.

Donna kicked the corpse. "You fucking loser. I'm not that big a deal."

Happy holidays. Christmas for crucifixion-heads, Hanukkah for hebes, Kwanzaa for spooks simmering for secession. Ho, ho, ho — holiday cheer at Hillsboro and Sawyer.

Donna and me. Let's dig on our dead. Let's honor ourselves. Let's celebrate our cessation.

We had two months together. It was goooood. We got singed by circumstance. We got rigorously reawakened.

The media made good. The "Suicide Season" survived and moved into myth. Cool Cal caught the outside edge. Joe Tierney toted him up to terminal cancer. The pain pounded him. Cal couldn't take it. He opted for self-immolation.

A viable verdict. No castration by canine, no death by Donna D.

Call it cosmetic. Cal killed himself. His Hot-Prowl Hell died with him. Leotis Lauter got memorably murdered. It was rap-music related.

Monster Mack-Mack was making time with Leotis's lady. It was one trippy triangle. It was baaaad jig juju. Leotis caught Mack-Mack at Mohammad's Mosque #6. Mack-Mack pulled a machine gun. Mack-Mack mowed him down. Leotis leeched up 26 rounds and rang off to Allah. He's currently couched with Khalid Khareem.

Daisy Delgado made him for the Gary Getchell snuff. She filed Murder One postmortem.

It's all tied up. There's a dozen declared dead in Hot-Prowl Heaven or Hell.

I had two months with Donna. Prosaics pried us apart. I caught some Cold Case murders. She caught a mid-season series. She played a Homicide cop.

We sat in my Saturn sedan. We traded gifts. We stared at Stephanie's house. She gave me a cashmere coat. I gave her Monster Mack-Mack's machine gun, moved from an evidence vault.

The house held us. Time tripped us up. Then to now and patterns past. Stephanie unavenged. A dead daughter older than us. Our finite future.

We talked. We tossed some tears. We said I-love-yous. I got lonely and Donnafied with Donna right there. Unbreachable crimes, unreachable women—and me.

Jungletown Jihad

eaven's still forever. Time still stings you and makes you bop backward. Intervals intertwine. The hot-prowl holocaust and shattering shit six months later.

Donna. Me. A short shove to March '05.

Another murder mandate. A cold-case contretemps. My yearning. Her reluctance. The urge to merge. Donna. Me. Toxic terror. Jungle juju. Ring my retrospection back to this:

Los Angeles Times, March 1, 2005.
COLD CASE SQUAD INVESTIGATES
ROBBERY MURDERS
By Miles Corwin

The LAPD's Cold Case Unit is now actively investigating three brazen homicides that occurred during the holdups of Southside liquor stores in the spring of 2001. Detective David Slatkin, the unit's officer-in-charge, told the *Times* that a recent tip may prove "quite valuable."

On the afternoon of April 29, 2001, two men entered the Liquor Heaven store at Normandie Avenue and Martin Luther King Boulevard in South-Central Los Angeles. They robbed the store at gunpoint and shot proprietor Dong Quan Lem to death. A stockboy crouched unseen behind the dairy case described the men as "young Arab types. You know, like those guys you see waving sticks and stuff in Iraq." The killers escaped. The stockboy provided LAPD detectives with a description of them, and assisted the detectives in creating Identikit portraits.

The robber-killers struck again on May 16. They entered the Liquor World store on Jefferson Boulevard and Vermont Avenue, robbed the establishment and fatally shot owner Jim Wong Kim. A pedestrian eyewitness saw the killers escape. She described both assailants as "male Arabs with mustaches like that no-goodnik Saddam Hussein." She confirmed the Identikit portraits as accurate and added, "Both men looked very mean."

LAPD detectives expanded their investigation. They followed up on numerous leads and checked with Federal agencies for information on armed robbers with possible terrorist ties. Nothing conclusive resulted, and the robber-killers struck again on June 9.

Their target was the Liquor King store on Imperial Highway. They made the proprietor, Kwan Paul Park, unlock an office vault and hand over a week's cash receipts. After Park complied, they shot him fourteen times and escaped out a back door. A parking-lot witness said both men yelled, "Praise to Allah!" and "Free Palestine!" He embellished the two prior suspect descriptions, stating, "Both guys looked wasted, like they was on dope or on the sauce. That, and they sure looked crazy and mean."

The LAPD stepped up its investigation, spurred by urgings from Asian-American civil-rights groups. An attempt to locate Arab-terrorist "sleeper cells" followed. Arab-American civil-rights groups protested the LAPD's "heavy handedness" and "fascist methods" in interrogating Arab-American citizens.

Arab League spokesman Gazi Alli called the investigation a "pogrom" and a "Zionist conspiracy."

The investigation continued, unsuccessfully. The September 11 terrorist bombings diverted the flow, as Federal agencies began a massive post-attack investigation of their own, aimed at uncovering terrorist cells in the Los Angeles area. LAPD detectives constantly monitored the FBI Task Force's progress, but turned up no salient leads on the robbery-murder men. The investigation stagnated and assumed "open file" status.

Detective Slatkin told the *Times*, "Our investigators have checked out over 400 tips, and Chief Tierney has now assigned the job to the Cold Case Unit. We're making it our number-one priority. We're about to check out an informant who has pledged to give us some important information. He seems to be plugged in to the Arab criminal network, so we're guardedly optimistic."

Will the informant offer up data on terrorist activities? Detective Slatkin thinks not. "We think this is street crime, pure and simple," he said. "The shouted slogans are most likely obfuscation. We're treating this as a series of heinous, but nonpolitical, crimes."

Daily Variety, March 2, 2005.
COP FLOP: "HOMICIDE HEAT" FIZZLES.
DONAHUE SETS ON STAGE.
By Bruce Balaban

ABC has pulled the plug on the Donna Donahue starrer *Homicide Heat* after a scant six episodes. The L.A.-set cop-u-drama moped to miserable market shares and flat-out flopper-ooed. The show, which featured La Donahue as LAPD Detective Daisy Delphine, sunk despite proud production values, Ms. Donahue's *sin*-tillating performance as a promiscuous diva cop and its status as LAPD Chief Joe Tierney's

favorite TV program. El Jefe's bereft, but don't look for Divine
Donna at the unemployment office or Brentwood breadlines.

No, she's sternly stuck on the stage. She wants to eschew
indie cheapies, sexploitation yukfests like *Exit to Ecstasy* and
overblown oaters like *San Laredo*. Her plan? To commission a
playwright and bomb the boards as pill-popping poetess Anne
Sexton.

Sexy Sexton succumbed to suicide in 1974. Deep Donna
digs on her as a kool kindred soul. "I've had two seismic
eruptions in my life," she said. "One in '83 and one last year. I
want to transmogrify them into my role as Sexton."

Doe-eyed Donna does Sexton—whoa! It wends as one wild
one-woman show. That Shakespeare shtarker is dead—ditto
torrid Tennessee Williams. Who does Dishy Donna—currently flogging Barko Bits dog food with her Rhodesian ridgeback Reggie—see as her scribe?

"There's a young playwright I've got my eye on," she said.
"He's stuck on '70s culture, especially the SLA–Patty Hearst
thing, but I think I can get him hooked on Sexton."

That sounds like savvy and sagacious Sextonism. Mean-
while, look for Dogophile Donna at the Barko Bits booth at
the Beverly Hills Kennel Club trials. She'll also be a presenter
at this month's Oscar fest, and *that's* no dog of a show.

Los Angeles Police Department/Psychological
Evaluation Report/Official Routing Only: Commander,
Robbery-Homicide Division & Personnel Division [file
inclusion]. Reporting psychologist: Alan V. Kurland,
Ph.D. Subject: Jenson, Richard W./Detective 3rd-
Grade/currently assigned to Cold Case Homicide Unit.
Date of submission: 3/6/05.

Sirs:
Between the dates 2/21 and 2/26/05 I conducted three one-
hour sessions with Detective Jenson, who was referred to me

(compulsory) by Captain Walter D. Tyndall, the Commander
of Robbery-Homicide Division. Captain Tyndall's reason for
referral was his personal assessment of Detective Jenson: i.e.,
that he was suffering from nervous exhaustion and "some sort
of ongoing personal crisis."

I found Detective Jenson to be a person of acute intellect
and substantial insight, marred by the presence of Obsessive-
Compulsive Disorder (OCD), which by its debilitating long-
term nature has led Detective Jenson into a state of
excitability, pathological work habits and a disturbing need for
mental stimulation. The underpinnings of Detective Jenson's
compulsiveness appear to be his romantic attachment to a
1965 murder victim (Stephanie Lynn Gorman, DOD 8/5/65,
DR #65-538-991), an unsolved crime recently investigated by
the Cold Case Unit, and his occasional involvement with a
well-known actress (who Detective Jenson refuses to name),
an intermittently intimate relationship that dates back over
twenty years.

Detective Jenson stated that he has eschewed marriage
and long-term relationships with other women out of a sense
of devotion to this woman, because "with her, everything is
possible," "she's constantly with me, anyway," and "I'll never
take a soft line on love." Detective Jenson further stated that
he has written two "novella-length" memoirs about his "wild-
ass love" for this woman, and that they were both stylistically
influenced by the alliterative prose style of *Hush-Hush* magazine. When queried about the content of the memoirs,
Detective Jenson said, "It's private shit. And, no, you can't
read them." He went on to describe his writings as both
"odes" and "hymns to the few times I've fully loved and felt
incandescently alive." Implicit in those statements: both
memoirs described Detective Jenson and the unnamed
woman in moments of violent intrigue. It should be noted
that Detective Jenson's admitted grandiosity and hoarding of
"my righteous secrets with this woman" are consistent with

the defining psychological guidelines of Obsessive-
Compulsive Disorder.

There are other deeply compulsive aspects of Detective
Jenson's fixation. He stated that he "only digs women who
look like her," "falls into" relationships with look-alike women
and "axes them when they fall short of her." Detective Jenson
also employs "snitches" who direct him to the woman's whereabouts so that he may "show up, accidentally on purpose."
When pressed on the desperation inherent in this, Detective
Jenson stated, "So fucking what? I'm a cop. I use informants,
and any man who won't make a fool of himself for a woman is
a fucking fruit."

Detective Jenson's intransigence also extends to the
Stephanie Gorman case. The victim (a 16-year-old girl from
West Los Angeles) has, in Detective Jenson's words, "constel-
lated my need to yearn, live in the past, fuck myself up on
unknowability and maybe get some righteous revenge." With
uncanny self-perception, he pointed to his use of informants
and his hours parked outside Stephanie Gorman's former
house. "It's a meditation," he said. "It makes me feel tender. I
sit still and figure things out about myself. I don't have to fuck
women to love them."

At this time, Detective Jenson is not amenable to entering
therapy or taking medication that might serve to curb his
obsessive-compulsive behavior. His physical condition—based
on his last LAPD examination—is excellent, and his work
performance is unimpaired. Detective Jenson (who has killed
five armed suspects in the line of duty) does not seem to suffer
from the post-traumatic stress disorders common to police-
men. When asked about the state of nervous exhaustion and
"ongoing personal crisis" described by Captain Tyndall, he
replied, "If you're not on the edge, you're taking up too much
space." Detective Jenson has, despite his excitability, pathological work habits and need for stimulation, a grounding in the

realities of his life. At this time, I believe there to be no cause
for his suspension from duty. I would further recommend a
second evaluation in six months' time.

Respectfully,
Alan V. Kurland,
Ph.D.

1.

The informant:

Habib Rashad/male Arab/age 36/4823 S. St. Andrews.

We humped the Harbor Freeway southbound. Cops call it the
"Coal Chute." It's a jungle-bunny juggernaut and a sleaze sluice.
It coonects Darktown with White Man's L.A.

Tim Marti drove. I daydreamed. Donna Standard Time tapped
me. *Homicide Heat* — tanksville. No more impromptu set visits.
No more Donna done up fetishistic: LAPD badge, gun, and cuffs.

The blues blasted me. Donna deprivation, Stephanie still
stamped unsolved and DEAD. My torch flared and billowed
bipartite. Said torch now torqued Tim's kid Brandon. My crush
created his crush. He dug Donna delirious. He prized Stephanie
as his prom date pristine.

Darktown dipped by. Shit shacks, shine stands, Afriqued
AMEs. The Coal Chute ran elevated. I saw liquor-store layabouts
lap Olde English 800. I saw hos pander poontang and cats
cliqued up outside rib cribs.

The '01 murders. Three dead, Arab suspects, Southside locations. Habib Rashad — Southside habitué.

He called the chief's office. He said he had major shit. Joe
Tierney bought in. Terrorists tickled Tierney. He hosannaed for
Homeland Security. He called the Cold Case guys in.

Three liquor-store snuffs. Brutal, brazen. Terrorist tie-ins —
don't bet on it.

We hit the 10 freeway westbound. I Donna-dreamed. We mated in Malibu. We soixante-neuf'd at Sofitels. Reggie Ridge-back romped rambunctious and furred us up.

Tim took the Normandie exit. We whipped west and south. There's the address: a weathered wood-frame pad.

We parked curbside. Jigaboos perched on porches checked our fuzzmobile out. We bopped to the front door. Tim rang the bell. A full-drag dune coon opened up.

Designer threads. A Husseinesque house smock. A boss bur-noose from Bin Laden's Boutique.

Tim laffed. I said, "Ahab the A-rab. Where's your camel, moth-erfucker?"

Daddy-o deadpanned us. We bopped in unbidden. The living room: a mad mini-mosque.

Pricey prayer rugs. Wild wall tapestries. Freaky framed photo-graphs—Al Qaeda-ish cats with big beards. All-star ayatollahs. Sacred Saddams and holy Hassims. A camel caravan supreme.

Rashad said, "I have information. I give, and you give me good deal."

Beanbag chairs beckoned. Tim and I plopped in. Rashad paced. His burnoose billowed. Fuck this Scimitar Sid.

The digs diverted me. Hookahs heaped on side tables. Char-treuse shawls covered with camel or cat hair. Those wall pix—beady-eyed Bedouins.

Tim said, "The liquor-store jobs. Give on that, and we'll talk to the D.A."

Big bugs rocked across the rugs. They lugged lamb hunks and shish-kebab shards. Southside centipedes loomed large—L.A. Laker–like.

I said, "Is this terrorist shit we're dealing with? Did those guys have some kind of political motive?"

Rashad shook his head. "They wanted to show courage to a radical Islamic group. You know the term 'sleeper cell'? They wanted to secure funds from the group and form a cell, but they had no intention of performing terrorist acts. They just wanted to enjoy themselves with the money. You know the term 'party hearty'?"

I *saw* it. Murderous Muslims maraud the Sunset Strip. Camels corralled by the Viper Room. Lamb roasts right by the Roxy.

Rashad paced. His house smock swirled. His sandals slapped. Shit—a shot shook/a side window shattered.

It ratched Rashad. It ricocheted. It hit a hookah and hammered his head twice. It chewed his cheekbones, his brains breezed, his scalp scattered.

I dove. Tim dove. We rolled and ate prayer rug. Bugs crawled with falafel crumbs.

Rashad palsied and pulsed pole-axed. He flew. He flatlined. He dropped DOA.

I got up. Tim got up. We reached for our roscoes and ran out the door. Getaway car—a purple Pontiac peeling out.

We ran. We got our car. Tim caught the key and goosed the gas. We tore tread, reamed the rims, and ripped rubber.

We gained ground. We pounced on the Pontiac. We sheared shots off. We blasted the back window out.

Glass shrapnelized. Our towelhead target boded, backlit.

I fired. Tim fired. We tore towel fabric. His burnoose burned. His hair flared and flamed the headliner.

He screamed. I *heard* it. He alakazamed to Allah. We banged his bumper. We climbed close in. His beard broiled down to bristles. His face went on fire.

The Pontiac pulled right and popped over the curb. It hit a hydrant, stalled and stopped. Local losers poured off their porches. They whooped wild and cheered.

The guy jumped from the car. His face was a four-alarm fire. A porch punk pulled a hose over. He laughed loud and lobbed water up.

The guy sizzled and fizzled. The guy sputtered sparks and dipped dead.

THE SHOOTING TEAM SHOWED. Ditto the lab. Ditto the coroner's car and six bluesuits.

They roped the street off. They perused the Pontiac. Fire Face—high up in *hafiz* heaven. The coroner's cats cased his stiff.

Filed fingertips. Scar tissue over print surface. One U.S. passport. Saudi Arabia stamps/Habib Rashad's name/Fire Face's unfried features. Sexy secular threads: color-*coon*ordinated Tommy Hipnigger.

Local louts loitered. Porch punks paraded. They hopped house to house and shared Schlitz malt liquor. Lab guys popped the Pontiac's trunk. They found a Mach 10 machine gun, a copper kettle caked with couscous, four bug microphones.

Bug mikes—whoa, why dat?

The shooting team shoved shit at Tim and me. You shot that sharp sheik. Yeah, he killed Scimitar Sid—but *justify* it.

We laid it out. The liquor-store snuffs. Rashad—righteous informant. He's out to name names. He's prepping his prelude. *Bam*—the sheik shoots, Sid leeches lead.

The shooting guys *got* it. Internecine intrigue. Camelhead conspiracy. Some panicked Pan-Arab Pax.

We tossed the pad. We roamed rooms, combed cubbyholes, and found this:

Personal papers. Proud proprietor Rashad—owner of Falafel Fan, 34th and Vermont.

Mucho mattresses stuffed in storage closets.

Hate tracts. Arabic script. Gross graphics of insidious Israelis. Dig their fat fangs and big beaks. Dig their kike Cadillacs. Dig their six-point-star-meets-dollar-sign regalia.

Five .44 Magnums. Fifteen 40-caliber Brownings. Appropriate ammo.

Pandemic porno vids. Torrid and topical titles. *Darsheika Does*

Damascus, Syrian 69, Golan Heights Gang Bang, Sexy Sad-damites, and *Cairo Cuties.*

Four spackle-coated cameras. Surefire surveillance cams.

Link it large: the bug mikes and the cameras.

Print techs whipped through and worked walls and windows. Tim and I rocked room to room and recorded details. A coroner's canoe rolled Rashad and Fire Face off. I contemplated my kills, line of duty.

The Garcia brothers—wicked wetbacks/choice cholos. Huey Muhammad 6X—rapacious rape-o. Shondell Dineen and Webster Washington—blasphemous black hoods. My bold body count—now six total.

My cell phone rang. The display lit up. A Donna snitch snared me.

I hit On. "It's Jenson."

"Hi, Rhino. It's Tom. You know, at Raleigh Studios."

"Yeah?"

"She's on Stage 6. She's doing this dog food commercial."

DIG THE DICHOTOMY: dead dune coons to Dangerous Donna.

I drove to Raleigh Studios. I circled Stage 6 and parked. *Rowf* fucking *rowf*—there's Reggie Ridgeback's huckster howls.

The barks bid me inside. I cut down corridors and caught the commercial. There's the director. There's the crew. There's Reggie and Donna.

A flag fluttered behind them. Reggie rowfed in red, white, and blue dog duds. A right-wing conglomerate hawked Barko Bits. Donna parsed out patriotic pap.

"Hi. This is Donna Donahue, with my dog, Reggie. Like all Americans, I'm concerned about the specter of terrorist attack. I stay healthy and vigilant by eating a well-balanced diet, and I feed Reggie Barko Bits All-American Dog Chow. I want a vigilant watchdog who's alert 24–7. Barko Bits' special blend of meat, vitamins, and minerals keeps Reggie up on his paws and sniffing out terrorist suspects. Speak, Reggie! Tell us how *you* feel about Barko Bits All-American Dog Chow!"

Reggie went "Rowf!" Reggie dipped through his dog duds and dug into his dick.

He bit, he licked, he tongued himself tumescent. Donna howled. The director yelled, "Reggie, you fucking lowlife, lay off your shvantz!"

Reggie ignored him. Reggie dick-dug deeper. The crew yukked. I noticed a cool cat standing stage right. He oozed male-model machismo. He was fagged-out in Ferragamo and artfully arrayed in Armani. Resentment ripped me. He vibed Donna boy toy.

The director yelled, "Cut! Let's take five for now!"

Boy Toy bopped toward Donna. Reggie *gggrrrowled* at him. I hopped on stage. Donna hugged me. I said, "Who's the fruit?" Donna said, "He's a playwright, and I'm not sleeping with him."

My resentment rippled off. I un-machismoed and magnanimized. I Donna-disengaged and braced Boy Toy.

"I'm Rick Jenson. Donna and I go back. I'm on LAPD, and I just dusted an A-rab."

Donna laffed. "Rick's a xenophobe, and he tends to brag to impress me. It works sometimes."

Boy Toy bristled. "I'm Donny DeFreeze, and I'm not impressed. I support the PFL and all Middle Eastern wars of liberation. I told Donna this commercial was beneath her, but she insisted. She has a codependent relationship with her dog."

Reggie growled. His fur furled tailbone and torso. It was deep dog dislike and instant indictment.

I said, "Donny DeFreeze? Like that SLA fool 'Cinque'? Don't tell me. You think he's cool and relevant to this time of internal repression, and you regret that you were born white."

Donna poked me. Reggie flared his flaps and flashed his fangs. DeFreeze detoured and mowed down a mike stand.

It toppled. I picked it up. Donna reached for Reggie and restrained him.

"Donny's going to write my Anne Sexton show. He's written some plays and spec scripts that caught my attention."

Boy Toy/Butt Banger/Budding Bolshevik Bard—fuck him six ways from Sunday.

"Watch out for Donna. She's more dangerous than you'll ever know. And watch out for Reggie and me, because we're right behind you."

Reggie growled. His dick shot from the shaft. He vibed dog defiler and ridgeback rape-o.

Donna said, "Rick, you asshole."

DeFreeze simpered sissified. His lips pursed perverted. Spit bubbles bipped out and spun.

"My best work hasn't been produced yet, but I think you'll find it shocking when you see it."

Cryptic. Cruel. Fatalistically faggy. This hard-eyed homophile hiss.

I flipped his tie in his face. I stepped off the stage. Donna said, "Rick, you shit."

I walked outside. I caught the crew with crullers and coffee. I saw a lipstick-red Lamborghini parked adjoining. The license plate read "DeFrzz."

DIG THE DICHOTOMY: dog dissent to dog den delight.

I drove to Dave Slatkin's dog shelter. I hooked up and homed in with his hounds. A canine cacophony warmed me—six brindle pit bulls full of love.

We shared oki pastrami burritos. We crafted a cross-species group grope. I pulled out a pallet. We all snuggled up.

I talked up Reggie's resentment. I said Donna deftly demurred.

This DeFreeze dipshit was writing her Sexton show. She couldn't opt to offend him. She couldn't call him on his Commie jive. Yeah, I was an asshole. I should have shut up.

The hounds heard me out. I told them I toasted a camel jockey. I mentioned the mattresses. Southside sleeper cell— maybe. We'd re-toss the crib tomorrow. More shit might turn up.

I dozed. Dog farts fanned. DeFreeze reprised and dug at me. He vibed parasitic pantywaist with molten mean streak. I didn't want him working angles on Donna.

I called the DMV and plied a plate run. A clerk caught the "DeFrzz" stats and coughed up a make. The lipstick Lambo: long-term rental from Khalid's Kustom Cars/Khalid Salaam, owner.

It fit the prick's profile. Appropriate an appearance and hit Hollywood. Dun someone like Donna Donahue. Trap them and transfuse yourself. Latch on like a leech. Pile on like a piranha.

I dozed. I drifted. I slipped into slumber. Hound heartbeats held me. I felt this big canine caress.

I dreamed. Shondell Dineen and Webster Washington whipped through my wig. The '92 riots. Nihilistic nostalgia. The sack of Sal's Market, South-Central.

Dineen's dinged with needle tracks, smug and smacked-back. He's caught with a case of Cutty. Webster's wearing a "Shaq Attack" sweatshirt. He's got ten cartons of Kools and a shitload of Schlitz malt liquor.

They've got guns. They're just out of the joint. They've got prison shoes—San Quentin sandals.

There's Sal's Market. They're bopping out with booty. I'm going in.

SURPRISE!!!!!

I've got a Remington pump. One spread spritzes them. The Cutty cascades. The Schlitz shvitzes. Their collective last word is "motherfucker."

I woke up. Donna Standard Time stung me. Let's kommune with a kindred soul. Let's kall Brandon Marti.

I dug through dogs and filched the phone. I dialed the Marti pad.

Brandon grabbed it. "Uh, yeah?"

"It's me, kid."

"Oh, hi, Uncle Rhino."

Fleas flipped on the pallet. Pit bulls scrunched and scratched.

I said, "Did your dad tell you about the Arabs?"

"Uh, yeah. He said you popped Glaser slugs and fried the guy's face. It sounded really cool."

"The shooting board should clear us. The guy just iced our witness."

"Uh, yeah. My dad said it was a good kill, but these stupid A-rab civil-rights groups might protest."

"Let them. We've got right on our side, and—"

"You want to talk about Donna. I can always tell by your voice."

I sighed soft. "You know me, kid."

Brandon coughed. "My dad says you're a loser in love. He said it's okay for me to moon for Donna, because I'm a kid, but you should know better."

A pit bull licked my face. Burrito breath blew.

"I've been places your dad's never been. I think he's jealous."

"Maybe. Or maybe you're just on to something he doesn't understand."

"I'll buy that."

"My English teacher gets it. He wrote his doctoral thesis on Donna. He's really into her hold on men and all that. He said I could read it, because I'm a Donna guy, too."

I yawned. "Make a copy for me, will you? You can drop it off here at the shelter."

Brandon yawned. "Okay."

"Goodnight, kid. Sweet Donna dreams."

"Goodnight, Uncle Rhino. Good luck with the A-rabs."

I hung up. I got loser-in-love lonely. I was too tired for a Stephanie stakeout. I wanted to Donna-diminuendo and sleep.

Donny DeFreeze dinged me. I decided to dig up derogatory dish. Let's loop his life. Let's look for larceny. No sale?—we'll frappé and frame his ass then.

I dozed. Hurricane-hurled hazel eyes hammered me.

2.

The media mauled me. The radio rocked with it.

We caught the Coal Chute. Dave Slatkin drove. Tim ran the radio. This fucking fedayee Gazi Alli filleted me. It was civil-rights shit shorn of shape and reason. Two sharp Shiite sharifs— dead. Boo-hoo—two super Sufis. Rhino Rick rampages. He's tripped-out and trigger-happy. He's deep depressed. LAPD just shot him to a shrink.

I bounced in the backseat. Gazi gored my goat. Some personnel punk leaked him my package. Tim made the jackoff sign. Dave ditzed the dial. Some ballsy bitch ballyhooed the upcoming Oscars.

I groaned. Donna was set to attend. She was boyfriend-bereft now. She might take Dipshit DeFreeze.

We cut off the Coal Chute. We caught side streets to Saint Andrews. Bluesuits bloomed on our block. They cordoned back a camelhead cadre. Many Moors mingled. They shucked with shines and mouthed multicultural mayhem. They growled grievance in some spunky Spook-Arab Pact.

We parked outside the cordon and coursed through on foot. We rolled through Ramadan cut with Kwanzaa. Black Muslims materialized and mau-maued us with their eyes. Anti-Zionist zingers zipped by:

"Islam—not Israel!"/"Stop the LAPD Jew Jihad!"/"Gen-o-cide, gen-o-cide, LAPD and the Jews can't hide!"

We walked through. We made tracks through mini-Ramadan and parted the Red Sea of Resentment. We barged biiiiiig. We shot out sharp elbows. We ripped through reefer smoke and toppled tallboys of Olde English 800.

There's the Rashad rancho—let's duck inside.

We did it. We laid up with some lab guys and print techs. They told us this:

Per prints—we latched on to some latents. We got Rashad's prints, we got glove prints boocoo. Match the mattresses to the glove prints—you craft a crash pad. Figure fingerprint-known felons. They gloved and hid their hands. Figure fuckheads with felonious intent.

Per the Pontiac—we impounded it and pounced on the panels. We found fourteen K in cash. We print-wiped inside and outside. The shooter's filed fingertips showed up—scuffed skin marks.

We flung floor mats. We found mucho matchbooks. They came from "gentlemen's clubs." Dig: Sandi's Sandbox, Lani's Lapdance, the Chrysanthemum Club. We found soiled clothes, dishes, and detergent in the trunk. We think Fire Face slept in his car.

A patrol sergeant dipped in and debriefed us. He told us this:

Patrolmen polled the locals. Said locals laid out Rashad. Many men popped by the pad. All Arabs, all hours. Some locals vibed terrorist trouble and buzzed the Feds.

Dave called his Fed connection and tracked the tips. His connection coughed up a conclusion. Yeah, we checked it out. No, we nabbed no known suspects. Habib Rashad—forget him—he's some falafel fuck.

Dave, Tim, and I huddled hard. We bounced the bug mikes in the Pontiac to the spackle-specked cameras in the pad. We talked. We threaded theories. We culled no conclusive shit at all.

I called the U.S. Passport Office. I fielded favors. I learned this:

The Pontiac passport had Fire Face's features and Habib Rashad's name. The address of record: Rashad's falafel hut.

A lab guy laid a morgue mug shot on us. There's Fire Face with his scorched skin scraped off. His face—now feature-firm and fit to make IDs off.

Tim called Pac Bell and racked up Rashad's phone records. He got short-shrift shit. Rashad buzzed his Falafel Fan biz repeatedly. Rashad rang nobody else.

Suspicious. Sleeper cell slippery—yeah, probably.

Dave, Tim, and I huddled hard. Rashad *had* to make more calls. Conclusion: He called from pay phones.

We walked outside. We genuflected to the genocide chanters and made them mad with the sign of the cross. We borrowed a black-and-white and whipped to Western Avenue—the nearest pay-phone-filled street.

We walked phone to phone and nabbed numbers. We found fifteen phones in a four-block stretch. Tim called Pac Bell back.

He gave them our pay-phone stats. He requested a readout on phone numbers called. The clerk said she'd have readout results tomorrow. She'd call the Cold Case Squad.

My phone rang. I read the display. Rob the snitch/Starbucks/Beverly Hills.

Call it Donna communing with coffee. Call me too work-wigged to go.

We drove back to Rashad's rancho and dropped Dave off. Jigs chucked chicken wings and rib bones at our car. It was a bar-b-q bombardment. A multitude of malicious Muslims mean-mouthed us.

"Gen-o-cide! Gen-o-cide! LAPD and the Jews can't hide!"

FALAFEL FAN: A hajj hut at 34th and Vermont. A dervish dive from the get-go. A counter and picnic tables out front.

We parked and walked up. We gaped and guffawed at the menu: the "Palestine Pita," the "Soul Souvlaki," the "Shiite Shish-Kebab."

Baaaaad bow-tied Muslims at tables. Slicksters slurping up

"Muhammad's Meatball Sub." A mean mosque mastiff behind the counter. He's spanking a spatula, he's grinding griddle grease, he's stirring steak chunks in lentil sauce.

We cut around the counter and dipped in the door. Grease granules griddle-hopped and grabbed me. Daddy-o did not deign to look at us. Call him one *cooool* Camelite Cal.

I said, "LAPD."

Tim pulled out pix: the Fire Face morgue shot/the '01 killers' Identikits.

Cal speared his spatula. He lanced lamb and stirred steak. He glared at us. He glanced at the pix. His eyes racked up recognition. He said, "No. I do not know them. I tell you truth, now you leave."

Tim said, "Habib Rashad's dead. Who gets this place now?"

Camel Cal shrugged. "I get place. Mine now. Rashad my cousin. He was good man. He *Hafiz*."

I flashed the matchbooks: Sandi's Sandbox/Lani's Lapdance/Chrysanthemum Club. Camel Cal glanced and glowered. More recognition racked up.

"You guys hang out there, don't you? You, Rashad, the dead guy in the picture."

Cal shook his head. "No. Such places are for infidels. Good men never go."

Tim said, "Shit, *I* go. I don't see the big deal."

"You infidel. I see you two in newspaper. You shoot man who shoot Rashad. You 'trigger-happy.' Arab League say that."

I laffed. "Come on, man. He killed your cousin."

"All Arabs my cousins. We unite against infidels. We spit on you."

Tim laffed. Cal spit on the griddle. The loogie landed, sputtered, hissed.

I said, "Bugging microphones and surveillance cameras. We found them at Rashad's house *and* in the shooter's car. I think the two guys knew each other, and I think you know them *and* the liquor-store guys, *and* a fuckload of other Arabs up to no fucking good."

Cal spit on the griddle. Cal spanked his spatula in griddle grease. His face flushed. His heartbeat hammered and vibrated veins. Tim bellied up to him.

"Here's what I think. This dump is a message drop for Arab criminals. They get their mail here. They leave messages here. Your fuckhead friends come by for the fucking cat-meat couscous, and you—"

Cal swung the spatula. It caught Tim's coat collar. It snared. It snagged. Tim kicked Cal in the balls.

He jackknifed. Tim judo-chopped him. He aimed at his Adam's apple, all applied force. I jumped in. I nabbed Cal's neck. I kicked his legs loose. I bent him backwards. I scorched his scalp on the grill.

He screamed. I bent him back. Hair frizzed and frazzled. I burned his long locks down to a crewcut.

Tim tossed the place.

He spilled spice racks. He dumped dishes. He climbed through a closet. He ripped through Ramadan robes, shot through shelves and nabbed mail.

Cal's hair sizzled. His crewcut burned down to a butch.

MAIL:

We popped to Parker Center and went through it. It indicated infidels and hajjite horndogs.

Flyers for gentlemen's clubs/matches to our matchbooks, plus the Honey Bunny and Dawn's Dugout. Outcall hooker ads—grabber graphics, clipped newspaper stock. Skin magazines/dog-eared pages/vivid ads for 1-800-VIAGRA. Gun shop inventories, insidious. Buy-by-mail Mac10s and Magnums.

Whoa!—Lani's Lapdance meets Cool Coed Outcall meets Pan-Patriot Guns. Fetishistic fotos—gone girls in garters. Stacked

Stewardess Outcall. Viagra vertiginous. Six down-and-dirty dick-enlargement ads.

Dave, Tim, and I huddled. Dave sicced SIS surveillance on the Falafel Fan. We left Camel Cal shorn like a sandal-clad Samson. He might rabbit or free-form freak out. He might lose it and lead us to the liquor-store cats.

Pac Bell—no callback yet. No make on the pay-phone calls. The shooting board—tapped for Tuesday next. Call the kill kosher—I knew we'd walk. Our prime priority: Prowl the gentlemen's clubs.

We laid out our list. We divvied destinations. I got the Honey Bunny and Sandi's Sandbox.

I solo-sailed to the City of Commerce. It was all industrial interspersed with stinky strip malls. Lap-dance lairs were laid out next to nail nooks and fast-food joints. It was murky multicultural. Hopped-up Hondurans, kool-kat Koreans, Sufis and sushi-heads. White Man's L.A., where you at?

I hit Sandi's Sandbox. Listless Latinas lap-danced and stripped to strobe lights. The audience was the *Coon*ited Nations—immigrant duskies in deep despair, digging on 4:00 p.m. dark.

I badged the boss. He flipped me a flashlight. I roamed the runways and paraded my pix. Lap-dance Louies and Lolitas looked at them. I lashed up one long no, nix and *nyet*.

The Honey Bunny buttressed a Burmese burger barn and a mex *mariscos* dive. I badged in bold. The doorman sulked subservient and seated me ringside. The dump was dead dark. The runway bristled in bright light. A white wench wiggled to dated disco music. My eyes stung, stigmatic. I blinked and got full sight.

I saw one long lap-dance loop around the runway. Girls girded themselves over chumps in chairs and hip-humped it home. I dunned the doorman for a flashlight. I looped the loop and laid out my pictures. I lashed through a line of loser longing. The girls saw my pix, the geeks saw my pix, no one coughed confirmation up.

"I don't know them." "Who are they?" "We don't get many A-rabs here." "Who's that guy with the burned-up face, he sure looks funny." "Oh, *ick*. They look like Saddam Hussein."

I returned to my ringside rack. I felt beat-up and *bush*whacked and slapped by my slink though Saddam and Gomorrah. I dug for Donna. I shut my eyes for showtime. I shut out the Junkie Jill on the runway and dunned Donna up.

She laughed. We held hands in Holmby Hills. We tossed treats to Reggie Ridgeback. She hammed it up on *Homicide Heat*.

Somebody tapped me. A corpulent Korean and a nifty nude Nadine stood next to me. I coughed and called up my cop self. I said, "LAPD."

The guy said, "A-rabs, huh? I see some in here." The woman said, "I'm from Tel Aviv. Oy, Arabs I know from, believe me."

I showed my pix. Identikit killers and Fire Face—now dig on it.

They stood still. They stared. They studied. They *both* tapped the pix.

The guy said, "I see guys like the guys in the pictures in here. Maybe two, three months ago. They spend lots of money."

Tel Aviv Tanya said, "I danced for the man with the peeled face. It was like last week. He said he was depressed, he feared his death, tsuris like that. Oy, did he party hard, and spend money. I said, 'Honey, for you there's no tomorrow,' and now you show me this."

I gulped. "Credit cards. Did they use—"

The guy cut in. "Cash only here. Credit cads not okay."

Money—where from? Three heists in '01, chump change takes all. The Falafel Fan—minor moneymaker. Rashad: "no intention of performing terrorist acts"/"just wanted to enjoy themselves"/ "You know the term 'party hearty'?"

Maybe—a rift—*real* terrorists vs. party pigs. *But*—Fire Face

"was depressed"/"he feared his death"/" 'for you there's no tomorrow.' "

Say that says suicide shit?

My cell phone rang. The display dilated. Pat at Pacific Dining
Car—that means Donna's there.

Tanya said, "I did the Arab in his car. He was hung like a
Hebrew National salami."

DONNA DINED SOLO. She noshed noodles and char-
broiled chicken. She saw me and flipped me off.

"Rick, you fuck. You were a shit with Donny."

I barged into her booth. "Are you doing him?"

"No, but I may do him just to mess with you."

I laffed. I sipped her seltzer. I shagged a shrimp in Alfredo
sauce.

"What do you know about him?"

Donna sighed. "He's rich from dot-com investments. He's living in the old Clark Gable house in Malibu, Casa de Suenos.
He's writing spec scripts and trying to break into the business."

"Where did you meet him?"

"At a party. I saw him talking to Lou Pellegrino—you know, the
'Private Eye to the Stars.' He'd heard that I wanted to do an Anne
Sexton show, and so we started talking Sexton. He has a Web site,
in case you're interested."

Pellegrino: strong-arm goon, shakedown sharpie. Slick sleaze-
monger. Ripe-rumored extortionist. Pint-sized pit bull/longtime
lapdog for the Hollywood elite.

I said, "Reggie hates DeFreeze. What does that tell you?"

"Reggie is a *dog*. I don't credit him with ESP. I'm not some
addled pet owner."

I freed French fries and wrapped them in relish. Tasty shit—
yum yum.

"*I* hate DeFreeze. What does that tell—"

"That you're my best friend and *very* occasional lover. That you hate him on GP. That the LAPD just sent you to a shrink, that you killed a man in the line of duty, and you're running a little raw right now."

I laffed. I held Donna's hands under the table. My pant python perked up.

"It's been six months. I keep waiting for something to happen that will stir us up again."

Donna squeezed my hands. "You can't *will* it. And *I* can't keep shooting people and getting embroiled in your crazy life all the time."

Sadness slid up and slammed me. My python sidled south and *de*-perked.

"Twice in *twenty-one* years? That's not *all* the time."

Donna sighed. "I'm almost fifty years old. How did *my* life get so wild and fucked up?"

I HIT A mocha mecca on Mariposa and Wilshire. I jacked up some java. The joint was serve-yourself-cyberspace—two terminals, pay-as-you-play, computer hookups.

I Internet-invaded. I walked Web sites. I hit Donny DeFreeze name combinations. I pulled the punk's page up. Dig—DeFreezeworld.net.

Script scrolls. Excerpts from:

"Eldridge Cleaver, Revolutionary Rapist": "You don't understand, baby. Dis be de '60s. Every time I rapes a white woman, it be a blow against The Establishment and The Man."

"Black Panther Shootout—People's Revolt Against LAPD": "You gots to dig it, baby. Dis be 1969. We be waging war on de pigs."

"SLA Insurrection—Southside Gundown with LAPD": "Listen to me, baby. Dis be soul brother Cinque DeFreeze talkin'. It be 1974 now. We's kidnapped Patty Hearst, now it be time to lay some race war on Mr. Charlie."

"Palestinian Payback: The End Justifies the Means": Listen, my Islamic brother! It is now 2003! The time has come to smite the American insect! Hear me now, my fedayee!"

"Harvey Glatman, Sex-Fiend Saint": "You fuzz don't get it. It's 1958, diggit? Those three kool kittens I strangled prophesy the '60s. I predict some king-size chaos, you sound me?"

Puerile pap. Punk pontification. Anticop communistic. *Niggerdly* nostalgic. Left-wing lunacy.

Glamour Girl Slayer: Harvey Glatman, posing as a fashion photographer, bound, raped, and murdered aspiring starlets. *(Los Angeles Times Collection, Department of Special Collections, Charles E. Young Research Library, UCLA)*

Harvey Glatman—glaring non sequitur. Glatman glommed three women '57–'58. He posed as a photographer. He leeched off lonely hearts listings. He photo-fucked and vilely violated his victims. He was a rope freak and a bondage buffoon. He dumped his devastated damsels in the desert. His fourth victim fought him off. He fried 9/59 at Big Q.

?????

The A-rab stuff stung me. A dune-coon coonection dug in.

DeFreeze rented a lipstick-red Lamborghini. It was one cool coontach—let's coontemplate this.

He rented it from Khalid's Kustom Cars/Khalid Salaam, owner.

?????

I MAINLINED MORE mocha and made tracks for Malibu. I knew Casa de Suenos. I worked off-duty security there, circa '77. It was a spanking-white Spanish pad by the sea.

Sea breezes bristled. Night air nudged my noggin. Coffee coursed through me. I popped up Pacific Coast Highway. I saw the pad, pulled a U-turn, and parked.

There's the casa. Let's be casual. It's perched on PCH, two doors down.

I walked over. I lugged my evidence kit. I popped by the porte cochere. There's the lipstick Lamborghini. There's a boss Bentley sedan. There's a beaming Beemer. The plate reads "Lou P."

Probably the property of: prick private eye Lou Pellegrino.

Be bold now—bring it on brazen.

I laid my kit on the Lambo. I prepared print powder. I tricked up transparency strips. I powdered the driver's-side door and lifted two latents.

I stashed the strips. I closed my kit. I loped around the pad left to right. A walkway whipped back to the water. I walked it and watched window light. I kicked up mounds of mortar dust. I perv-peeped that light.

I saw cheezy furniture—rock-bottom rental stuff. I saw loads of leftist wall pix. There's sick Cinque. There's rape-o Cleaver. There's blasphemous Black Panther shots.

I bopped back to the beach. I ducked by a deck. Bedroom light bounced.

There's demented Donny DeFreeze. He's full-out fucking on a futon. He's making it with a mid-60s mama. She's careful-coiffed. She's wrinkle-ridged. She's age-addled but fuckable-fit.

She's got her eyes shut. Donny's drilling her draconian. His eyes hop with hate.

3.

I shot to the shelter. Pit bulls pounced. A dog daisy chain developed. Donny DeFreeze diminuendoed and disappeared. I settled in for an eight-dog nite.

I fed the pits burrito bites. Brandon Marti made good on that manuscript. I found it on a shelf.

Her Lonely Places: Donna Donahue Deconstructed by James Ellington.

The pits piled on. A terrier territory enclosed me. I scrunched up a dog-dandered pillow. Let's rack out and read.

Ellington wrote elegant. His Donna jones-jumped. He rocked home wild riffs.

"Per Donna Donahue's physical force. It is manifestly powerful and stems from facial features that suggest strength of character, kindness, decency, and a concurrent playfulness and reticence. Here paradox reigns. Suggestions run bipartite. 'I am an open book'/'It's an open book I'll never let you fully understand.' "

Ellington elaborated. He riffed on "mid-range celebrity" synced to "television viewer demographics" synced to a "rapidly fluctuating media culture that feeds off a fickle yearning for the newness and nearness of youth." He states: "Ms. Donahue retains an implacable hold on men as she ages and her presence more and more strongly suggests a sensuality grounded in wisdom." Her never-married status denotes her as an "opportunist of love" who operates from a "passion for the moment" undercut by a stern desire "never to dilute her oneness through subservience to any man," a reluctance perhaps influenced by "astute childhood readings of the Donahue family dynamic and early awareness of parental dysfunction."

Woo hoo! Call this cat one deep Donnaphile!

"Los Angeles is a media center and rumor mill. Two oft-told bits of Donna Donahue lore pertain to her participation in chains of violent events in 1983 and last fall in 2004. The details recounted in rumor—varied and wholly disparate in nature—all relate to her sporadic involvement in covert investigations initiated by the Los Angeles Police Department."

Ring-a-ding! Rip it to Rhino Rick! Lay it on LAPD!

Ellington riffed on that rumor. Donna had scintillating secrets. She staked a clandestine claim on her own heart and held hungers back. She pulsed for possibility. She downscaled and dimmed her romantic expectations. She lived as a lightning rod. She wished up wild and wicked webs and waltzed through them worshipful and wistful for more. She feared her spirit to spark cataclysm. She prized the prosaic in calamitous counterpoint.

Ellington nailed Donna. Ellington nailed the distance between us. Ellington nailed *me*.

I MARCHED THROUGH the manuscript. I dog-eared Donna-deep pages. Pit bulls slipped into slumber beside me. I slid into sleep.

A-rabs assaulted my ass. Some shit-for-brains Shiites fucked me with fatwas à la Salman Rushdie. Donny DeFreeze cornholed a camel. Saddam Hussein handed Harvey Glatman a harem and strands of stranglers' rope. Sleazy sleeper cells. Lurid lap dances. Rhino herds gorge on Palestinian pitas and Muhammad's Meatball Subs. That sissified psychologist says, "Rhino, you're sick."

Demons descend on Donna. Some asshole ayatollah damns

her with a death decree. Big-toothed bats bombard her. Surreptitious serpents surf up her legs.

I stirred. I stood. The pit pile disbursed. I saw *Her Lonely Places*. It hit me *haaaaaaard*. That text télls why she'll never love me from here to heaven's heights.

I lost it. I lobbed dog crates at the west wall. I dumped dog dishes. I kicked kibble bags. I bombed the back wall with bags of Barko Bits All-American Dog Chow.

The pit bulls loved it. They hopped, howled, and humped me. They licked me and laid on their love.

THE TIRADE TIGHTENED my wig. I dusted off dog dander and drove downtown.

I hit Parker Center. I laid the Lambo prints on a print tech. He promised rapid results. I talked to Tim and Dave. We down-and-dirty discussed our visits to the gentlemen's clubs.

I talked up Tanya's tale. Tim and Dave dittoed me. They canvassed and caught the same feedback. Fuck—party-hearty Arabs/death talk/deep depression. Slide me, Slick—is this sleeper-cell shit?

And—where did they dig up their *dinero*?

Dave dished out a hot lead. Danielle at Dawn's Dugout—not at work yesterday. A boogie barkeep said she's got some ace A-rab tips. Rhino, you roll on that—she shifts on at 6:00.

Our landline lit up. Tim took the call. Ping—Pac Bell reports. They ran the pay-phone calls. They got an instant incongruity. Four days, 49 calls to 432 East 49th Street/Hassan Sufeer, the Sufi subscriber.

DARKTOWN AGAIN— *Coo*necticut and Jigaboo Junction.

We caught the Coal Chute code 2. We climbed in close to the old SLA-shootout pad. Donny DeFreeze ruminations ripped me—the punk rang me wrong.

We hit the house. It was pulsating peach stucco stuck on sink-ing cinderblocks. We rang the doorbell. We racked up no response. We shoulder-shoved the door in.

Dig this—the dive's deserted.

No pricey prayer rugs. No camel-furred furniture. No couscous or kebab casserole ware in the kitchen. No mattresses, no minarets, no mini-mosque accoutrements.

We tossed the pad. We closet-climbed. We rolled room to room. We crawled crevices and crannies. We found this:

Takeout-food debris. Stale stuff stuck in Styrofoam containers. Putrefied pita pockets, picked-at pizza, moth-munched meatball marinara.

Escort-service brochures. Bright fotos. Wild wenches with whips—white women all. Bleached blondes blooming in pink peignoirs. Comely Caucasoids to whore with hordes of dark-skinned scoundrels.

A strand of rolled-up rope, flaring out a floor beam. Blistered and blood-bleached.

Scary. A scalding find. Scorched skin that tore off at a touch.

We room-to-room rocked and re-tossed. No more shit showed up. Dave buzzed the Feds. He said we sailed through this safe house—grok this grave alert.

We bopped outside. Porch monkeys perused us. We hopped house to house. We canvassed. We blew block to block. We paraded our pix and caught this:

The house—a hajj hive and camel cave from jump street. Two Arabs in attendance—the coarse cats in the Identikits. Wild-ass white women wending by, all hours of the nite. The A-rabs—"dey moves out yesterday."

Call it cold:

Two mosque minions *morte*—Rashad and Fire Face. The insidious Islamics learn this and leave for the lurch.

My cell phone rang. I caught the call. The print guy delivered on Donny DeFreeze—match-up and major rap sheet.

WE DROVE BACK to Parker Center. The print guy shot me the sheet. CII on Donny DeFreeze—real name Jomo Kenyatta Perry.

Born in Berkeley, 12/8/72. Father unknown. Mother: sulky SLA succubus Nancy Ling Perry.

Named after monstrous mau-mau Jomo Kenyatta. Hellbound-hatched before the Patty Hearst snatch. Two extortion busts, Alameda County.

Nancy Ling Perry, a member of the Symbionese Liberation Army and participant in the 1974 robbery of the Hibernia bank in San Francisco. Killed in the SLA shootout. *(Photo courtesy of the LAPD)*

He beats both beefs. They're fruit shakes. He's a shakedown shill. He keesters cats while his comrades catch it on camera.

He humps homos. They're closet clowns in deep cover. The cops catch on. The fruitcake Freddies freak and refuse to cooperate.

The rap sheet ran rife with rumors. "Subject is said to have moved to the Los Angeles area." "Subject is said to harbor strong left-wing, anti-American sentiments." "Subject is said to strongly identify with radical groups of the 1970s, particularly those of the black-nationalist ilk."

Despicable Donny. Noxious negrophile. Leftist-loser legacy. Butt banger. Pro-Sambo, anti-Uncle Sam. This jejune jungle bunny manqué, "Jomo Kenyatta."

My thoughts jumped and jumbled. Donny. Donna. Lou Pellegrino—*Hollywood* shakedown man—

DAWN'S DUGOUT: A dank dump in the soiled San Gabriel Valley. A raunch ranch off Rosemead Boulevard.

I ambled in ambivalent. I was terrorist-torqued and ditzed on Devil Donny DeFreeze. I wanted to clear my multiple murder case. I wanted to rid Donna of Dirty Donny and bop back bold to her bed.

The Dugout defined the word "dive." Down-and-dirty divas danced disco despair on a wraparound runway. Horndogs huddled at ringside tables. Said tables tilted and tipped. The horndogs pounded their puds under tabletop cover. Their hamsters hopped in their hands.

I badged a big bouncer. He bid me back to the dressing room. Danielle lounged on a lavender loveseat. She wore a white bikini. She skimmed skank in the *National Tattler*. She was all augmentation and titillating tattoos.

I said, "LAPD." She said, "Whatever it is, I didn't do it."

The bouncer bopped off. I straddled a stray chair and eyeballed Danielle. She was hickey-hived and herpes-sored and rug-burned from ruts on shag carpet. She was twenty-two going on dead.

She popped a pimple on one patella. Pus puffed putrescent. I noted her needle-notched arms.

"I said, 'Whatever it is, I didn't do it.' I tested clean my last three times. You can ask my PO."

I shook my head. "It's not about you."

"*So.* So, like, who *is* it about?"

I pulled my pix. "A barman here said you had some recent dealings with Arabs."

Danielle tossed her *Tattler.* Danielle rolled her eyes righteous. Danielle rubbed her rug burns rough.

"These two guys kept coming in and throwing money around. They, like, kept spending these fortunes. I lap-danced them, like, maybe fifteen times, but I wouldn't *do* them, 'cause I didn't like their vibe."

I flashed Fire Face. Danielle nodded no. I showed the Identi-kits. Danielle yipped and said, "Yes."

"Those are the guys?"

Danielle flipped them the finger. "Like I'd do two A-rabs, after 9/11 and all."

"Did you talk to them?"

"Yeah, about these 'adult movies' they were making. I said I don't do fuck flicks, 'cause, like, my dad might see them. He rents all this, like, sex shit on the Internet. He's sort of a perv, but he's my dad, and I love him."

I said, "What else did you talk to them about?"

"*Nothing.* They wanted me to do them, I said no. They wanted me to act in these fuck flicks, I vibed bad shit and said no. I can read vibes and auras, and, like, these guys were no good. All this was like last week, and they haven't been back."

An intercom popped. "Danielle, you're on in two minutes."

I stood up. Danielle stood up. She slithered and slipped off her bikini. She silicone-sizzled and bounced in the buff.

We floated back floorside. More horndogs hand-humped, more tables tipped. The door dipped. A man walked in. He was sweaty and swarthy and beaky Bedouinesque. Danielle said, "Fuck, that's—"

HIM. This mosque monster, this camelhead killer, Mr. Identikit—

He saw me. His hands hopped and held heat. Ten feet between us. These two Glocks gleamed.

He fired. Muzzle smoke smacked me. Powder particles parsed out, *pfffft.* The shots shattered chandelier glass. Danielle ducked. The horndogs horror-howled.

I pulled my piece. I fired fast. My shots whipped wide. They striated off a straight line and struck a stereo rig. A sound system exploded. A disco dirge dimmed and died.

I fired. He fired. Muzzle light blazed and blinded us. Shots shivved and ripped runway wood and dinged off course in the dark.

Ricochets rang wrong, banged the bar and broke bottles. Lap dancers lurched off laps and laid on the floor. Nude dancers dove off the runway.

I fired. He fired. Blinding blasts, nuke noise, chandelier shrapnel. Hammer clicks, empty clip, *his* hammer clicks.

I ran to him. I rubbed my eyes. I tipped tables and nailed nude women in the dark.

I GOT MY sight back. The A-rab got away. A shooting team showed.

They yelled. They yodeled this "you again" number. It was Sheriff's jurisdiction. Twelve deputies dipped by—puerile patrol pups all.

They horned out and hit on the dancers. They stood around and strung together statements. A Sheriff's crime-lab crew crawled the floor and spun up spent shells.

I ducked out. I dunked down to Darktown. Dusk dimmed East 49th Street. The porch-monkey parade was indoors.

I slid up to Sufi Sufeer's safe house. I picked the lock and slipped in. I re-tossed the rooms *rapidamente*.

I tore though the first toss and rang up no new results. I walked the walls and worked the wood for fake panels. I tapped. I honed my ears for hollowness. I roamed room to room. I hit solid wood, warped wood—whoa, what's this?

The living room. Thorough thumps/hollow hits/one panel pulsates.

I probed and pried up a loose piece of wood. The edge caught and cut my fingers. I yanked, I pulled, the panel popped free.

Inside: a hollowed-out hidey hole. One shelf of hidden booty.

More rope. Blood-blistered again. More scorched skin that tore off at a touch.

Polaroid pix. Fucked-up fetishistic. Bound-and-gagged women. Naked and nervous-eyed. Scared and skin-scorched in rough wraps of rope.

Stringy stretch marks. Awful augmentations. Hickey hives, needle notches, rude rug burns—lap-dance-Lola types.

I POUNCED on a pay phone. I dialed Dave at home. He knew about Dawn's Dugout. I shared Danielle's fuck-film revelations. He said the shooting board scheduled a second session with me.

You shoot too much. You got shrink-wrapped by Doc Kurland. Your latest shootout sure says shrinkage to me.

Dave digressed. The Feds kicked back on Hassan Sufeer: no wants, no warrants, no known terrorist ties. A Fed forensic team was set to surf the safe house tomorrow. I said *I* re-tossed it. I found more bloody rope. I found fetish fotos. It vibed tie-ins to gentlemen's clubs.

Dave said he'd call the clubs and try to clear clues. He'd stress fuck flicks, fetish fotos, and misogynistic mayhem. Put the pix on my desk—we'll canvass clubs with them.

I hung up and headed to Parker Center. I felt Donna-deprived, Donna-depressed, Donna-driven. I ran the radio. I stuck to all-news stuff. Some Sheriff's shit shouted per the "Dawn's Dugout Disaster."

Danielle mauled the mike. "I was, like, talking to this LAPD guy. We talked about these A-rabs, and this A-rab just walked in the door! I want to say hi to my dad, and, like, reassure him that I never did the A-rab, because I remember 9/11. Is that okay?"

I turned it off. A notion nudged me. It blistered me, blossomed, and bloomed.

The bound-and-gagged pix—fucking familiar. Let that Rhino remembrance ring.

The memory moved sideways. It dipped to Dave Slatkin. Dave—savvy pseudo-psychic/crime historian.

His photo stash. Sex-crime sensations. Sick shit shorn from old '50s files.

I *knew* it now. I couldn't quite *say* it.

I hit Parker Center. I dove on Dave's desk. I drove through his drawers and found IT.

Filched file forms. Bound-and-gagged women. 8/1/57, 3/8/58, 7/20/58. Judy Ann Dull, Shirley Ann Bridgeford, Ruth Rita Mercado.

Identical poses. The '50s meet the millennium. Harvey Glatman's three vics.

My brain broiled. Fotos. Fuck films. Bug mikes in Fire Face's purple Pontiac. Habib Rashad's pad—surveillance cams, spackle-spotted—there. A spray of spackle-type mortar by the Donny DeFreeze pad.

Donny DeFreeze—shakedown man—fruit shakes in Frisco. Donny pours the pork to that mama-san in Malibu. Donny, aka Jomo Kenyatta.

He's left-wing. He wickedly worships Arabs. He rented his lipstick Lambo from Khalid's Kustom Cars. He spat out a Harvey Glatman spec script.

Donna—where does she—

I called her house. I buzzed her cell phone. I got two machines. I made for Malibu meeeeean and *maaaaaaaad.*

CASA DE SUENOS—call it Hell House or Shakedown Shack now.

I parked on PCH. I saw the lipstick Lambo. I saw Lou Pellegrino's boss Beemer. I saw a Rolls Corniche in the porte cochere.

No Donna-mobile Mercedes. Surf sounds and salty air.

I cut around the casa. I looped left and back. I dipped up to the deck. There's the bedroom. I window-watched.

There's Jomo-Donny. There's a shakedown-sharp two-way mirror. There's a movie-biz matriarch I met at Ma Maison. I was bodyguarding Bad Bill Clinton, Secret Service adjunct. This limousine liberal Lorna Lowenstein was there.

Donna dished dirt on her. She threw political parties and pined for penis in her senescent seventies. Her hubby hustled teenage talent at some agency. The marriage was meshugina. He banged bun buddies on the Boys' Town Strip.

I watched Jomo jump her geriatric bones. I saw her lips latch his love muscle and leech. I saw them sidle sideways and suck soixante-neuf.

It was licentiously leftist and corrosively communistic. Lorna loved it. Jomo simmered in self-loathing and munched muff with homoized hate.

I bopped to the back door. I picked the lock and let myself in.

I hooked down a hallway. Let's catch the camera cubbyhole. Let's lay out Lou Pellegrino. Let's—

My back. Something sharp and shivlike. Shivers and this needle-nuclear *hush*—

IT'S AFRICA OR ARABIA. Trans-Zulu Airlines transports me. The cargo hold's cacophonous, carniverous, and cannibalistic. I'm this rhino reposed with four-hump camels and four-foot pygmies.

We bolt down Barko Bits Dog Chow. A mau-mau minstrel show materializes and makes us mew meek. Stephanie Gorman blanches in blackface. Donny DeFreeze scores a skin-tone transfusion and jigs out as Jomo for real.

We lurch and land. My line-of-duty dead disembark in a dirge. There's the Garcia brothers. There's Huey Muhammad 6X. There's Webster Washington and Shondell Dineen.

They tug my rhino horn and torment me. I tear loose and light out for L.A. I hoof-hump hundreds of miles. A loopy landscape liberates me.

It's some doofus dystopia. Sand dunes meet Mount Kilimanjaro. Spear-chucking spooks spill crockpots of Christian-missionary stew. I graze gratefully. The sacrilege satisfies me. I cultivate communion. I willfully whip down white wafers. The spooks spill a second helping. I grunt, growl, and gorge.

I sigh and psychedelicize. I see Russ Kuster and Osama Bin Laden. Donna peppers a Palestine pita. Mount Kilimanjaro morphs to Darktown L.A.

There's Fire Face and Habib Rashad. There's cross-cultural confusion. Osama opens the Muezzin Market. It caters to coons and comes up with deep discounts on welfare-check day. The store stocks malt liquor and Kool cigarettes. Osama offers offal— hair-o-wine, crack cocaine, choice chicken wings. Reggie Ridgeback rips through ribs and coughs up collard greens. Danielle dances at Dawn's Dugout and digs on her "Dad."

I jerked. My knees struck a steering wheel and ditzed a dashboard. My eyes popped. My periphery pulsated. I caught *my* car seat. I squinted and squared up a windshield. I saw a dawn beach.

The motherfuckers Mickey Finned me. It made me *maaaaaaaaaaaaaaaaad*.

4.

My head hurt. My bones burned. I felt sideswiped and psyche-deli*fried*. My mad mood magnified.

I couldn't juke Jomo-Donny just yet. I B&E'd his beach pad. I left myself open to legal meshugas. I had to hand Donna hard truths on her scurrilous scribe. I had to jiggle the Jomo/Arab *coon*ection.

Dawn bristled into bright daylight. I hit Holmby Hills and slid my sled up Donna's driveway. Her Mercedes was missing. She probably bombed out for her morning mocha.

I waited in the backyard. I popped up to the patio and perched. Reggie ran over. I raked his ridge and ruminated romantic. Rhino Rick and Donna, let's rock.

Mickey Finn dregs drifted through me. They made me muse poetic. I called up quotes from *Her Lonely Places*. Let's send a cell-phone selection of lit-lifted love.

I punched in Donna's number. Her voice-mail message melted me mellifluous. I parsed out paraphrases.

"You retain your implacable hold on men as you age and your presence more and more strongly suggests a sensuality grounded in wisdom."

"You're my 'opportunist of love.' You have a stern desire never to dilute your oneness through subservience to any man."

My phone fucked up. The connection cut off. Reggie reclined by my feet.

I talked to him. I tried for James Ellington eloquence. I said, "I'm afraid we'll never happen again. She only capitulates to me in fits and starts. Things might be getting crazy like they did those two other times, but twice in twenty-one years can never sustain me."

Reggie nuzzled my knees. I notched it up. I said, "It kills me. I always have to rely on outside events to bring us together. If I could think of a formula, or a phrase, or any kind of strategy that would hold us through plain old everyday life, I'd be the richest, most grateful motherfucker on earth."

A breeze sent me scents. There's sandalwood soap. There's almond after-bath. There's mocha melting off morning breath.

I turned around. I saw Donna. She said, "Okay, sweetie. For a little while, at least."

WE DID IT AGAIN. We threw ourselves into *Rick-Donna* 3.

We tried to tame time. We lay down and lasted long. Time tricked us and trumped us before. Every touch told time to stay away and let us make these moments meld.

Donna brought me a new body. She'd softened in the six months since our last *then*. This *then* became our new *now*. We kissed, caressed, tasted. Her hips flared and flattened and rolled into her ribs. I spanned the whole spread with my hands.

She tasted. I tasted. Sandalwood soap, after-bath balm, my up-all-night sweat. I swirled. Her tastes nabbed me new. Preciously private—my brave bride a third time—thrill me both *then* and *now* new.

We tricked time. We trailed our kisses and caresses and took our tastes new places and waited and went wild with the new. We fell into our meld in a soft sync. Her hurricane-hurled hazel eyes led me through.

SLEEP. SLIDING GLASS. One-way wall peeks aimed at *us*.

I woke up. I felt fur. Reggie Ridgeback rolled and chucked his chin on my chest.

Donna sat over me. She wore a salmon satin wrap. I looked

around. I found the phone. Reggie's head was heavy. Donna held my hands.

"Tell me. Something's wrong, or you wouldn't be here at seven a.m., looking like you slept in your car."

I yawned. "It's about DeFreeze."

Donna said, "Of course it is. You've got that 'Where's the phone, I've got to call Dave Slatkin' look, and we only get back together when there's some dead people involved."

I yawned. Reggie yawned. Donna said, *"Tell me."*

I said it simple, sotto voce, stock-still stoic and *slooooooooow.*

"DeFreeze is an extortionist. He was shaking down fags in San Francisco, and he's extorting rich old women here. He's very probably involved in my Arab snuff case."

Donna squirmed and squeezed my hands. Donna said, "Fuck"—sloe-eyed and *slooooooooow.*

"Do you believe me?"

"Of course. I was starting to think he plagiarized this Anne Sexton script proposal he showed me, and you just confirmed it."

"I'm sorry."

"I'm not. Jesus, and I was going to take him to the Academy Awards next week."

I yawned. Reggie yawned. I raked his ridge. Donna said, *"Fuck."*

I filched the phone. Donna ducked from the room. I dialed Dave.

"Cold Case Unit. Detective Slatkin."

"It's me."

"Shit. Where have you—"

"Don't ask. Have you—"

"Yeah, I canvassed the gentlemen's clubs and showed those fetish pix around. There were no dancers missing, but I got more IDs on our Identikit guys, and more confirmations that they tried to get the girls to appear in so-called adult films."

Insidious. Shit circles and surfaces surefire—

"Rick, are you there?"

"I'm here. Dave, do you know Lou Pellegrino?"

"Sure. He's this fuckhead PI."

I yawned—fuck—that mean Mickey Finn.

"He sandbagged me. Have Tim put a stationary tail on his office."

"All right. But will you exp—"

"Yeah, I'll explain when I see you."

Dave sighed. Dave read the sign—Rhino on a roll. I hung up. I rolled Reggie off me. I dipped into the den.

Donna watched TV. News footage filled the screen. I saw the smog-smacked San Gabriels. I recognized a ridge line. A crime-lab crew crawled for clues. A Sheriff's dick talked.

". . . we've got slight decomposition of the bodies, and we've tentatively ID'd all three women as prostitutes employed by the Cool Coed and Stacked Stewardess outcall services. Further examination of the bodies revealed that—"

The cop-ese coursed into gibberish. A cold sweat swarmed me. The fetish fotos. The safe house. Falafel Fan. The outrageous outcall brochures.

Donna tapped me telepathic. Her hard hazels hurled.

"It's us. Isn't it?"

"Yes."

"Is this *Brave New World 3*?"

"Yes."

Donna smiled. "Let's try not to kill anyone, *please*."

SMOG SMOLDERED AND hid the hills. We mowed through Monrovia and made the scene.

I badged us by the cordon. We moved by the meat wagon. I craned a look and caught the corpses within.

Three women. The ones from the bound-and-gagged pix. Nude. Neck abrasions—rope-wrap burns for real.

It was a glaring glut of Glatmanism. It was DeFreeze depravity. It socked me soul sick.

Donna looked in. Donna called up old Catholicism and signed the sign of the cross.

The safe house. The blood-blistered rope. *Scorched skin that tore off at a touch.*

I bug-eyed the bodies. I saw slight sunburns. Make it movie-camera lights. Probable overlighting. Fucked-up filmmakers. Awful A-rab amateurs. The Identikit Islamics. The gentlemen's clubs—"Come on, baby. You make film with us."

A thought snagged me. *Snuff films.* Some terrorist tie-in. Camel jockey conundrum. Party-hearty Palestinians vs. real Jihad-ites.

Donna tipped some tears out. I stared at the corpses and called up Stephanie G. Deputies dipped by. Detectives dug in the dirt by the dump site. A coroner cornered a ranking cop. He caught Donna sidelong. He righteously recognized her. His eyes said, "Say what?"

Vivid voices overlapped. Cop talk cascaded: "time of death," "rectal temperature," "last seen alive," "dumped after dark."

Two detectives saw us and sidled over. I didn't want to share my shit. I steered Donna off.

She said, "How much of this is Donny?"

"I don't know."

"Let's take him down."

I said, "Not yet."

SHE HAD TO hear the horror. I dished the dirt on Donny and tattled the tie-ins. Donna delivered *her* dirt. She figured the fuck for a fag. She slowly slipped to the fact that he didn't dig sexy Anne Sexton. She told him to scoot her some script pages. He deftly demurred. She grokked something grave. He might be wickedly working her. He's ugly, he's usurious. His motives run ulterior.

We winged west. I cell-phoned Dave Slatkin and shorthand shored up my case. Dave said he'd set SIS out to tail Jomo-Donny. I said whip a wiretap, too. Hotwire his house and seize his cell-phone calls. Dave said he'd dun Deputy D.A. Daisy Delgado. She'd write warrants quicksville.

I hung up. Donna said Lou P.'s the linchpin. I said yeah, he's the shakedown shit supreme. I buzzed Tim. I caught his cell service. He'd left me a voice message.

"I'm in the garage at Pellegrino's building. It's 9166 Sunset."

We nudged north. We sailed out Sunset. We bopped to the building and sunk into a subterranean garage.

There's parking slots and deep Dempsey Dumpsters. There's Tim by a telephone bank.

He caught our car and came over. He saw Donna and curtsied—cute.

He leaned in her window. "Jesus. Are you two doing it again?"

Donna laffed. "For a little while, at least."

I said, "We're getting married."

Donna said, "Fuck you."

Tim laffed. "Pellegrino's been coming down and tossing shredded paper in the Dumpsters. He's made three trips so far."

Donna said, "He's creepazoid. He whipped it out on a friend of mine. She said he was hung like a cashew."

Laff time—Tim and I howled hard. I heard foot scuffs. I scanned the garage. There's loutlike Lou P. by the Dumpsters.

I got *molto* maaaaad. I careened from the car and ran toward him. He shoved shreds in a Dumpster. He saw me. He did a deep double-take and spun into a sprint.

The elevator enclosure—he's getting near.

I ran. Tim tore tracks. Donna flew on flat heels. Lou lurched and lost ground. I bolted onto his back belt loops and brought him down.

He blitzed the blacktop. He graced the ground and groveled. Genuflections, gesticulations—*please don't hit me.*

I didn't *hit* him. I whipped my wide-welt wingtips in. I rammed his ribs. I laced his legs. I banged his back. He wiggled and whimpered and plied me with please-don't-hit-me pleas.

Tim tore up and torqued me off him. Donna dug in and shoe-shot him a boss bang to the balls. It was fetchingly feministic. She hated wienie waggers and Mickey Mouse misogynists.

Lou P. pulsed punklike. I dragged him behind a maroon Mercedes and two whitewashed walls. The space was contained and cubbyholed. Let's lay down the law.

Lou looked up and pissed his pants. We stood over him and straddled him stern. Donna kicked him in the cojones. He wiggled, whimpered, and whizzed anew.

Donna said, "You whipped it out on a friend of mine. That was for her."

I said, "Donny DeFreeze. Roll on the motherfucker, before I get *really* mad."

Lou looked up. He saw vicious vigilantes and the loose-cannon law. No rapid right of writs and redress here. No mitigation mercy pleas, no O.J. jive justice, no sissy civil rights.

He looked at us. He quelled his quakes. He rubbed his bruised balls.

He said, "Donny's fucking psycho. He's batshit on certain shit, like he's non-compos-fucking-mental. I set him up with these old babes. They were heavily biz-connected, you know, industry-type wives with gelt. The plan was photo shakes. You know, I shoot the old girls and Donny in the saddle, and we threaten to show the pix to the husbands if the old girls don't pay out."

Tim said, "Keep going. Why's this clown 'psycho'?"

Lou rubbed his ribs and nursed his gnashed nuts. He sniveled and snitched snakelike.

"It was the crazy shit he talked. He said he needed money for this 'holy war.' I saw him talking to these Arab guys at his crib, and that scared me. I don't know, I just felt heat coming down. Then you snuck into the house while I was filming Donny dicking this old dame, and I sandbagged you. I figured you was a PI, then I saw your badge. I talked Donny out of icing you."

Donna said, "He was writing a script for me. Did he ever mention my name?"

Lou leered. "He dropped these hints. He said he had this 'plan' for you, but he didn't give out no details."

Tim said, "Kick loose some names. The women, who you collected from, and how much."

Lou licked his lips loathsome. "This Jane Pearlstein cooze. Her old man's a *macher* at Paramount, and we took her for forty K. The second mark was Sharon Michaelman. Her husband's a big biz lawyer, and she coughed out sixty K total. Lorna Lowenstein was the last. I ain't put the bite on her yet. This has been a good fucking gig. I like old snatch. I get off on the wrinkles. I might let Lorna pay me off in trade. Fuck, I thought this might happen. I was tossing all my paper on Donny."

I bent down. I bored in and beady-eyed him. I sunk into my psycho cop persona. I'll state it straight: It wasn't much of a stretch.

"You'll be talking to DeFreeze. You don't let on that we braced you. We've got his phones tapped, so we've got your talks with him nailed. If he brings me up, you tell him I'm compromised. I'm considered a wack within LAPD, and I'll lose Donna if I follow up on him."

Lou nodded numb. Lou sniveled snitchlike. Donna kicked him in the balls.

"In the name of all oppressed women, fuckhead."

LORNA LOWENSTEIN let us in. The pad was a palazzo. Her husband was out. The maid was off. The setup served us superb.

Donna knew her. They surfed the same social circuit. We came sans Tim. That served to simplify. She vibed out our vile visit. Her eyes racked up something's wrong. Donna dipped by uninvited. I was unshaven, unkempt, and a cop.

We sat down. The living room loomed large. Fucking Beverly Hills—high-ticket hebe haciendas.

La Lowenstein looked at us. I reran the shakedown show at Casa de Suenos. Lewd Lorna leeches that love tool. Lurid Lorna flares her fly trap. She leaps lizardlike and licks.

Donna said, "It's about Donny DeFreeze."

Laydown Lorna lowered her eyes. "Yes?"

I said, "He's an extortionist, Mrs. Lowenstein. His partner made films of the two of you. He planned to threaten to expose you to your husband."

Lachrymose Lorna—her tear ducts dipped on and dripped.

"I would have paid."

Donna said, "You won't have to now."

I said, "He's a major suspect in some other crimes. I'm sure we'll get him for them before he has the chance to extort you."

Loser-in-love Lorna—lured into the lurch. Wet-eyed with tear-torn mascara.

"The age difference. I should have known, but I was having too much fun."

Donna handed her a hankie. Donna shot me a shush now, you heathen look.

"Did he ever discuss someone who had a so-called plan for me?"

Lorna held her hankie. Lorna hid her eyes. Tears channeled down to her chin.

"He said he had a powerful friend with a big thing for you, and that you were taking him to the Oscars. I'm on the awards committee, and he asked me lots of questions about the show."

My cell phone vibrated and popped in my pants. I took it out. A text message ditzed display diodes and mapped.

"D.S. to R.J.: Go to Falafel Fan now."

Libidinous Lorna said, "My husband has fun with his boys. Why can't I have fun with a sexy young man?"

———

WE FREEWAY FLEW. We took the 10 and soared surface streets south. We came in code 3. I ran my red light and sounded my siren.

We threaded up 34th Street. We veered on Vermont. We pounced on pandemonium. We saw this:

A blitz blaze of black-and-whites. A cordoned-off corner. Coroner's canoes. A flat-out felony-car flotilla. Falafel Fan—crossed by crime-scene ropes. Cops—a sizable sidewalk contingent. Witness types winding around them. Dig—the cops are culling them and showing them pictures.

I stopped the car. I got out. I smelled soul souvlakis and Palestine pitas. I threaded the throng. I tore around the tables and caught the counter.

There's Camelhead Cal. Tim and I griddle-groomed him two days ago. We sizzleized and Samsonized him. We burned his hair down to a butch.

He's dead now. He's flat on the floor. He's alight with Allah or crackling crisp in Christianized hell. His face is shotgun shorn and shaved. It's a blood bloom. It's pellet-pitted double-aught deep.

I turned around. I saw Dave. He said, "We've got four eyewit IDs. It's the guys from the Identikit pix."

I GOT it. I got it again. I got it *goooood*. It's a hellbound holy war. It's sex-crazed secularists vs. jacked-up jihadites. It's some dune coon D-day. It's a ghetto Gettysburg in Jigtown L.A.

I saw Donna. She sat on a black-and-white. She signed autographs for cops and cruel cats in Crips colors. I walked over. A fat fuck in a "Tupac Lives" sweatshirt swatted his legs and laffed.

Donna signed his county jail release slip. She wrote, "Brave New World 3. Love, Donna D."

5.

The wire room—a boss bunker beside Parker Center.

Wall-to-wall widgets. Tall tap devices. Switchboards and colored cords plied and plugged in. Confiscated couches covered in cat hair. Four headsets—for Donna, Dave, Tim, and me.

We listened. We caught calls lewd and listless. Daisy Delgado delivered that warrant. We juked Jomo-Donny. We full-on phone-tapped him.

SIS fucked up the Falafel Fan surveillance. Camel Cal got shotgun shaved in spite of it. The media materialized and maimed us. Falafel Fan, Habib Rashad, Fire Face, Dawn's Dugout—what's this A-rab aggravation and Shiite shit? Dead dames dumped in the San Gabriels—collateral carnage or corrosive coincidence?

Chief Tierney tallied our dervish dead and dithered disingenuous. Ha, ha—holy war—not in my city. Terrorist tie-ins—no way. Those *baaaad* body dumps—undeniably unrelated.

Dave phoned the Feds. They jumped on our Jigtown Jihad theory. They said they'd cull camelheads in custody. Said camelites might cough up intelligence. They'd hold them for LAPD.

We sat four across. We caught calls. Our headsets hopped heat. I held hands with Donna. Sandalwood soap and almond after-bath assailed me.

Calls. Switchboard lights lay out numbers and cull up caller ID.

Jomo-Donny to Lorna Lowenstein. Message-machine mush. "Darling, I miss you so much. I ache for our next rendezvous."

Jomo-Donny to Donna. Message-machine machinations. "Donna, hi. It's Donny. I'm thinking about the Oscars. I'm honored that we're going together, and I'm making progress on the Sexton script. Call me. 'Bye."

Jomo-Donny and Sandra Saperstein, horny Hollywood wife—dig this ditzy extract:

"I can't tell you how I miss you, Donny."

"I miss you, too, doll."

"I'm going to get a peel at the Georgette Klinger Salon. They say it takes years off a person."

"What's forty-nine years between lovers, doll? You've got pizzazz, and that's what counts. I see you as ageless."

Jomo-Donny and Claire Samovitz, another Shakedown Sheba—hold for this rapture riff:

"It was good last night, doll. You were the best."

"Oh, Donny. It was like my prom date, back in . . . oh, well . . . some time ago."

"Time's for the bourgeoisie, baby. Brother Cinque said that. We've got the *moment*, and that's where it's at."

"Oh, Donny. You give the best head."

Jomo-Donny to pay phone/some A-rab-voiced asshole/sick seditiousness:

"The target, Assan. If we concentrate on the target now, all will be well."

"I understand, Jomo. We must assume that the police know we killed the infidel at the Falafel Fan. We must hide until the moment. The target is everything."

Jomo-Donny to pay phone/another A-rab asshole/sexed-out sin shit:

"I cannot go to the clubs, Jomo. There is too much heat. I have become addicted to lap dances, my brother. I know that my end and my final reward are near, but I crave the bounty of the flesh until that moment I greet Allah and his virgins. I need white pussy and chilled cocktails to sustain me."

"You will meet Allah soon, my brother. You must curb your urges and think of the target. Eternal poontang will be yours in paradise."

Jomo-Donny to Lou Pellegrino/rancid riffs on *me*:

"We should have whacked that Jenson fuck."

"You don't whack cops, Donny. It just ain't done."

"He's a fuck. He humiliated me in front of Donna."

"He's a weirdo. He's considered a freak around LAPD, and I've heard he's got two shooting boards coming up. He's got these shootouts hanging over him, and he can't move on you, because he's got this sick thing for Donna Donahue, and he'll fuck it up if he fucks you over."

Jomo-Donny made more calls. Jomo-Donny buzzed Bigtown Pizza. Jomo-Donny called Khalid's Kustom Cars and Larry's Lamborghini Service. Jomo-Donny called two more horny Hollywood Hannahs. They talked Oscar shit. They replayed recent ruts. Both babes boded borderline senile. They grooved and grokked Jomo-Donny on their greased slide to the grave.

Shakedown shit. "Target" talk—totally terrorist. Lou Pellegrino—coerced and compromised—our punk puppet now.

Jomo-Donny—mosque mastiff manqué. He's one insidious Islamic. He's indictable now. *But*—we need to shore more shit on the "target."

I held Donna's hand. I heard her heartbeat. I hammered out a plan and unhooked our headsets. Tim and Dave dumped theirs.

Tim said, "I know that look. You've got a brainstorm."

I said, "We send Donna in wired. She meets the fuck for dinner and pumps him on the 'target.' He's a risk freak, so he might divulge."

Dave said, "I'm in."

Donna pored through her purse and pulled out a pearl-gripped Python. The big barrel glistened and gleamed.

"I'm in. Pacific Dining Car, tonight. I've been jonesing for a good steak."

Tim filched a field phone. We hooked on our headsets. Donna dialed Dipshit Donny.

Three rings, one pickup pop. Demon Donny's "Hello?"

"Hi, it's Donna."

"Hi, yourself. I was just going to call you."

"How about dinner tonight? The Dining Car, on me."

"No, on *me*. I want to talk some serious Sexton."

"Eight, then? Some good wine, some good talk."

"*Film* talk, doll. I've got some ideas for an erotic thriller you'd be great in."

Thriller? *Threat*. Donna's .357 Purse Python. Rope. Horror hebe Harvey Glatman. The body-dump babes. Snuff films. Blood-blistered rope. *Scorched skin that tore off at a touch*.

Donna hung up. Mark it mission accomplished. Dave and Tim applauded. Hurricane-hurled hazel eyes hammered me.

Donna said, "*Brave New World 3*. If it goes bad, I'll kill him."

THE FEDS CULLED camel fuckers in custody. Said camel-heads confirmed the contretemps. There's a holy war inside a holy war—hear me, hafiz!

Donna dipped off to a dog-food commercial. Dave, Tim, and I huddled at the Fed facility. We hogged a whole office. A fat Fed named Fields debriefed us. He said he'd interviewed eight inbred Islamics. They issued identical shit. He held one hajjite back to talk to us. In the meantime, dig this:

We've got wild-ass A-rabs up the wazoo. We've detained these dune dusters on full felonies and Minnie Mouse misdemeanors. There's an ugly underground undulating all over L.A. These louts are looking for laundered loot, courtesy of Al Qaeda. It's fucked-up funding for sleeper cells—real and fake. Some camel cads want to blow up buildings and mow down monuments. Some jihadite jackoffs want to couch the cash and party dawn to dusk.

The latter losers live for lurid liaisons with white wenches. They blitz Blonde Bombshell and Blue-Eyed Babes outcall. They live in lap-dance lairs. They pounce on porno bookstores and buy beaver boox. They rampage through rock clubs. They slip Round-reeled Ritas Rohypnol and rape them. They quiver on Quaaludes, they creep out on crack cocaine, they vibrate on Viagra. Their full-on fundamentalism has flared and flip-flopped. Islam—

ick—we're Americans now. Fuck the corny Koran. We're swarthy swingers. We're sold-out Secular Sids.

We dug it. We chortled in our chairs. Fields ducked out and bopped back with a beaky Bedouin. The cat was cuffed. He wore a white jumpsuit. He looked wicked and wary and witheringly smart. He knew Ramadan from ram-a-lam-a-ding-dong.

Fields said, "This is Gamal Abboud, aka Abe Goldberg. He was trying to pass as a yid to score Jewish chicks. He's a panty sniffer. Hollywood Vice caught him slamming the ham in a back aisle at Victoria's Secret."

Abboud said, "I'm an American. I support George W. Bush *and* John F. Kerry. I support a woman's right to choose *and* school vouchers. I'm an apostate. Fuck that Islam shit."

Tim tittered. "You picked up some American vices."

"I'm an American. I respect diversity. You've got your bag, I've got mine. We're free to be you and me. I love white women and dry martinis. Your scene is your scene."

Whoa—he's one wild Wahhabi turned loose libertine! He's culture-corrupted. He's a vice vandal. He's Ameri*coon*ized!

I said, "Americans are good snitches. They curry favor with authority and rat their friends off to save their own skin. You dig my drift, sahib?"

He dug it. He salaamed and saluted. Critters crawled through his beard.

"I'm an American. I understand my civic duty as a stool pigeon. We're free to be all we can be. I'm free to suck up to authority in exchange for political asylum."

Dave dug out the Identikits. Fields chose a chair for Abboud. We served up a circle. Our knees nudged. Abboud picked his nose and nailed a nice nugget. A big beetle bipped through his beard.

He squinted. He squared up the pix. He said, "I know them."

I said, "Names?"

"I don't know."

Dave said, "Who *are* they?"

Abboud said, "Terrorists. They stay mobile and sleep in their cars. There is supposed to be a big attack soon, but I don't know the target. It's a suicide mission. Those Shiite pigs have been living it up, because they know they will die soon. I've seen them at gentlemen's clubs."

Tim tore in. "How do you *know* this?"

Abboud licked his lips. A bug bopped off his beard and tangoed on his tongue. He bit him and ate him. Bug juice bipped.

"The Internet. Lap-dance Lou's Chatroom. All the expatriate Arab swingers log on. Lap-dance Lou is really Ephraim Ben-Gazi. He's also known as 'Date-Rape Dani Dayan.' He deals Rohypnol and Viagra. The swingers post notes to each other and reveal things they should keep secret. They're good Americans impaired by alcohol and drugs."

I said, " 'The target' implies a big operation. Where's the money coming from?"

"Two sources. The manager at Falafel Fan was laundering cash from Al Qaeda, but he kept blowing it at the clubs, which is why the zealot faction killed him. His cousin Habib Rashad laundered cash and blew it, which is why he was killed. They became good horny Americans, and—"

I cut it. "The second source. Give on *that.*"

Abboud leered licentious. "It's a white American with Arab sentiments. He's extorting rich women and making 'sin films' for distribution to Muslim biggies in Afghanistan and Iraq. I've heard they are quite misogynistic."

Jomo-Donny. Dead outcall hos. Snuff films. Harvey Glatman glowers. *Scorched skin that tore off at a—*

Dave dug in. "Where were the films shot?"

Abboud said, "I heard it was a loft. The warehouse district, maybe North Alameda."

Tim stood up. His chair tilted and toppled.

"I'll call the squad and have them check building ownerships. There's just a few loft blocks over there."

Dave nodded. Tim rolled from the room. Fields fidgeted, Fed-like—LAPD lifts his Sufi suspect for our collateral case. Donna dreams drilled me. I become her hellacious hero. I take on terrorists and trounce them. Rhino Rick reigns as the new Rudy G. Righteous Republicans raise my banner. I run for governor. I smugly smear Schwarzenegger as the sex-soiled and steroid-stung stinker he is. I marry Donna. We bloom in bliss and raise rambunctious rhinoettes. I'm Ronald Reagan redux. Fat cats find me and finance me. I prowl primary states and nab the nomination. I proudly pry up the Presidency.

Dig Donna as First Lady! Dig our *looooooooooooooooooooooong* lovemaking in the Lincoln Bedroom! Dig our *ruuuuuuuuuuuuude* Rose Garden ruts!

I fantasized. Abboud apostatized, motor-mouthed and meandered. It's priapic prophecy. A-rabs assail L.A. It's cocktail-lounge carnage. It's the date-rape diaspora. Dani Dayan dumps Rohypnol and wacks out the water supply. Rape-os come up comatose and rack out too ratched to rape. Falafel Fans fan out—freaky franchises all. They mulch McDonald's and burn down Burger King. Chief Tierney lays lap-dance lessons on LAPD. Lady cops cough up cooze to A-rabs citywide.

Tim ran into the room. Tim rocked it out.

"The building at 412 North Alameda—it's registered to a Harvey Glatman."

WE LAID TRACKS. We ribbed rubber to the address. It's a four-floor loft space just north of Japtown.

We filed into the foyer. We found mailbox slots. "Glatman" glared out. The fuck's on floor four.

The lift crawled, creaked, and left my lunch lurching. A hallway hooked to the door. I buzzed the bell. No answer. Tim laid lock picks into the latch. The jamb jumped, the door popped.

We walked in. We hit a snug snuff-film set. We crept the Weegeeish walls and crawled this cruel creepspace.

White wallpaper. Filthy fetish pix. Babes bound-and-gagged. Insidiously intercut with vicious victim shots.

Judy Ann Dull, Shirley Ann Bridgeford, Ruth Rita Mercado— Harvey G.'s desecrated dolls. They're hogtied. They're horror-struck. They're hoarse from screaming. It's death divvied up from detective-mag decks. It's nihilistic pop art.

More pix—all rancidly recent—strict stretched-neck strangulation shots. Familiar faces—the body-dump vics—devastated dears three across. Rope-burned and ravaged. Burned from arson-hot arc lights right on this spot.

Still more pix—'70s sensations—Donald DeFreeze and Dark Donny's mad mom, Nancy Ling Perry. There's his negrophile namesake—Mr. Mau-Mau himself—Jomo Kenyatta.

We fanned out. We flew across floor space. We found:

Donald DeFreeze was a leader in the Symbionese Liberation Army and was thought to have masterminded the 1974 kidnapping of Patty Hearst. *(Photo courtesy of the LAPD)*

Mattresses—shorn of sheets and shoved in a corner. Movie cameras, big boom mikes, lenses, lens caps. Rolls of rope on a table. Gristle gracing the strands. Blood blisters with neck hair notched in. A heaping hamper close by. White sheets popping out. Rope imprints rendered red and dried-blood maroon.

Tim said, "That 'erotic thriller'—he'll bring Donna back here after dinner and make his move."

Dave said, "We'll close-tail her and keep her safe, but she's got to get a make on the target."

I said, "She'll get him to talk. Then we'll let her kill him."

6.

Donna went in wired. We perched in the Pacific Dining Car parking lot.

She went in at 8:02. Jomo-Donny joined her at 8:06. He left his lipstick Lambo with Luis the car-park cat. Donna ditched her Daimler-Benz streetside.

We lay low. We waited in Dave's Dodge Dart. We wore free-frequency headsets. Dave pulled Donna's Purse Python. He figured she might wax wistful and whack the freaky fruit on GP. We gave her a scurvy script to work off. Donna, do this:

Stress stressed-out Rhino Rick Jenson. He's on a right-wing rampage. He's a zorched-out Zionist xenophobe hopped up on home security. He sheared shots at two innocent Arabs. It's his Palestine pogrom. He went to work stagger-stoned. He said Muslim motherfuckers Mickey Finned him. Nobody bought it. The shooting board shot him a reprimand. He got relieved of duty.

My headset itched. Wire warp whipped down my ears and wiggled loose wax. Static stammered, crystals cricked, voices vizzed.

Donna: ". . . and he's been under a great deal of stress. The chief made him take a month off."

Jomo-Donny: "He's the kind of fascist who gives fascists a bad name."

Donna: "He's not a fascist."

Jomo-Donny: "Don't be naïve. He's the kind of fascist who hounded the SLA and Harvey Glatman to their graves."

Donna: "Who's Harvey Glatman?"

Jomo-Donny: "I call him the 'Sex-Fiend Saint.' He offed three chicks and presaged the '60s. He was hip beyond hip."

Donna: "Let's talk about the Sexton script."

Jomo-Donny: "At my loft, okay? I want to take some pictures of you. It'll juice my creative process on the Sexton thing."

Donna: "What about this 'erotic thriller' you mentioned?"

Jomo-Donny: "It ties in. You'll dig it. It's a real sainthood scene."

Static stung me. Crystal cricks went *crrrrrrrrrr*. I hooked off my headset. Tim and Dave did the same. *Crrrrricks* headset-hopped and caromed the car.

We waited ten seconds. We hooked on our headsets. Fuck—no voices, no crystal crack, no static sticks. Just dead decibel air.

I looked at Dave. Dave looked at Tim. Tim looked at me. Telepathy tapped three ways. We dumped our headsets and hauled.

We ran into the restaurant. We whipped past waiters. Diverted diners looked up—say what? We barged to Donna's booth. We saw half-chomped appetizers—cold crab and calamari.

There's the wire. There's the body mike. They're flat on the floor. The casing's cracked and smashed to smithereens. There's the back door.

We ran outside. We dipped past Dumpsters and winged past winos on gourmet garbage hunts. We hit 6th Street. There's the curb. Donna's Daimler-Benz—gone.

We reconnoitered. We reconsidered. We reconstructed the scene. Jomo-Donny wised up to the wire. He won't lead us to the loft. He laid out loft talk. He knows we heard it. He won't whip Donna there.

He's malevolent. He's mobile. He's got Donna roped or restrained, Mickey Finned and made meek, sedated, or subdued.

Tim said, "She'll fight. He's got no idea how resourceful she is."

I said, "Where the fuck will he take her?"

Dave said, "He'll pull a Glatman. I *know* it. Glatman failed with his last victim. He drove her through Orange County. She got the drop on him there. He'll try to duplicate it and succeed."

I saw Donna devastated. I saw Donna dehumanized. I saw Donna decimated and dead.

It made me *maaaaaaaad* . . .

THE COAL CHUTE — code 3. Dave drives. I panic-pulse. Tim cell-phone sizzles.

He calls SIS. He issues interdictment orders. Stake out that loony loft. Make Malibu and catch Casa de Suenos. Don't be timid. Don't time it too tough. We're talking TERRORIST. Try not to trip up. We don't want to waste him. He knows the TAR-GET. He's got Rhino's dear Donna D.

We sailed southbound. Tim called Communications and came on curt. He described Donna's Daimler-Benz. He ran through the route most likely: the 405 Freeway down to desert cutoffs east. Alert all agencies, all units. Approach. Don't apprehend. We're talking TERRORIST. He knows the TARGET. Don't dive in except to save Dear Donna D.

We *soared* southbound. The Coal Chute *coon*ected with the 405. I dipped into Donna delirium. I delved decades back. It's '83 again. There's the Donna dead. There's the Hollywood Fuck Pad. There's the late great Russ Kuster.

It's '04 again. Hail the Hot-Prowl Rape-O. There's Rick and Donna deep in love. There's homicidal hound Reggie. Fangs for the memories — he's ripping rapist genitalia.

Southbound: Surf City exits, the lights of Long Beach, that muggy mock-Vietnam, Westminster. I eyeball-scanned. Tim eyeball-scanned. We caught cars winging every which way. West-minster whips into Huntington Beach. Huntington Beach be-comes Fountain Valley.

Cars—one mad maze. Headlights hit. Rays reflect. Tailpipes cough carcinogenic. Old fogeys in Fords. Choice cholos in Chevys. A pint-sized Pearl Harbor of Jap makes and models—one big banzai.

Headlights hit. Rays reflect. License plates light. Big Beemers, mauve Miatas—whoa now, what's—

THIS:

Donna's Daimler. Backlit bold. I see it. Tim sees it. Dave sees it. We're almost bumper-to-bumper. The Benz is backlit *biiiiiiiig*.

Jomo-Donny's driving. Call Donna comatose. See the center console. Her head's lolling on the leather. She's sprawled off her seat.

We climbed close. Our lights lit the Benz *biiiiiig*. Donna didn't move. Don't let her be dead—*please*, God, *please*.

We climbed closer. We clung. We tailgated tough. Jomo-Donny reacted and reached for his rearview mirror. Donna's head slid slightly. Donna came off the console and caught him up.

She pulled his hair. She raked his eyes. She bit bold and latched long and leeched his left earlobe off. She maimed the malignant mama's boy Mike Tyson-like. His hands fanned faggottish. Donna ripped the rearview mirror off its mounting. Donna hit his head with it. Donna chopped his face. Donna chewed his cheeks up.

The Benz buckled and bent right. A Jap jalopy braked brisk and dipped damage-free. A Chevy chugged off and out of the way. Donna yanked the wheel hard right.

The car lurched and leaped lanes. The car gored a guard rail. The car hurtled and hit a huge inflated safety bag.

HOMELAND SECURITY.

It justified jerry-rigged justice. It mandated mucho mayhem. It took us to torture techniques.

We deflated the bag. We dug Donna's Benz out. We cuffed the Donna-decimated Dipshit DeFreeze and dumped him in Dave's Dodge Dart. Donna said her wire worked loose at the restaurant. Jomo-Donny jumped her and juked her with a sedative shot.

Traffic tripped around us. We caravanned off the freeway, huddled and hubbubbed. We wrapped ourselves in a rationale of rogue justice. Let's fuck the Feds and move past mainstream LAPD. Let's make like the Mossad and get down like the Gestapo. Let's jingoize joyfully.

I called Phone Book Tom Ludlow. I briefed him. Tom tore in torrid. His tour in Nam napalm-nudged him nostalgic. The My Lai massacre made him misty. He said he took torture toys home with him. Yeah, Rhino—I'll roll. We'll rendezvous. We'll run a confession session. We'll jack this Jomo up with some jolts.

We rolled to the Wrangler's Ranch Motel. We rented a room. We racked Jomo-Donny to a radiator pipe. His face bloomed blood. He sputtered, he spit, he spun in his chair. He launched leftist lunacy. He popped PC pap.

He called us Fatuous Fascists, Cruel Crypto-Nazis, Insects for Israel. We were Prick Pro-Lifers. We were Horrid Homophobes. We were Hideous Hillary Haters, Consorts of Condoleezza Rice, and Bullies for Bush.

We laffed. He lunged in his chair. He rolled his wrists. His cuffs cut and bore down to the bone.

Knock, knock—there's Phone Book Tom.

Dave got the door. Tom wore too-tight field fatigues. He was gussied up gorgeous. His costume called out Khe Sahn, '68. He carried a cord-covered box. Wires wiggled off of it. Dig those tight testicle clamps.

I said, "Hi, Tom."

Donna said, "I like the outfit. It reminds me of a Vietnam flick I did."

Dave said, "Hook the cocksucker up."

Tim said, "We need *results*. Remember, this is Homeland Security."

Jomo-Donny sputtered and spit. Jomo-Donny kvelled and kvetched.

"Dittoheads for Dick Cheney!"

"Rush Limbaugh Rustics!"

"Impede the Imperialists!"

It tickled Tom. He giggled. He guffawed. He uncoiled cords and plugged his box in.

"You're starting to look like Victor Charles. You *comprende, muchacho?* That means the fucking VC."

Sparks spun off the clamps. Current coursed *kerrrrack.* I said, "Give up the target." Jomo-Donny said, "Viva PLF! Viva gay marriage! Viva Robert Mapplethorpe and freedom of expression! Viva National Public TV!"

I nodded. Tom nudged Jomo's knees. Tim claimed the clamps and crotch-crimped him crisp.

Voltage voomed. Jomo jumped behind a jillion jolts. Jomo jittered and hopped in his hot seat.

Dave de-clamped him. Donna said, "That's for Lorna Lowenstein, shitbird."

Jomo jittered. Jomo jiggled. Jomo jolt-jumped. The volts voodooized him. He pissed his pants. His hair hiked à la Don King.

I said, "*Give on the target.* The place, the details, the date."

Jomo jiggled. Jomo jerked. His pissed pants roiled with residual voltage and stormed up some steam.

"Viva Yassir Arafat! Viva Harvey Glatman! Viva misunderstood serial killers worldwide!"

Tim claimed the clamps. Tim crotch-crimped him. Jomo juice-jumped and screamed.

I said, "Give on the target."

Donna said, "That's for stringing me out on my Sexton play, you shit."

Dave popped a Pepsi Lite. The can coughed up carbonation.

Dave shook it and spritzed Jomo's balls. The Commie cord-conduit *screeeeamed*.

Tom tittered. Jomo jiggled. He did the Wired-Up Watusi, the Castrato Cakewalk, the Twittering Twist.

I said, *"The target.* Give it up, quick."

Jomo jolt-jumped. Jomo japped Donna with evil eyes. Jomo made misogynistic.

"Osama Bin Laden's got a thing for you, baby. That's right, the big guy himself. He's holed up in Afghanistan watching *Hospital Hearts* reruns. He paid me two hundred K to make a snuff film with you."

Donna flared florid. Donna popped pale and grew green at the gills. She pawed the Pepsi can. She claimed the clamps. She spritzed and crimped. She made a mini-mushroom cloud climb off the clown's clawed balls.

He screams. His hands hike. He pounces on his pockets. He pulls a pill. His hands hitch. He pops the pill in his mouth.

Cyanide or strychnine/a diagnosed death dose/the fanatic's fallback, oh fuck—

Jomo jumped. Jomo ratched the radiator loose. Jomo coursed with current, palsied with poison, *coon*vulsed and kicked off.

I looked at Dave.

Dave looked at Donna.

I looked at Tom.

Tom looked at Donna.

I looked at Tim.

Tim looked at Donna.

Telepathic telegrams Teletyped and fanned out five ways. Donna said it first.

"The target. It has to be the Academy Awards."

7.

Yeah, the fucking Oscars. It had to be JEW.

The Oscars. Hollyweird's nite of nites. Major media meshugas.

The Sheeny Shangri-la, the Mockie Matterhorn, the Kike Kili-manjaro. More Jews than the Old Testament.

We phoned the Feds. We shared out shit. We refused to reveal our source. The Feds fielded full-on security. They cordoned off the Kodak Theater. They bombarded it with bomb dogs. They perused for purloined passes. They freely frisked celebs running up the red carpet. They moved in metal detectors. They marched among movieland *machers*. They bopped around backstage. Choppers churned above the building. Their belly lights burned down. Glare blazed Hollywood Boulevard.

I went as Donna's date. LAPD laid out loads of cops inside. We wore moth-munched, fucked-fitting tuxedos. Walkie-talkies went at our waists. We settled in for the sicko ceremony.

I yawned. We'd bombed through big busy days. We faked a fag snuff on Deadly Donny. We dumped him in a dive motel room by the Boys' Town Strip. We created a cruel crime scene. It consisted of coarse queer regalia. We laid in loads of Judy Garland LPs. We came up with cocaine and K-Y jelly. We trashed the room. It reeked of rump-ranger rampage. We pulled this shit in Sheriff's jurisdiction. We figured they'd snag the snuff as fruitus interrup-tus and short-shrift the case.

We liaisoned—LAPD to the Feds. We cooncocted coontin-gency plans to detain dissident A-rabs. The Feds coonducted massive coontainment sweeps. The sweeps swept L.A. A-rab civil-rights groups bombed out big boo-hoo. They coonsidered the sweeps racist and reactionary. The average Angeleno reacted with coontempt. They loved the law-and-order lashing of loose liberties.

We settled in our seats. My tux pants bound my balls too tight. My cummerbund cut me. Donna wore daffodils on her delphine-blue gown. We held hands. My eyes clung to her cleavage. She promised me primo love later. My trouser trout trilled over it.

The show started. It smacked me smarmy and smug. It snared me up snoresville. It pulverized me into pulp. It was humanistic hoo-haw served up coongratulatory.

Best DocuDrama—a draw—the Holocaust ties with AIDS. Natterings of "Never Again!" and hosannahs for homo marriage. It gored my goat and pricked my Protestant pride. If God wanted men to mate with men, he'd have created Adam and *Steve*.

Donna delivered the Best Sound Award. Two tall techies swooned swishy and sailed sound bytes to their "partners." Donna decked me, devastating. Her slit-leg gown sliced my soul. Stage lights stung her hazel eyes and hurled heat at my heart.

The show shoved on. Donna dipped back to her seat. I laid low and leered at her legs. Awards, applause, speeches—specious and sparkless—sententious sentiment that sent me away. It withered me and whipped me and went on and on. Limo liberals mocked my man George W. Bush. Antigun gonifs chewed that champ Charlton Heston. I started to righteously root for a terrorist attack. Dig—Donna and I die and hit heaven on high. We clamor to our cloud. We evict evil A-rabs who flew heavenward on a fluke. We make love and romp with Reggie Ridgebacks 1, 2, and 3. We lunch at Lou's Cloud Room with Stephanie Gorman. We stone Stephanie's killer down deep in hell.

The show shoved on. Losers lurked and simmered insincere, noxious with noblesse oblige. Winners winged wondrous words of thanks, hot-aired and wholesale. Best Song nominees soared soporific. It was one long course of canned corn.

It went on forever. It twirled past the twelfth of never. It was faigelah fanfare and hard hucksterism supreme.

Then it stopped. Donna woke me up. I was listing into her lap. I was dreambound and slapped with sleep. We were high up in heaven. We held Oscars for Best Killer-Lovers. Reggie Ridgeback writhed at our feet.

SECURITY DE-SECURED. The cop contingent called off code 3. The Fed force disarmed and dispersed. The choppers churned away. The bomb dogs got carted back to their kennels.

Limousines looped the Kodak. Losers and winners and proud

presenters preened and prepared for parties. Donna loaded us into a limo. We spun out for Spago. She wanted one hour there. Some laughs, some lox pizza, lots of love later—okay?

The restaurant rocked. A sound system socked songs—nudnik nominee encores. Movie *machers* moved and made *mockie-evellian*. It was Dealmakers' Dystopia. It was stark star-fucking. The *Jew*nited Nations *coon*venes.

Table talk tattled all around me. Terrorism titters. Tough tales of studly studio heads. Loose-lipped liberal libels. The latest line on losers nominated and nudged out.

I watched Donna work the room. She shot table to table. She trudged trouper-like. Tonight's talk was tomorrow's paycheck. She pranced and preened like a pro.

Waiters whizzed by. I glutton-glommed glorious grub off their trays. Piquant pizza bites, gourmet goat-cheese puffs, cholesterol-clumped strands of steak. Conversations came and went. Words wafted. Percentage points, back-end bids, two busboys who never showed up.

I yawned. This last wild week whipped my ass and drugged me out to dry. Shiite shootouts, torture tiffs, Donna jihad-jeopardized. Hajjite hegemony, dune-coon demimondes, my L.A. lap-dance loop. I was hungover on homicidal heroics. I wanted to dun Donna for long-term love and salve my soul in the sack.

The restaurant rocked. I felt stuck and stifled. The concept of cool air called to me. I walked out to Canon Drive and dropped around to the alley.

A breeze bristled. It felt gossamer good. I stood between Dempsey Dumpsters and deep-breathed. *Aaaaaaah*, life! Movie madness and Muslim mayhem! *Ooooooooonly* in America, *laaaarge* in L.A.!

I stood there. Cool air cocooned me. My starched shirt wilted in the wind.

I *smeeeeellleddd* something. It noodled my nostrils. Some scent sent sanguinary . . .

I pivoted left. I peered in the Dumpster. I saw two wire-worn wetbacks. They're dead. They're garroted garish. Piano cord cut them—wire whips windpipe-deep.

White coats. Flecked food flaring. Neat nametags. St. Peter, meet Juan and Jose.

Muchachos muertos. Missing busboys. Oscar-nite obfuscation. Our movie *macher* mini-target *right here.*

I ran into the restaurant. Table talk tattled. The joint jumped like Jerusalem and tittered like Tel Aviv. I eyeball-orbed. I surfed celebrities. I took in tuxedos and scanned skin. I saw Donna dunned for autographs back by the kitchen. Two Bedouinesque busboys besieged her. They're wearing white coats. They've got neat nametags. They're the camel cads from the Identikits.

I ran over. I tipped tables and tore through tuxedos. I saw big bulges on the busboys. Their posteriors popped out. Call them body bombs on Suicide Sids.

I ran. I knocked over nudged-out nominees and homo hunks holding Oscars. Donna saw me. The bomb boys saw me. Telepathy tapped out four ways.

The Shiites pulled shivs. Donna pored through her purse and pulled her Python. The shivs shot out. Donna pirouetted and popped the punks point-blank.

Magnum loads mangled their faces. Hollow-points hacked up their heads. Big bullets bid the Bedouin beasts back to hell.

The restaurant reverberated. Table talk scrolled into screams. I looked at Donna. Donna looked at me. The dune devils death-throed and toppled a table. Their body bombs tick-tick-ticked.

I jumped. Donna jumped. We whipped off their white coats and wigged wires loose. The bombs did not detonate. The bombs tick-tick-ticked and sent seconds sounding off a built-in clock.

The red line rested at midnight. My Timex tallied 11:59.

Telepathy tapped us. We ignored ignominious screeches and screams.

We smiled at each other. We struck a style statement. It was ostentatious and Oscar-worthy. We bopped the bombs to the kitchen. We defused and dunked them in a barrel of bouillabaisse.

That's how Donna Donahue and I saved Hollywood—and the world.

Tim and I tossed Casa de Suenos. We found plans to destroy major monuments and media magnets throughout Christendom and beyond. Disneyland, the Vatican, Grauman's Chinese. The Taj Mahal, Dodger Stadium, the Eiffel Tower. The Dome of the Rock, the Flagship Sizzler Steakhouse, the Dalai Lama's pad. The world would have been full-on fucked without us.

We turned Devil Donny's notebooks and computer disks over to the Feds. It resulted in boocoo busts. Homeland Security rounded up 16,492 murderous Muslims. They got trial-trounced in numerous kangaroo kourts.

L.A. owed Donna and me. L.A. dug deep and delivered. We spared lives at Spago. A horde of Hollywood Hebes helped us out.

The L.A. County Grand Jury called our killings justified. The shooting board cleared me on my shootouts. The media hailed Jenson and Donahue as "Sexy Secular Saviors." Hollywood heaped us with a corporate carte blanche and a free-wheeling free lunch.

We developed Homeland Heroes. Donna's starred for sixteen seasons. I part-time produced and moonlighted on my moments off LAPD. Donna and I got righteously rich. Republicans ran me for governor. A demon Democrat defeated me in 2012. He was a half-A-rab/half-black fag fanatic. He delved into my dubious ties to the Enron Corpo-

ration. He ballyhooed me as a bagman for President Jeb Bush.

Donna and I pulsed as part-time lovers. We reconnected for rigorous rug rolls on Christmas and our birthdays. I stayed on LAPD until age 75. I never found Stephanie Gorman's killer.

I described my death in Hollywood Fuck Pad. I detailed the second Rick-and-Donna cataclysm in Hot-Prowl Rape-O. This true story concludes my memoirs of our messed-up and magnificent love.

I'm dead. Donna's still alive. I telepathically tap her via Reggie Ridgeback 12. I often serve up summaries of my life on earth. I always tell her my last living thought was You Were The One.

**Order further James Ellroy titles
from your local bookshop, or have them delivered
direct to your door by Bookpost**

☐	**Brown's Requiem**	0 09 964901 2	£6.99
☐	**Dick Contino's Blues**	0 09 941011 7	£6.99
☐	**The Big Nowhere**	0 09 936661 4	£6.99
☐	**American Tabloid**	0 09 989320 7	£8.99
☐	**The Cold Six Thousand**	0 09 989330 4	£8.99
☐	**Clandestine**	0 09 922622 7	£6.99
☐	**Silent Terror**	0 09 953970 5	£6.99
☐	**L.A. Confidential**	0 09 936671 1	£7.99
☐	**White Jazz**	0 09 964940 3	£6.99
☐	**My Dark Places**	0 09 954961 1	£7.99
☐	**Crime Wave**	0 09 927999 1	£6.99
☐	**L.A. Noir**	0 09 925509 X	£10.99

Free post and packing
Overseas customers allow £2 per paperback

Phone: 01624 677237

Post: Random House Books
c/o Bookpost, PO Box 29, Douglas, Isle of Man IM99 1BQ

Fax: 01624 670923

email: bookshop@enterprise.net

Cheques (payable to Bookpost) and credit cards accepted

Prices and availability subject to change without notice.
Allow 28 days for delivery.
When placing your order, please state if you do not wish to receive any
additional information.

www.randomhouse.co.uk/arrowbooks

arrow books